Donated by
Ian Thomson

Not for loan

The Past, Present and Future of the European Union

This is IEA conference volume no. 138

The Past, Present and Future of the European Union

Edited by

Alan V. Deardorff
University of Michigan

palgrave
macmillan

in association with
International Economic Association

First published 2004 by
PALGRAVE MACMILLAN
Houndmills, Basingstoke, Hampshire RG21 6XS and
175 Fifth Avenue, New York, N.Y. 10010
Companies and representatives throughout the world

PALGRAVE MACMILLAN is the global academic imprint of the Palgrave Macmillan division of St. Martin's Press, LLC and of Palgrave Macmillan Ltd. Macmillan® is a registered trademark in the United States, United Kingdom and other countries. Palgrave is a registered trademark in the European Union and other countries.

ISBN 1–4039–3486–X

This book is printed on paper suitable for recycling and made from fully managed and sustained forest sources.

A catalogue record for this book is available from the British Library.

Library of Congress Cataloging-in-Publication Data
International Economic Association. World Congress (13th : 2002 : Lisbon, Portugal)
The past, present and future of the European Union / edited by Alan V. Deardorff.
p. cm.
Papers presented at the 13th World Congress of the International Economic Association held in Lisbon, in September 2002.
Includes bibliographical references and index.
ISBN 1–4039–3486–X (cloth)
1. European Union countries – Economic policy. 2. Monetary policy – European Union countries. 3. European Union countries – Economic integration. I. Deardorff, Alan V. II. International Economic Association. III. Title.

HC240.I6447 2004
337.1′42—dc22 2004044371

10 9 8 7 6 5 4 3 2 1
13 12 11 10 09 08 07 06 05 04

Printed and bound in Great Britain by
Antony Rowe Ltd, Chippenham and Eastbourne

Contents

The International Economic Association

A non-profit organization with purely scientific aims, the International Economic Association (IEA) was founded in 1950. It is a federation of some sixty national economic associations in all parts of the world. Its basic purpose is the development of economics as an intellectual discipline, recognizing a diversity of problems, systems and values in the world and taking note of methodological diversities.

The IEA has, since its creation, sought to fulfil that purpose by promoting mutual understanding among economists through the organization of scientific meetings and common research programmes, and by means of publications on problems of fundamental as well as of current importance. Deriving from its long concern to assure professional contacts between East and West and North and South, the IEA pays special attention to issues of economies in systemic transition and in the course of development. During its nearly fifty years of existence, it has organized more than a hundred round-table conferences for specialists on topics ranging from fundamental theories to methods and tools of analysis and major problems of the present-day world. Participation in round tables is at the invitation of a specialist programme committee, but twelve triennial World Congresses have regularly attracted the participation of individual economists from all over the world.

The Association is governed by a Council, composed of representatives of all member associations, and by a fifteen-member Executive Committee which is elected by the Council. The Executive Committee (2002–05) at the time of the Lisbon Congress comprised:

President:	Professor János Kornai, Hungary
Vice-President:	Professor Bina Agarwal, India
Treasurer:	Professor Jacob Frenkel, Israel
Past President:	Professor Robert Solow, USA
President-elect:	Professor Guillermo Calvo, Argentina
Other members:	Professor Maria Augusztinovics, Hungary
	Professor Eliana Cardoso, World Bank
	Professor Duardo Engel, Chile
	Professor Heba Handoussa, Egypt
	Professor Michael Hoel, Norway
	Professor Jean-Jacques Laffont, France
	Professor Andreu Mas Colell, Spain
	Professor Kotaro Suzumura, Japan
	Professor Alessandro Vercelli, Italy

Sir Austin Robinson was an active Adviser on the publication of IEA Conference proceedings from 1954 until his final short illness in 1993.

The Association has also been fortunate in having secured many outstanding economists to serve as President:

Gottfried Haberler (1950–53), Howard S. Ellis (1953–56), Erik Lindahl (1956–59), E.A.G. Robinson (1959–62), Ugo Papi (1962–65), Paul A. Samuelson (1965–68), Erik Lundberg (1968–71), Fritz Machlup (1971–74), Edmund Malinvaud (1974–77), Shigeto Tsuru (1977–80), Victor L. Urquidi (1980–83), Kenneth J. Arrow (1983–86), Amartya Sen (1986–89), Anthony B. Atkinson (1989–92), Michael Bruno (1992–95), Jacques Drèze (1995–99) and Robert M. Solow (1999–2002).

The activities of the Association are mainly funded from the subscriptions of members and grants from a number of organizations. Support from UNESCO since the Association was founded, and from its International Social Science Council, is gratefully acknowledged, particularly for specific help for the Lisbon Congress.

Acknowledgements

The Congress was held from 9 to 13 September 2002 in the Centro Cultural de Belém, Lisbon, at the invitation of the Ordem dos Economistas de Portugal, and was attended by 1100 registered participants.

The Opening Session was addressed by the President of the Republic of Portugal, HE Senhor Jorge Sampaio, and by the newly-appointed Minister of Finance, HE Senhor Manuela Ferreira Leite; the IEA President, Professor Robert M. Solow, delivered a paper, 'Is Fiscal Policy Possible? Is it Desirable?' The programme comprised twenty invited lectures and three invited panels – on 'Growth in Developing and Transition Economies' (arranged by the Global Development Network), on 'Poverty Dynamics and Insurance' (organized by the European Development Research Network) and on 'The Turkish Financial Crisis' (prepared by the Turkish Economic Association). There were 198 contributed papers, a selection of which have been included with Invited Lectures in the four volumes of the Congress proceedings:

Bina Agarwal and Alessandro Verceilli (eds), *Psychology, Rationality and Economic Behaviour: Challenging Standard Assumptions*
Alan V. Deardorff (ed.), *The Past, Present and Future of the European Union*
Edward Graham (ed.), *The Role of Foreign Direct Investment and Multilateral Corporations in Economic Development*
Robert M. Solow (ed.), *Structural Reforms and Macroeconomic Policy*.

Studies generated by the Global Development Network are published in Gary McMahon and Lyn Squire (eds), *Explaining Growth: A Global Research Project* (IEA Conference Volume no. 137).

The scientific responsibility for the selection of papers was in the hands of an International Programme Committee chaired by Robert Solow, with the following members:

Bina Agarwal, India
Maria Augusztinovics, Hungary
Victor Becker, Argentina
Miguel Beleza, Portugal
Enrique Bour, Argentina
Juan Camilo Cardeñas, Colombia
Elinana Cardoso, Brazil
Vitor Constâncio, Portugal
Vittorio Corbo, Chile
Jacques Drèze, Belgium
Jean-Paul Fitoussi, France
Marc Flandreau, France
Augustin Fosu, Kenya
Jacob Frenkel, UK
Hans Gerbach, Germany
Gene Grossman, USA

Seppo Honkapohja, Finland
Peter Howitt, Canada
Andrea Ichino, Italy
Firella Kostoris Padoa-Schioppa, Italy
Valery Makarov, Russian Federation
Andreu Mas-Colell, Spain
Mustapha Nabli, Tunisia
Ademola Oyejide, Nigeria
Adrian Pagan, Australia
Luis Servén, USA
José Silva Lopes, Portugal
António Simões Lopes, Portugal
Hans-Werner Sinn, Germany
Kotaro Suzumura, Japan.

A National Scientific and Organizing Committee was convened by the Ordem dos Economistas de Portugal, under the chairmanship of its President, António Simões Lopes, who, with Amilcar Theias, Carlos Queiroz and Luisa Ahrens Teixeira (Executive Director of Mundiconvenius) formed an Executive Committee:

Mário Abreu
Luis Miguel Beleza
Daniel Bessa
Miguel Cadilhe
Teodora Cardoso
Eduardo Catroga
Maria José Constâncio
Vitor Constâncio
Vitor Pereira Dias
Erlânder Estrela
João Ferreira do Amaral
José Freire de Sousa
José Silveira Godinho
Manuela Ferreira Leite
Emâni Rodrigues Lopes
Isabel Almeida Lopes
Manuel de Oliveira Marques
Manuela Morgado
Isabel Almeida Mota
José de Almeida Serra
Francisco Soares.

The IEA is most grateful to the Ordem dos Economistas de Portugal, the Banco de Portugal, the Caixa Geral de Depósitos, the European Commission, the Fundação Calouste Gulbenkian, Portugal Telecom and other sources in Portugal which generously ensured most of the funding of the Congress. Among 46 other funders, mention must particularly be made (in alphabetical order) of the Banca d'Italia, the Bank for International Settlements, the European Central Bank, UNESCO and the World Bank. Cultural events were supported by the Fundação Calouste Gulbenkian for a concert at its Headquarters, by the Casino do Estoril for a Gala Dinner at the Casino, by the SECIL Corporation for a dinner for speakers at the Convento da Trindade. A Welcome Cocktail was offered on the opening evening at the Maritime Museum, Belém, and the publishers of the IEA conference volumes, Palgrave-Macmillan, gave a reception on the second evening to commemorate the Fiftieth Anniversary of the series, hosted by Amanda Watkins and Pooja Talwar. The Instituto Vinho do Porto provided a lecture and tasting of port wines. Day tours within the region of Lisbon were arranged in the three days after the Congress for participants and accompanying persons.

The logistics of the Congress were efficiently handled by the staff of Multiconvenius, co-ordinated by Luisa Ahrens Teixeira, its Executive Director. The staff of the Ordem dos Economistas do Portugal furnished additional assistance under the management of Carlos Quiroz.

The President of the IEA, Robert Solow, was Congress Editor. The IEA editorial team comprised Maureen Hadfield and Michael Kaser; the latter was responsible for the present volume.

List of Contributors

Alberto Bagnai, Università di Roma, Italy
Rossella Bardazzi, Università di Firenze, Italy
Michele Boldrin, University of Minnesota, Minneapolis-St Paul, Minn., USA
Alan V. Deardorff, University of Michigan, Ann Arbor, Mich., USA
Maurizio Grassini, Università di Firenze, Italy
Arjan Lejour, CPB Netherlands Bureau for Economic Policy Analysis, The Hague, Netherlands
Matthias Lutz, Universität St-Gallen, Switzerland
Richard Nahuis, CPB Netherlands Bureau for Economic Policy Analysis, The Hague, Netherlands
Romano Prodi, President of the European Commission, Brussels, Belgium
Robert M. Stern, University of Michigan, Ann Arbor, Mich., USA
Roberto Tamborini, Università di Trento, Italy
Nuno Valério, Technical University of Lisbon, Portugal

List of Abbreviations and Acronyms

BTM	bilateral trade model
CC	Candidate Country
CCN	Chapters of Combined Nomenclature
CEEC	Central and East European country
CEPII	Centre d'Etudes Prospectives et d'Information Internationales
CEPR	Centre for Economic Policy Research
CES	constant elasticity of supply
CET	Common External Tariff
CGE	computable general equilibrium
CU	customs union
DD	difference-in-differences
DG	Directorate General (EC)
DPM	demographic projection model
EAGGF	European Agricultural Guidance and Guarantee Fund
EC	European Commission
ECB	European Central Bank
EFTA	European Free Trade Association
EIC	European Integration Consortium
EMS	European Monetary System
EMU	Economic and Monetary Union
ERDF	European Regional Development Fund
ESF	European Social Fund
EU	European Union
EU-6/9/15/25	EU of 6/9/15/25 members
FA	fiscal authority
FDI	foreign direct investment
FEDER	Fondo Europeo Desarollo Regional
GDP	gross domestic product
GE	general equilibrium
GTAP	global trade, assistance and production [model]
IBO	Interdepartmentaal Beleidsonderzoek (Netherlands)
IGC	Inter-governmental Conference (EU)
i.i.d.	independently and identically distributed
IM	internal market
IMM	interindustry macroeconomic model
Inforum	Interindustry forecasting [model] (University of Maryland)

INTIMO	Interindustry Italian Model
ISPA	Instrument for Structural Policies for Pre-Accession
MA	monetary authority
MMM	multisectoral macroeconomic model
NAIRU	non-accelerating inflation rate of unemployment
NBER	National Bureau of Economic Research
n.e.c.	not elsewhere classified
NTB	non-tariff barrier
NUTS	Nomenclature Communautaire des Unités Territoriales Statistiques
OECD	Organisation for Economic Co-operation and Development
OEEC	Organisation for European Economic Co-operation
OPEC	Organization of Petroleum Exporting Countries
PHARE	EC programmes for CEECs
PPP	purchasing power parity
PPS	purchasing power standards (ESA index of Eurostat)
R & D	research and development
ROW	rest of world
SGP	Stability and Growth Pact
TFP	total factor productivity
TRAINS	Trade Analysis and Information System
UBS	Union des Banques Suisses
UNCTAD	United Nations Conference on Trade and Development
WIFO	Austrian Institute of Economic Research
WTDB	World Trade Data Base

1
Introduction

Alan V. Deardorff
University of Michigan, USA

This volume collects the best of those papers dealing with the European Union that were presented at the Thirteenth Congress of the International Economic Association held in Lisbon in September 2002. Chapter 2 is the address to the Congress by Romano Prodi, President of the European Commission, who sets the tone for the other contributions by describing and evaluating two of the greatest past and future accomplishments of the EU: economic and monetary union (EMU), and the forthcoming enlargement of the EU to include ten more countries from Central and Eastern Europe. Other authors deal in detail with various aspects of these and other issues, using a mixture of theoretical, empirical, and other tools.

Regarding the euro, Chapter 3 addresses the stability of macroeconomic adjustment under the Stability and Growth Pact of the EMU, while Chapter 4 examines the available empirical evidence of price convergence. Regarding enlargement, Chapters 5 to 9 examine likely effects on current member countries and/or the new entrants. These include both macroeconomic and microeconomic effects, as well as overall impacts on growth and welfare. Rounding out the collection are two chapters not specifically about the EMU or enlargement, Chapter 9 providing the beginnings of a macro-econometric model that is expected to grow in coverage and usefulness along with the EU itself, and Chapter 10 providing a political perspective on how the institutions of the EU are likely to evolve. Together, the volume seeks to provide a broad-ranging sample of the major issues confronting the EU and of the research that is ongoing to address these issues from multiple perspectives.

Romano Prodi, in Chapter 2, describes and evaluates what he views as the two greatest accomplishments that have been undertaken in recent years by the EU: the creation and adoption of the euro, and the forthcoming enlargement of the EU from 15 to 25 countries. Regarding the euro, President Prodi describes the process by which it was implemented and the rationale for it. He acknowledges the views of sceptics who predicted failure, but then documents the extent to which the euro is already a marked success. Regarding enlargement, he records the steps that were taken first to assist the former communist countries in their transition to markets, and then the criteria that were set out for their ultimate inclusion within the EU. This, too, he views as a success, although in comparison to the euro, the project is still in process.

President Prodi's contribution is followed by two chapters dealing with the euro and EMU. These address questions of, first, the EMUs macroeconomic viability and, second, its microeconomic success in integrating markets. Both chapters, nevertheless, convey rather negative messages.

In Chapter 3 Roberto Tamborini uses a theoretical model of monetary and fiscal policies to examine the viability of the EMU and its policy assignments. Due to restrictions on the use of fiscal policies and the delegation of monetary policy to the European Central Bank, centralized monetary policy is, in effect, assigned to symmetric shocks – those that affect all EU countries more or less equally, while decentralized fiscal policies are left to deal with asymmetric shocks. In a model based on the familiar aggregate supply and demand framework of theoretical macroeconomics, Tamborini shows that this assignment is unlikely to be efficient. This is true, even though he uses favourable assumptions that preclude a number of policy dilemmas which would otherwise pose additional problems. Further imposing on policy choice the constraints of the Stability and Growth Pact (SGP), he finds that precisely those conditions that motivated the SGP tend to make it more binding and thus undermine the ability of the policy assignment to achieve its goals.

In Chapter 4, Matthias Lutz examines whether the EMU has caused a convergence of prices across the EMU countries, as it was commonly expected to do. For this purpose he draws on four different datasets of diverse prices before and after the initiation of the EMU, in both EMU and non-EMU countries. Using a 'difference-in-differences' technique, he looks for evidence that the standard deviation of prices in EMU countries fell, from its inception to after, by more than in non-EMU countries. Results are mixed, with approximately as much evidence of a relative rise in price dispersion as there is evidence of its fall. Lutz concludes that, at least on the basis of the very limited evidence available so far, we cannot conclude that the EMU has caused prices to become more uniform across participating countries.

There are four chapters on various aspects of EU expansion.

The first, by Deardorff and Robert Stern, Chapter 5, looks initially empirically and then theoretically at the proposition that European integration has raised the growth rates of participating countries. Simply looking at the data on the performance of current EU members before and after they joined the EU does not suggest any lasting effect on their rates of growth, although it does appear that the larger of the original members experienced a boost in their relative GDPs per capita in the years after forming the European common market, and that some of the smaller members benefited similarly, but with a delay. A review of the empirical literature on the growth effects of the EU provides a mixed signal, some studies finding positive effects on growth, others not, although the authors give reasons to be sceptical of the former conclusion. Thus they infer that the more important effects of European integration may have been not on long-run growth, but rather on somewhat shorter-run increases in per capita income that vary, especially in their timing, with country size and the order of entry. They therefore use the last part of the chapter to present a simple theoretical model, incorporating increasing returns to scale, that may help to make sense of these patterns.

The theoretical case for growth effects of economic integration depends in part on models that permit countries' growth rates to diverge permanently over time. But these same models then predict that different countries within an integrated bloc may also diverge unless appropriate policies are used to counteract that. In Chapter 6, Michele Boldrin reviews work that he and others have done elsewhere, evaluating the empirical implications of models of both converging and diverging economic growth. The main purpose here is to illuminate the case for structural and regional policies in the EU, the case for which is routinely that, absent these policies, the integration of markets in the EU will lead to divergence, richer countries and regions becoming richer and poorer ones remaining poor. The theoretical case for these policies therefore rests on models in which regions diverge, either because economic growth is based on externalities and economies of scale that favour some regions over others, or because similar mechanisms lead to agglomeration of economic activity in some places at the expense of others. Boldrin argues that the empirical support for these models is lacking and that, on the contrary, evidence favours models of convergence of one sort or another. He also notes the growth experience of countries in the EU and the fact that it does not seem to have been affected positively by the receipt of structural and regional funds. On the contrary, he sees these funds as fostering a climate of dependence that causes recipient regions to become mired in low productivity, high unemployment and reduced labour participation.

Turning in Chapter 7 to the more immediate and better understood effects of economic integration through reductions in barriers to movement of goods and people, and also international transfer payments, Arjan Lejour and Richard Nahuis examine the likely effects on Central and Eastern European Countries (CEECs) of acceding to the EU. The authors' primary tool for this purpose is the WorldScan CGE model, which they use to calculate the effects of tariff changes, internal market and migration on consumption, GDP and terms of trade of Poland, Hungary and a group of five other CEECs, cumulating to the year 2020. As inputs to the model, they draw on several sources, including their gravity-model estimation of the effects of the internal market on GDP. They also supplement the model with separate calculations of the effects of structural and cohesion funds on these countries, though they find these effects to be small in comparison with the effects of economic integration. Their results indicate that the largest effects will arise from inclusion of the CEECs in the internal market of the EU, which they model as reducing the real costs of both exports and imports between countries. This accounts for more than half of the gains estimated by their model, the total of which is an increase by over ten per cent in per capita GDP of the CEECs in 2020, and an even larger increase in per capita consumption. Their model also includes effects on the EU countries, which are found to be essentially negligible, and mostly due to immigration.

In the last of four chapters dealing with effects of EU enlargement, Rosella Bardazzi and Maurizio Grassini in Chapter 8 use the INFORUM multi-sector trade model to estimate the effects that EU enlargement will have on sectoral performance of a particular current member country of the EU: Italy. Their analysis takes as given that enlargement will cause expansion of the acceding countries and first examines the sectoral effects of this expansion, through trade with Italy directly and also indirectly with the EU-15, on Italy's sectoral rates of growth. They then also incorporate the removal of remaining tariffs and non-tariff barriers. The results of these various scenarios indicate that, while the overall effect of EU enlargement on the Italian economy will be small, there will be distinct and noticeable effects on sectoral performance and thus on the structure of the Italian economy. A broader lesson of this analysis is that all of the EU-15 economies stand to experience such structural effects as a result of enlargement, some through their direct trade with the acceding countries, and others indirectly through their trade with current members.

The final two chapters deal with issues that are not directly related to either the adoption of the euro or to expansion of the size of the EU. The first addresses the macroeconomic behaviour of the EU, while the second addresses the political forces that may shape the constitutional restructuring that the EU may be currently undergoing.

In Chapter 9, Alberto Bagnai uses a dynamic macro-econometric model of the EMU bloc of countries interacting with a comparable model of the United States, together with separate equations for other major countries and regions, to simulate the effects of several shocks and policy changes on variables of the EMU. The baseline solution of the model has real GDP in the EMU growing at an increasing rate, rising to 2.79 per cent in 2007; a depreciation of the euro of 9 per cent by that year; and a persistent government deficit rising to close to 3 per cent of GDP. The experiments with the model include: an increase in rest-of-world demand that stimulates EMU growth but causes further depreciation of the euro; an increase in rest-of-world export (i.e., oil) prices that causes a temporary drop in EMU GDP and a gradual appreciation of the euro along with a sustained increase in EMU unemployment; and an expansionary EMU monetary policy that provides only a temporary boost to EMU GDP but, by lowering interest payments, causes a decline in the fiscal deficit relative to GDP. The model and these results are only preliminary, since of necessity it is estimated from pre-EMU data, but it is nonetheless illustrative of the macroeconomic forces that may operate in the EMU and the interactions that may connect the EMU economies to those of its trading partners.

In the final chapter (10), Nuno Valério asks about the likely future evolution of the EU in institutional and political terms. The current structure has nation states ceding part of their sovereignty to a supranational authority, but at the same time largely retaining their national identities and aspects of their autonomy. The question is whether the evolution of the EU will retain this hybrid structure or will instead either converge to a fully federalist single state, or instead disintegrate back into independent nations. Valério looks at historical parallels to the integration process, including especially the long process of German unification in the nineteenth century. From this and other examples, he concludes that the current structure is unlikely to be stable and that, of the options that are likely to be available, further integration leading to a European federal state is the most desirable.

2
The Euro and Enlargement*

Romano Prodi
President of the European Commission, Brussels

First I wish to thank you all, and Professor Robert Solow in particular, for your invitation. As some of you may know, before becoming Prime Minister of Italy and later President of the European Commission, I was professor of industrial economics for 25 years. Being here with you today, therefore, takes me back to my younger days.

As joyful as this occasion may be, my speech today inevitably starts on a sombre note. Tomorrow, 11 September, will mark the first anniversary of the terrorist attacks on the United States of America. Delivering death, destruction, pain and fear, those attacks propelled the whole world, both politically and economically, into an unknown and dangerous dimension.

We knew then as we know now that those barbaric and cowardly acts were directed not only against the United States but also against the values of the entire free world, and the freedom and security of every individual were under threat. Every free country, every liberty-loving people was called to play its part in the fight against terrorism, because the task of ensuring safety, well-being and peace is one that no State, no institution, no people, however big, powerful and respected it may be, can carry out alone.

In this new and supremely challenging phase of our history, Europe is ready, determined and able to play an active role as a force capable of spreading peace, stability and prosperity far beyond its borders. The enlarged, economically strong and reformed European Union we are building has the resources to play such a role. From this point of view, 2002 is a tremendous year for Europe because of three main events.

A year that began with the successful changeover from twelve national currencies towards a single currency in an unprecedented logistical operation.

---

* Edited version of the address delivered at the IEA Lisbon Congress. It came about four years after the official beginning of the European and Monetary Union – and nine months after the physical introduction of the Euro into 12 European countries – and three months before the Summit of EU Heads of State in Copenhagen, which formally decided in favour of Enlargement to 25 countries from 1 May 2004.

The euro is now the main trading currency for more than 300 million people. The changeover has proved that Europe's people can indeed work together, with enthusiasm and firm resolve, towards a common goal and in support of an ambitious common project, and that they can make that project a reality. The euro symbolizes the determination of Europe's people to share a future together.

A year that has continued with the inauguration of a European Convention, whose mandate is to give the European Union a new constitutional treaty. I will not bother you with the details of the EU's institutional architecture. Suffice it to say that the challenge that lies ahead for the 105 men and women members of the European Convention, amounts to nothing less than ensuring that the enlarged EU is fully capable of operating with the maximum efficiency whilst retaining and, where needed, improving its transparency and democratic legitimacy. In this sense, the task is comparable to the one that faced their American counterparts in the 1787 Philadelphia Convention.

A year that I am confident will end with an historic decision to enlarge today's Union of 15 Member States to bring in as many as ten new Member States – thus finally reuniting the European continent. I refer to the three Baltic States (Latvia, Lithuania and Estonia), the four central European States (the Czech Republic, Slovakia, Hungary and Poland), Slovenia and the two Mediterranean islands of Malta and Cyprus. These are the ten countries that we are looking to have as new full members as early as 2004. To this group you must add Romania and Bulgaria, which are moving at a slightly slower pace, and Turkey, which is a fully-fledged candidate for accession but has not yet entered the formal negotiating process. In a few years the Union will extend to most of Europe, a family of nations with a population of more than 500 million people. It is our solemn duty to grasp this historic opportunity, to tear down the last shreds of the Iron Curtain and to unite east and west within a peaceful, free and democratic Europe for the benefit of all its peoples.

But a Union of 500 million people cannot function with procedures designed for a Community of six countries half a century ago. This is why we are now undertaking a reform of our institutions and the way they work. Let me turn, then, to the economic implications of the euro and of the enlargement.

1 The euro is today in our pockets

As 1 January 2002 dawned, the euro became a reality for the 300 million citizens of the twelve nations of the euro area, but the road towards it has been long and not always easy. Let me recapitulate the main steps.

1.1 From Bretton Woods to the European Monetary Union

A single currency has long been a dream for many Europeans. It is a dream that was initiated more than fifty years ago, at the end of a war that started in Europe, spread throughout the world and left our continent devastated. Out of the follies of nationalism and protectionism that had led to war grew a new determination: Europe's leaders resolved to ensure the economic and social progress of their countries by eliminating the barriers that divided the continent. This determination eventually led to the creation of the European Community in 1958.

Eliminating trade barriers was never regarded as sufficient to foster trade and create a true common market in Europe. Many always regarded exchange rate stability as an important condition for trade expansion. Since 1944, exchange rates had remained fairly stable in Europe and elsewhere, thanks to the Bretton Woods system. Together with the liberalization of trade, this situation permitted a rapid expansion of trade in Europe and elsewhere. As long as the Bretton Woods system operated smoothly, there was relatively little need for discussion of monetary unification in Europe.

In the late 1960s, however, cracks started to appear in the Bretton Woods system as it became clear that the dollar, the lynchpin of the system, was beginning to falter. Fearing the system's demise and the consequences of this for the European common market, the governments of the six EC countries decided to take action. In 1969, they gave Pierre Werner, Luxembourg Prime Minister and Finance Minister, the task of chairing a group of experts on the formation of an economic and monetary union.

The Werner Report was completed in 1970 and called for the completion of monetary union by 1980. The Report proposed a three-stage approach to monetary unification, leading eventually to irreversibly fixed exchange rates and a system of EC central banks. Pierre Werner was therefore one of the true spiritual fathers of the euro. He died in June this year after seeing his brainchild realized in the form of coins and notes.

In 1971, the year the Bretton Woods system broke down, the EC Council of Ministers endorsed the strategy proposed by the Werner Report and started to implement some of its recommendations. Shortly afterwards, a system for limiting bilateral exchange-rate fluctuations, known as the 'snake in the tunnel', was instituted. But the worldwide shift to floating exchange rates in 1973, ushered in by the demise of Bretton Woods, made the tunnel untenable. Soon EC countries were letting their currencies float independently. After a few years of great economic turbulence and of great stress for the free circulation of goods within the common market, EC governments resumed their efforts to achieve monetary integration. Abandoning the agenda set out in the Werner Report, in 1978 they endorsed the proposal by Chancellor Schmidt and President Giscard d'Estaing based on European Commission President Roy Jenkins' initiative to form a 'zone of monetary stability' in Europe by establishing the European Monetary System (EMS).

The EMS was the most significant and effective international exchange-rate arrangement since the breakdown of Bretton Woods. In fact, EMS was nothing short of a mini-Bretton Woods system. The franc, the lira and other

European currencies in the system were essentially fixed in relation to the mark, which floated against the dollar, the yen and other currencies outside the system.

EMS worked remarkably well throughout most of the 1980s, in spite of major shocks to the European economy. The group of leading European economists advising the European Commission on Europe's macroeconomic problems and prospects at that time included Olivier Blanchard, Jacques Drèze and Mario Monti. The group was led by one of the most talented political economists of our time, Rudiger Dornbusch, who died this summer at the age of 60. His death is a great loss to us all.

EMS became unsustainable in the late 1980s after the full liberalization of capital movements within the Community. As many economists soon realized, Europe could not have stable exchange rates, free capital movements and independent monetary policies all at the same time. The post-Bretton Woods period showed that Europe needed stable exchange rates. Given the already close integration of European markets in goods and services, large exchange-rate fluctuations were simply not acceptable. Therefore maintaining free capital movements called for a common monetary policy. Put very simply, the European Single Market required a single European currency.

1.2 Economic and Monetary Union: a policy assignment to ensure stability

Economic and Monetary Union (EMU) was Europe's ultimate response to the quest for stability. A single currency would be an instrument and a tangible sign that EMU members wholly embraced a culture of stability. This is the motivation behind the EMU project as set out in the Maastricht Treaty of 1992. This fundamental choice is crucial to understanding the originality of Europe's currency union. Europe's monetary union is unlike any other example of monetary unification, currently or in the past. There is no instance of a group of countries with a single currency controlled by a single central bank in which each State retains such a large degree of political and fiscal autonomy as in EMU.

Within EMU, monetary policy is centralized and entrusted to an independent central bank – the European Central Bank – with a clear mandate to preserve price stability. The European Central Bank is probably the most independent central bank in the world, enjoying all safeguards against political interference. This policy priority for the European Central Bank does not downplay the role of monetary policy in supporting the broader economic objectives of the EU, such as growth and employment. On the contrary, it recognizes the crucial importance of price stability in achieving those objectives.

Fiscal policy remains a national responsibility, but is subject to centralized EU constraints. Fiscal policy is conducted in a manner that takes account of the spillovers of national fiscal policies in an increasingly integrated economy and is consistent with the monetary policy objective of maintaining price stability. This is the motivation behind the Stability and Growth Pact. The Pact was adopted by EU countries in 1997, five years after the Treaty of Maastricht. It requires Member States to adhere to strict fiscal discipline while allowing them to respond to cyclical developments in their national economies.

The objective is to achieve a progressive reduction of government indebtedness through the maintenance of budget balance or surplus in the medium term. Budget deficits should not rise above 3 per cent of GDP. This macroeconomic framework is supported by structural reforms. Their goal is to improve the way the markets – all markets – function, thus enhancing flexibility in the euro-area economy, and ultimately increasing its potential growth and reducing structural unemployment. Though there is close policy co-ordination, responsibility for structural reforms remains with national governments. This process of structural reform goes under the name of the Lisbon process, because it was agreed by the Heads of States in this beautiful city in the Spring of the year 2000. Since then, the annual Spring meeting of the Heads of States focuses on assessing progress and the need for action with respect to structural reforms.

1.3 The claim that 'EMU is not an optimal currency area, so it cannot work'

This construction was bound to arouse criticism amongst some politicians and academics. Today, before this audience of distinguished economists and scholars, let me try to recapitulate them.

The most common criticisms revolved around the diversity of the EU countries, which exposed them to asymmetric shocks, and the lack of instruments to respond to such shocks.

The first claim was that wage flexibility was considered insufficient to accommodate shocks. Since – unlike the situation in the United States – there is virtually no labour mobility between EU countries, when a negative shock occurs, the result, it was claimed, would be a rise in unemployment.

The second claim was that without a sizeable central budget – as in all federal countries – and the deficit ceiling of 3 per cent of GDP, fiscal policy at national level would be stifled. Also, attempts to reduce budget deficits would create a recession. In essence, the criticism of EMU was that European countries were abandoning a policy instrument – national monetary independence – without replacing it with other tools, leaving countries exposed in times of crisis. To use a concept you will all recognize, sceptics concluded that the EU is not an optimal currency area and thus a single currency could not work.

The third claim argued that European countries had different social preferences which cannot be squared with a 'one size fits all' monetary policy and a single currency. Labour market rigidities, a too-small central budget and too-heterogeneous preferences were seen by many as an unlikely mix for the European and Monetary Union to work. Some – I remember a famous article by Martin Feldstein – even predicted escalating tensions and an early collapse of the new monetary regime.

1.4 Almost four years into the EMU: a success

While many academic economists were sceptical, it is worth noting that Robert Mundell, the father of the Optimal Currency Area theory, became one of the staunchest supporters of Europe's monetary union. What can we say now, almost four years into the new regime and nine months since euro notes and coins started to circulate in the twelve countries of the euro area? While the jury is still out on a number of issues, one can safely conclude that the EMU has succeeded in meeting the challenges it faced in the early years. I have no doubt that the EMU is a success and has already yielded results.

The euro area has already weathered a number of external shocks. The last three years have been a turbulent period. We had the Asian and the international financial crises in 1997–99, the oil price hike in 2000, the bursting of the information-technology bubble and the global slowdown in 2001 and 2002. Yet the EMU has proved it is able to withstand the consequences of these shocks. Monetary and fiscal policies have provided a broadly adequate response. This situation has greatly benefited from the stability *within* the euro area, which stemmed from the adoption of the single currency. Imagine how Europe would have fared in reaction to such events at the beginning of this decade had the euro not existed. Just remember the currency crises that beset Europe in the early 1990s! On this basis alone, EMU can be judged as an effective EU response to the challenges of globalization.

The 'stability culture' that has long been a hallmark of the German economy now extends across the euro area as a whole. The way in which the EMU functions will increasingly benefit from this. If one were to examine the economic history of European countries over the last forty years, one would see that most asymmetric shocks were actually due to policy mistakes. The stability-oriented macroeconomic framework of the EMU is set to reduce the risk of policy-induced shocks. The prevalence of this stability culture is confirmed when some relevant economic indicators are considered.

At the beginning of the 1990s, the twelve euro-area Member States had an average inflation rate of almost 5 per cent. Today their inflation rates have converged to an average of less than 2 per cent. After an extended period of devaluation *vis-à-vis* the US dollar, the euro exchange rate has also regained strength and I am confident this will be confirmed in the months ahead.

What about fiscal policy, currently a burning issue in Europe? The average budget deficit of the euro-area member states has declined from an historical high of 5.5 per cent in 1993 to less than 2 per cent of GDP. Spectacular turnarounds in fiscal performance have occurred in some countries. Between 1993 and 2000 Italy and Greece managed to reduce their budget deficits by

7 and 10 percentage points of GDP respectively. True, budget deficits are rising again today, partially as a result of the economic slowdown. But from an historical perspective, deficits remain low and several countries are actually comfortably in surplus. Peer pressure inflicts a political cost should countries miss their targets. And no country – as sceptics predicted in the run-up to EMU – has gone back to the old habits of fiscal profligacy.

Clearly, budgetary retrenchment will have to resume. A special effort is required in Germany, France, Italy and Portugal, the latter being the first country to exceed the deficit ceiling of 3 per cent of GDP in 2001. I believe the Stability and Growth Pact has served the EMU well. And if intelligently applied, it does not prevent countries from using fiscal policy for cyclical stabilization. On the contrary, it is precisely by ensuring sound public finances in good times that fiscal policy can have enough room for manoeuvre when times get worse. The past experience of countries with high deficits and a high public debt is telling. These countries had much less room for manoeuvre than countries with sound public finances and were forced to cut spending and raise taxes during recessions.

Progress is also being achieved in the area of market integration and structural reforms. Following the introduction of the euro, financial markets were bound to be the first to adapt. Well-operating financial markets are important if the EMU is to function smoothly: they allow portfolios to be diversified and risks to be spread, and as such, they contribute to reducing exposure to asymmetric shocks. The euro has spurred closer integration in the EU financial system: markets have generally become more homogeneous, new and innovative products and techniques have been developed and consolidation among financial intermediaries and exchanges has greatly intensified.

Let me give three examples. First, the unsecured money market is completely integrated in the euro area. Secondly, the euro corporate bond market has grown very rapidly, albeit from a small base: gross issues by euro area corporations have increased from €27 billion to €97 billion between 1998 and 2001, almost a fourfold increase! Thirdly, the trading infrastructure is consolidating rapidly. Three major poles have emerged for equity trading: London, Frankfurt and Euronext (which includes Paris, Brussels, Amsterdam and Lisbon).

Clearly, there are still many obstacles – regulatory, legal and technical – that need to be removed to complete the EU internal financial market. Implementation of the Financial Services Action Plan – a package of 42 policy initiatives aimed at improving the functioning of the EU financial system by 2005 – is the keystone of the EU strategy.

Labour markets are being reformed. A simple way to assess progress is to look at the employment trend since the beginning of the EMU. The acceleration in economic activity during the first two years had a beneficial impact on employment creation. But interestingly, job creation held up reasonably well even during the downswing. In the first three years of the EMU, some

6 million jobs were created in the euro area versus 3.5 million in the United States. Thus GDP growth has translated into higher employment growth. The explanations for this job-rich growth lie in structural changes in the labour market that have led to a higher share of part-time jobs and temporary contracts in total employment. A protracted period of wage moderation has reversed the trend of replacing labour with capital that was detrimental to employment in the early 1990s.

Nevertheless, a lot still remains to be done. Unemployment has declined from over 11 per cent in 1997, but at some 8 per cent it remains unacceptably high. On the supply side the participation rate, in particular of women, has increased, but it is still very low compared to the best performers in the EU – the Nordic countries and the United Kingdom – and the United States.

The plan for a co-ordinated strategy of structural reforms, agreed by the EU leaders here in Lisbon two years ago, is providing further impetus for the reform effort. It is a plan that, building on the stability achieved in the past few years, aims to promote better functioning markets and increase growth potential while maintaining or even strengthening the equity foundations of the European Social Model.

1.5 An international role for the euro

The creation of the euro was bound to have important repercussions not only within Europe but also internationally. Since its inception on 1 January 1999, the euro has established itself as the second most important currency after the US dollar on the world financial markets. There are three main factors that support the use of the euro as a major international currency. The first is the size of the euro-area economy. The euro area accounts for about 16 per cent of world GDP and 19 per cent of world trade, only slightly behind that of the United States. The second factor that makes the euro attractive as an international currency is its stability. The euro's stability reflects the area's sound economic fundamentals and the stability-oriented economic policy framework of Europe's monetary union. The third factor is the ongoing integration of Europe's financial markets into a broad, deep and liquid pan-European financial market. Achieving this will greatly enhance the role of the euro in international lending and borrowing activity.

Let me briefly describe the achievements of the euro in its international use by the private and official sectors. As far as the private sector is concerned, the issuing of bonds, notes and international money-market instruments is a good indication of the standing of the euro in comparison to other currencies. Following the introduction of the euro, there was a huge surge in euro-denominated bond and note issues. In 1997, bonds and notes denominated in the legacy currencies of the euro accounted for barely 22 per cent of world issues, compared to 47 per cent for dollar-denominated bonds and notes. In 2001, the dollar was still the main currency of denomination for bonds and notes, with a market share of 47 per cent, but the euro's share had increased to 36 per cent.

An even more spectacular development took place on the money market. In 1997, money-market instruments denominated in the euro's predecessor currencies accounted for scarcely 17 per cent of world issues, compared to 58 per cent for dollar-denominated instruments. By 2001, the gap between the euro and the dollar had become relatively small: the share of issues in dollars had fallen to 42 per cent while the share of euro issues had climbed to 33 per cent.

Overall, therefore, euro-denominated debt issuance has increased enormously over a very short span of time.

Turning to the official sector, the euro is already widely used as an anchor or reference currency in the exchange regimes of non-EU countries. Over 50 countries operate managed exchange-rate arrangements that include the euro as a reference, either in isolation or in conjunction with other reserve currencies. The types of arrangements adopted by third countries range from currency boards to managed floats. These countries are located mainly in Europe and Africa. The main reason why these countries have adopted the euro as a reference currency is, obviously, their extensive trade and financial links to the euro area.

As a reserve currency, the euro accounted for 13 per cent of official reserves at the beginning of 2002. Admittedly it still played a much smaller role than the US dollar, whose share amounted to 66 per cent. The European Central Bank itself, by holding large amounts of US dollars, contributes to the prevailing role of the US currency as an official reserve currency. In the course of 2002, however, central banks in major Asian economies that hold large reserves seem to have raised their euro holdings. For instance, it was reported that Taiwan has increased its euro holdings to about 35 per cent of total reserves, up from 20 per cent. It is also estimated that a third of Singapore's US$ 80 billion reserves are held in euros. Meanwhile, it is generally assumed that some 10 to 15 per cent of the Bank of Japan's foreign currency reserves – the world's largest at around US$450 billion at the end of June – are held in euros. China is also reported to be making some adjustments to its foreign reserves holdings in favour of the euro.

In a short time the euro has gained quite a remarkable international status. Unfortunately, the euro's international status has not been accompanied by a sufficient role for Europe in the international monetary and financial system. I share the view of those who say 'It is time for the euro to grow up and play its proper role in the international monetary and financial system.'

So far, progress towards adequate external representation of the euro area and a single European voice in international forums has been hampered by several factors, including a lack of will on the part of EU governments. Soon, I hope, our countries will realize the need for a single European 'political voice' in the area of international money and finance, as has long been the case, and with great success, in the area of international trade policy.

2 Enlargement

Enlargement will be a decisive step in the process of political and economic convergence between eastern and western Europe that started in the early 1990s. As much as for the road towards the euro, the road towards enlargement has been a long and not always easy one.

2.1 The preparation for enlargement

A decade ago, just after the collapse of Communism, the countries of central and eastern Europe and the Baltic States embarked on the far-reaching transition from a command to a market economy. They started to reorient their economies towards the West and they made clear their desire to join the European Union. The European Union welcomed and supported the changes politically and swiftly put in place a framework to facilitate the transition to the market economy and membership of the Union. This involved two steps: the EU negotiated the progressive establishment of a **free-trade area** with these countries, and in December 1993 the EU heads of State and government spelt out the political and economic **criteria for membership**. I consider the consequences of these two decisions in turn.

2.1.1 The establishment of a free-trade area

The establishment of a **free-trade area** allowed integration between the current EU members and the candidate countries to take place at a fast pace during the 1990s. Let me quote a few figures that might be familiar to most of you. About 70 per cent of the candidate countries' exports goes to the EU, where it accounts for only about 10 per cent of the EU's total imports. Similarly, only about 12 per cent of EU exports goes to the candidate countries, but this amounts to about 63 per cent of their imports. This means that the EU is by far the most important trade partner for the candidate countries while the candidate countries are the second largest market for the EU.

The structure of trade has revealed strong complementarity. The EU is specialized in high-technology products while the candidate countries have moved from resource-intensive products and sectors to labour-intensive ones.

Since the mid-1990s, foreign direct investment in the candidate countries has risen steeply. Rapid increase of FDI into the candidate countries took place when private investors could expect that their capital would be placed in a tried and trusted environment. By the year 2000, annual flows (see Figure 2.1) had reached remarkable levels, sometimes close to 10 per cent of GDP (much higher than the level observed during the previous accession of Spain, Portugal and Greece). Between 1994 and 2000, aggregate investment flows from the EU to the candidate countries more than doubled (see Figure 2.2). FDI concentrated on key manufacturing sectors and services and on the financial sector. This process is bound to speed up the improvement

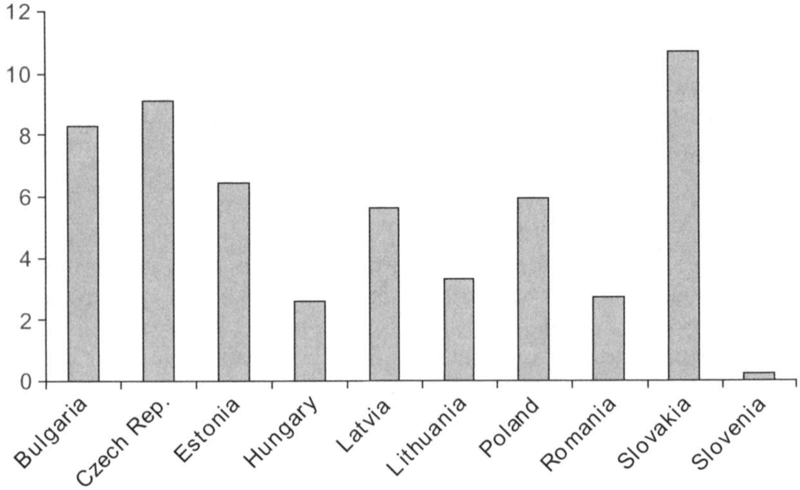

Figure 2.1 Foreign direct investment flows in the year 2000 (*Percentages of GDP*)

Source: European Bank for Reconstruction and Development.

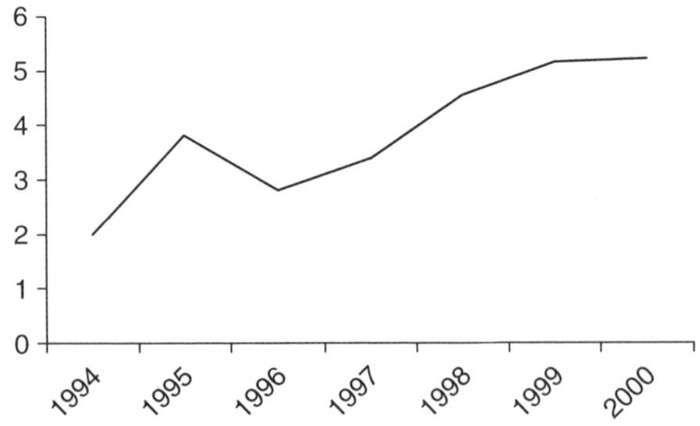

Figure 2.2 Foreign direct investment in EU candidate countries (*Percentages of GDP*)

Source: European Commission, New Cronos database.

of financial services, a key area for fostering growth. At the same time, such financial integration should increase financial stability.

FDI is usually accompanied in the country originating the FDI by fears of loss of production capacity and jobs. When FDI targets candidate countries it tends only to augment these fears because the prospect of Enlargement facilitates a market-induced harmonization of the production functions and therefore lowers most of the obstacles to deepen industrial relations.

However, when one looks at what really happened in the integration between current EU and candidate countries, one realizes that most fears were and are actually misplaced because FDI in candidate countries proved to be much more beneficial to the EU countries than FDI elsewhere.

Indeed, FDI in candidate countries was transformed over the last ten years in a significant way. Initially, it was a traditional financial commitment to exploit a lower cost of labour to produce low-end goods. As soon as FDI was followed by a transfer of technology, as soon as quality standards diffused, a very interesting process of industrial integration between the production in the current EU countries and in the candidate countries emerged. The low cost of labour is now exploited to produce labour-intensive components for high-end goods, which are finally assembled in the current EU and sold globally.

Far from undermining the main EU operations, FDI in the central and eastern European plants have thus provided EU manufacturers with a low-cost supply base and made an important contribution to their profits and competitiveness. At the same time, through the establishment of a large network of suppliers tied into their quality-control systems, FDI ensured that the entire modernization process reaches deep into the eastern and central European economies.

I draw a simple lesson from this: investment in the candidate countries does not harm EU firms (as many suggest). On the contrary, it helps maintain EU firms' competitiveness and jobs.

2.1.2 The political and economic criteria for membership

The **political and economic criteria for membership** set by the EU heads of State and government in 1993 can be summarized in four sets of criteria. The political criteria for membership required stability of institutions guaranteeing democracy, the rule of law, human rights and respect and protection of minorities. The economic criteria required the existence of a functioning market economy and the ability to cope with the competitive pressures and the market forces within the Union. The technical criteria required the capacity to adopt the so-called *acquis communautaire* (the entire EU body of law). Finally, there was also a fourth criterion to be respected by the current EU countries: Member States, by the time of Enlargement, should have made the necessary institutional transformation to allow the enlarged EU to work. The Nice Treaty, the Convention and the ICG starting in October 2003 are meant to respond to this last criterion.

Despite these criteria being judged in many quarters as excessively 'severe', between 1994 and 1995 all the countries concerned applied officially to join the EU. The EU accepted them as 'candidate countries' committed to undertake the necessary transformation in order to meet the criteria for membership and then become members. The process of political and economic transformation undertaken by the candidate countries with a view to joining the EU required a considerable effort from their citizens. Nevertheless I am convinced that linking this transformation to membership has spared candidate countries an enormous degree of internal conflict. Furthermore, to help the candidate countries to attain both the political and the economic objectives, through its common budget the European Union has provided and is still providing technical and financial support of around €3 billion per annum.

Great progress has already been achieved; more is still required between now and the date of accession and even more will be needed after they become members. In this perspective, the EU's imminent enlargement must be seen as fundamental in the lengthy process of political and economic integration encompassing the current EU members and the candidate countries.

2.2 The opportunity and the challenge of enlargement

In economic terms, enlargement amounts to integrating two areas with a very large gap in income and productivity: the candidate countries represent 28 per cent of the population of the present 15 Member States but only 5 per cent of their GDP. As the proverbial two-handed economist, I cannot refrain from saying that enlargement is both an unprecedented economic **opportunity** and a huge **challenge**.

On the one hand, the **opportunity** lies in the establishment of a large economic space encompassing around 500 million consumers. A space with great economic diversity that holds out the hope of a truly efficient pan-European industrial organization. Both the current and the future member countries have the human and physical resources to make the best out of the new opportunities that enlargement offers. I am confident that enlargement will produce substantial economic gains throughout Europe: these gains derive both from the better allocation of resources and from the boost to investment and productivity that will follow enlargement.

On the other hand, the **challenge** lies in managing a pan-European Single Market with 25 or more countries. Part of the challenge will derive from the increased economic diversity within the European Union. To function properly, the Single Market requires a set of common rules and policies in a number of areas. The candidate countries have already made much progress in adopting the EU rules. But the real challenge will come when the rules have to be applied in full, after membership.

Enlargement will see the intensification of the process – which is already well advanced – of economic convergence and integration that started at the beginning of the 1990s. Convergence and integration processes are not zero-sum games where one gains what the other loses. They are positive-sum games leading to a win–win outcome.

2.3 Enlargement and EU public investment

In order to foster convergence, new members will be aided by the EU by means of a series of financial instruments funded by its common budget. The provision of public capital to build, say, infrastructure and training facilities will increase the return on private investment, thus making FDI into the new member countries all the more attractive. Investment from the EU budget encourages the high inflow of private investment so as to foster growth. How big does this public investment need to be? As I said, the candidate countries' GDP is only 5 per cent of the GDP in the EU-15. This implies that a small effort by the present EU members will amount to a large hand-up for the new members.

In January 2002 the Commission presented a proposal for the first few years after enlargement. This proposal contemplates transfers of about €16 billion to the new members, which is equivalent to around 0.15 per cent of the EU's GDP and will result in 3 per cent of the GDP of the new members. It seems to me an effort worth making! Let me remind you that this effort of 0.15 per cent of our GDP accounts for about 1/6 (one sixth!) of what Member States spend annually on 'State subsidies to firms'. And when we talk about 'State subsidies' we are not always talking about investing in the future!

2.4 The enlargement: macroeconomic effects and impact on growth

It is interesting to know to what extent the growth of trade, private and public capital flows due to the quantum leap of enlargement will translate into higher real growth in both new and current EU member countries.

To answer this question, for a long time the Commission departments have been using a 'modified Solow model of growth accounting', for which we are all indebted to our host Robert! Different scenarios have been looked at with this 'modified Solow model'. The scenarios represent increasing degrees of structural reform undertaken.

Broadly speaking, all scenarios show that new members will draw the largest benefits, in terms of the boost to growth following accession. As expected these benefits will stem not only from financial transfers from the EU budget, but also and primarily from foreign direct investment, from the standard gains in total factor productivity and from integration into the Single Market.

Depending on the degree of structural reform undertaken, enlargement-induced additional growth for the new members ranges from 1.4 to 2.7 per cent (over a baseline scenario of 3 per cent growth). This relatively sizeable impact is also supported by the latent growth potential in the new members, due to the still relatively high proportion of total employment in low productivity sectors. As for the impact on the current EU-15, an increase in growth of the EU's second trade partner will translate into a positive impact for the EU itself. But to avoid disappointment, we must once again bear in mind the new members' relative economic weight as compared with the current EU. Since the new members will represent only 5 per cent of the EU's GDP and 12 per cent of EU exports, the impact of their growth on the EU as a whole is likely to be small (of the order of less than one percentage point cumulatively over the period).

However, a small aggregate figure for EU-15 masks large effects in some regions and countries. In particular Germany, Austria and Italy, the countries with the closest and strongest links with the new members, are set to see their growth boosted by around 0.5 per cent per annum. Let us not forget that, thanks to European integration and the Single Market, a boost in growth in Germany and Austria due to enlargement implies a benefit for Portugal and Spain also.

The trickle-down effect of benefits (the so-called 'indirect effect' or 'second-order effect') on all the EU countries is both a huge advantage of the internal market and a huge strength for our European economies. I would like to stress that this is also one of the strongest 'social shock-absorbers' on the market. Europe has the tools and the 'infrastructure' to spread economic growth to all regions and to reduce inter-regional differences between levels of development. Recent studies, some of which are also presented at this Congress, show that the indirect effects of enlargement in many regions and countries might be as sizeable as the direct effect.

To sum up, the impact on growth will be definitely greater in the new members than in the current EU, but those European regions and countries with stronger trading links with the new members will also see a boost in growth. In the medium term, the Single Market will allow the benefits to spread to the other EU countries and regions.

I am confident that, thanks to the Economic and Monetary Union, to enlargement and the necessary institutional reforms, Europe will be able to make a decisive contribution, both politically and economically, to safety, stability and prosperity throughout the world.

3

One 'Monetary Giant' with Many 'Fiscal Dwarfs': The Efficiency of Macroeconomic Stabilization Policies in the European Monetary Union*

Roberto Tamborini
University of Trento, Italy

1 Introduction

> My own judgement is that, on balance, a European Monetary Union (EMU) would be an economic liability. The gains from reduced transaction costs would be small and might, when looked at from the global point of view, be negative. At the same time, EMU would increase cyclical instability, raising the cyclical unemployment rate (Feldstein, 1997).

Feldstein's famous criticism of the EMU endeavour pointed out one of the key problems facing the new monetary institution: macroeconomic stabilization. The debate on this issue is still lively, for economists disagree on its theoretical or practical relevance while the historical evidence is too short-lived to help discriminate among different predictions. Nonetheless, downgrading the stabilization issue may turn out to be a mistake with implications stretching well beyond welfare considerations within each member country.

It is clear that the EMU has not been conceived and pursued with great determination for its own sake. Its founders viewed it as the first building block in a system of truly federal institutions in Europe. As is well known, European citizens have historically ranked protection against adverse conditions high on their political demand schedule. Hence phases of recession

* This chapter draws on a report prepared for the Italian Economic Society jointly with Francesco Farina, 'Macroeconomic stabilization policies in Europe under the new regime of monetary union', Società Italiana degli Economisti, XLI Riunione Scientifica Annuale, Cagliari, Italy, October 2000. I benefited from comments by the participants at the Italian Economic Society's meeting, and by Luisa Lambertini and Patrizio Tirelli in a seminar at the State University of Milan 'Bicocca, February 2001. I remain fully responsible for this chapter. Financial support by the University of Trento is gratefully acknowledged.

or inflation longer and wider than in the past may undermine the credibility of the promise of the 'EMU dividend', and may impair the political will to go ahead with deepening the European Union. At the same time, strong incentives to deviate from 'fiscal and monetary discipline' may build up, together with political pressures on the European Central Bank (ECB), causing a paradoxical self-defeat of the entire defensive system erected by the Maastricht Treaty.

As regards theory, according to the traditional optimal currency areas approach, the stabilization problem arises in relation to the peculiar institutional setup of the EMU. Member countries have relinquished independent monetary policy and exchange-rate determination in favour of a single monetary authority (MA), while their national fiscal authorities (FAs) have (self-)restrained domestic fiscal policy within the limits imposed by the Stability and Growth Pact (SGP). Hence, it is argued that two major obstacles may hinder stabilization policy: first, member countries may find themselves short of instruments in the event of individual shocks; second, national FAs may find it costly or impossible to co-ordinate their fiscal policies were it beneficial to do so *vis-à-vis* the policy stance of the MA. These concerns are by no means universally shared, however, since a substantial number of economists are ready to subscribe to the view that a 'monetary giant' surrounded by 'fiscal dwarfs' is a better guarantee of the independence of the central bank, of monetary and financial stability, of restricted growth of the public sector and of fiscal discipline. Therefore, it is argued, the so-called 'credibility *vs.* flexibility trade-off', or better a long-run stability *vs.* short-run stabilization trade-off, is either non-existent or is such that the benefits of credibility for non-inflationary long-run growth outweigh the costs of restrained flexibility in the short-run stabilization task.[1] This view favouring the present institutional arrangement is often supplemented by the idea, also put forward in some European Commission documents (e.g. Buti and Sapir, 1998), that the EMU regime allows for a simple and straightforward assignment rule between centralized monetary policy, aimed at stabilizing union-wide shocks, and national fiscal policies, aimed at stabilizing their own domestic shocks (see also Dixit and Lambertini, 2001).

The present state of assessment of economic policy and institution design in the EMU also reflects a line of research that has mostly focused on the assumption that the MA and the FAs may have conflicting preferences and/or targets in the inflation-employment dilemma. In particular, the FAs are typically portrayed as being less (or not) inflation-averse and more (or totally) unemployment-averse relative to the MA, and/or as having an output (employment) target greater than the equilibrium potential output (employment). Assuming that policy makers pursue their goals by means of aggregate demand instruments, the policy game may result in macroeconomic equilibria that are sub-optimal for the economy. Therefore, the EMU institutional design has almost exclusively been assessed in its capacity to prevent the distortions that may be created by 'undisciplined' policy makers.[2] Only recently has research started investigating how the EMU might perform under the stabilization profile once all policy makers have indeed been 'disciplined': examples are the papers by De Grauwe (2000), Dixit and Lambertini (2001), Buti, Roeger and Veld (2001). The question is important because hopefully the EMU is an enduring institution and in the long run actors' preferences may evolve under the effect of a given set of rules. If it is true that an insititution such as the SGP supports macroeconomic equilibria that are Pareto superior to those that would emerge under undisciplined behaviours by policy makers, one may expect that in the long run everyone will recognize the superiority of the disciplined behaviours in such a way that the undisciplined ones are wiped out from the system. Will that same institution then still ensure optimal macroeconomic equilibria?[3]

My purpose here is to contribute to this new point of view on economic policy in the EMU by examining whether, in the presence of disciplined policy makers, the co-existence of one single MA with many independent FAs and the simple rule assigning aggregate stabilization to the MA and domestic stabilization to the FAs (under the SGP constraint) can indeed ensure optimal stabilization for every member country. My analysis of the stabilization problem is organized as follows.

Section 2 presents a macroeconomic model of the EMU characterized as a two-country 'inter-regional' monetary system: that is, one with a single central bank but two independent FAs. Economies are hit by random shocks producing real and nominal fluctuations around potential output with a given rate of structural unemployment. With regard to the treatment of shocks, following recent works by De Grauwe (2000), Cooper and Kempf (2000), Dixit (2001) and Dixit and Lambertini (2001), the model goes beyond the traditional dichotomy between symmetric shocks (uniform for all countries) and asymmetric shocks (in one single country) and uses the degree of correlation of shocks across countries as the discriminating parameter. Only demand-side shocks are considered: in fact, these shocks rule out any policy dilemma and allow examination of whether the EMU institutional framework enables solution of the stabilization problem primarily at its pure 'technical' level (in a sense that is clarified below).[4] Consistently with this aim, the model displays a richer structure than is usually found in models focused on policy dilemmas and preferences of policy-makers. This feature turns out to be valuable when analysis is conducted of the mechanisms that transmit shocks and policy measures across EMU members – the so-called 'spillover effects' that play a major role in the debate on the pros and cons of the present insitutional framework, but are often poorly modelled.

Section 3 examines the stabilization problem in the EMU amid centralized monetary policy and decentralized fiscal policies in relation to different degrees of correlation of shocks across countries. As explained above, I assume that all policy makers are disciplined according to the rules established by the EMU treaties and pacts. This may be called a *pure stabilization regime*, where the central MA and the national FAs (i) share the same model of the economy and the same targets of inflation and potential output, (ii) wish to minimize deviations from target values of inflation and output with no 'inflation bias' in their objective functions (i.e., they abstain from using macroeconomic policies intended to manipulate the long-run equilibrium levels of inflation, output and unemployment). Can the EMU members be sufficiently sheltered against macroeconomic fluctuations in this ideal regime? As we see below, having disciplined policy-makers does not exhaust the problem of policy design, for the further problem of *the efficient choice and assignment of stabilization instruments* has still to be addressed. To this end, it is necessary to revive the traditional approach to the normative analysis of economic policy – associated with Tinbergen and Meade – centred on the principle of the *efficiency* of policy instruments. As is well known, in this approach the key to efficiency is the criterion of *optimal assignment* – which has inexplicably gone astray in the current debate on the EMU. It consists of *two* requirements: (i) a number of instruments equal to the number of objectives, *and* (ii) each instrument assigned to an objective in such a way that the cost-effect balance in the use of the instrument is optimal.

In the light of this analysis, the popular idea of assigning common shocks to centralized monetary policy and domestic shocks to decentralized fiscal policies turns out to be overly simplistic. It will be seen that there is indeed a matter of choice of the optimal stabilizer, which depends on the interplay between (i) the nature and extent of the spillover effects, and (ii) the degree of correlation of shocks across countries. There may be conditions such that centralized monetary policy is not the most efficient instrument even for symmetric shocks; and other conditions may exist such that national FAs are forced to stabilize asymmetric shocks when fiscal policy is not the most efficient instrument. Inefficiency typically implies 'excessive' use of the instrument. Thus, paradoxically, unduly large budget swings may emerge as a by-product of an institutional design aimed at minimizing fiscal activism. The consequences of this result are also discussed in consideration of the role of the SGP.

Section 4 summarizes the chapter and puts forward its main conclusions.

2 A macroeconomic model of the European Monetary Union

In order to examine the EMU in its stabilization capacity, we shall proceed on the basis of a theoretical approach whose main ingredients can be summarized as follows. (i) The real variables of the economy (output and employment) fluctuate in response to demand disturbances that for the sake of simplicity are treated as exogenous random shocks. (ii) Fluctuations take place around a long-period level of domestic output ('potential output') corresponding to full use of the factors net of any 'structural unemployment'. (iii) The economic system responds to shocks with variations in quantities, and not only in prices, because of imperfections in the organization of the labour market. (iv) Neither fiscal nor monetary interventions on aggregate demand are able to alter the level of potential output and the structural rate of unemployment permanently, but they can minimize fluctuations and their real costs.

Characteristic EMU features are also added, as explained in the subsequent paragraphs of the section.[5]

2.1 The model

The model depicts the EMU as an open system consisting of two countries with the following characteristics:

- production of a single good, either consumed or exported, which differs in each of the two countries; the good may be exported intra-EMU or extra-EMU;
- capital mobility;
- absence of labour mobility;
- structural symmetry;
- one national FA for each country;
- one MA for the EMU.

The rest of the world (ROW) is not specified except for the following characteristics in relation to the EMU:

- mobility of commodities and capital;
- absence of labour mobility;
- free floating currency regime.

2.1.1 Definitions

All the variables are defined in logarithms (unless stated otherwise) and they represent *stochastic deviations* from long-period equilibrium values in the EMU.[6] All shocks are i.i.d. with zero mean. For the reader's convenience the full list of variables is reported below:

Countries ($i = 1, 2$)

π_i change in the price level (temporary inflation)
y_i change in aggregate demand
g_i cyclical government budget
δ_i demand shock
z_i change in output
m_i^d change in money demand
m_i change in the money stock
λ_i money demand shock
μ_i money supply shock
q_i change in the terms of trade (effective real exchange rate)

EMU:

r	change in the interest rate
π, π^e	inflation and expected inflation
z	change in output
m	change in money supply
x, x^e	change, and expected change, in the euro exchange rate (euros per 1 unit of foreign currency)

ROW:

r_w	change in the interest rate
π_w, π_w^e	inflation and expected inflation

2.1.2 The EMU countries

The following equations ($i = 1, 2, j \neq i$) are given for each EMU country.

Aggregate demand

$$y_i = -y_q q_i + y_z z_j - y_r(r - \pi^e) - g_i + \delta_i \tag{2.1}$$

which depends on (changes in)

- intra-EMU and extra-EMU foreign trade in function of the domestic terms of trade, $y_q q_i$, of the other EMU country's output, $y_z z_j$, and of world demand shocks included in δ_i
- consumption and investment dependent on the domestic real rate of interest, $y_r(r - \pi^e)$
- government non-structural budget, g_i
- exogenous shocks δ_i

Terms of trade (effective real exchange rate)

$$q_i = \alpha(\pi_i - \pi_j) + (1 - \alpha)(\pi_i - (x + \pi_w)) \tag{2.2}$$

which is calculated as the weighted average of the intra-EMU terms of trade, $\pi_i - \pi_j$, and the extra-EMU terms of trade, $\pi_i - (x + \pi_w)$, where α is the weight of intra-EMU trade.

Aggregate supply

$$z_i = z_\pi(\pi_i - \pi e) \tag{2.3}$$

which reflects the labour market regime. A given amount of 'structural unemployment' (e.g. NAIRU) is assumed, together with a degree of nominal wage stickiness in the case of unexpected changes in the inflation rate, $z_\pi > 0$. With no loss of generality, it is convenient to set $z_\pi = 1$. Consequently, output and employment increase (decrease) with respect to the long-run equilibrium (potential output) in the presence of unexpected domestic inflation (deflation).[7]

Money demand

$$m_i^d = \pi_i + m_z z_i - m_r r + \lambda_i \tag{2.4}$$

which depends on (changes in)

- domestic price level, π_i
- output, $m_z z_i$
- rate of interest on bonds, $m_r r$
- exogenous shocks, λ_i

Domestic money stock

$$m_i = -y_q\alpha(\pi_i - \pi_j) + y_z(z_j - z_i) + \mu_i \tag{2.5}$$

In the absence of an independent MA, each individual country has only two channels of money creation: its intra-EMU balance of payments,[8] which redistributes a given EMU money stock, and the bank channel (i.e. the domestic banks' borrowing from the ECB) which has a counterpart in the EMU money stock.[9] Overall, the determinants of m_i are:

- intra-EMU foreign trade, which depends on the intra-EMU terms of trade, $y_q\alpha(\pi_i - \pi_j)$ (see equation (2.2) above) and on the other country's output, $y_z z_j$, net of the imports induced by domestic activity, $y_z z_i$;
- exogenous shocks including the domestic banks' borrowing from the ECB, μ_i.

Equilibrium of the output market

$$y_i = z_i \tag{2.6}$$

Equilibrium of the domestic money market

$$m_i^d = m_i \tag{2.7}$$

2.1.3 *The Union*

The following conditions must hold for the EMU as a whole.

Equilibrium of the money market:

$$(\Sigma m_i^d - m) + (\Sigma\lambda_i - \Sigma(-g_i)) = 0 \tag{2.8}$$

Monetary equilibrium is expressed in relation to financial general equilibrium (Walras law), where the demand for bonds is represented as a shock to the domestic demand for money of each country *vis-à-vis* the supply of bonds, which is equal to aggregate fiscal deficits.[10] Given the bond market equilibrium, equilibrium of the money market requires[11]

$$\Sigma m_i^d = m \tag{2.9}$$

$$2\pi + m_z z - 2m_r r = m + \Sigma g_i$$

Uncovered real interest parity

$$x = r_w - r + x^e \tag{2.10}$$

The euro exchange rate must be constantly aligned to uncovered interest parity with respect to the ROW. There is therefore appreciation $x < 0$ (depreciation, $x > 0$) if, *ceteris paribus*,

- the world interest rate decreases (increases), $r_w \lessgtr 0$;
- the EMU interest rate increases (decreases), $r \gtrless 0$;
- the euro is expected to appreciate (depreciate), $x^e \lessgtr 0$.

Let us assume that exchange rate expectations are driven by the expected inflation differential between EMU and ROW;[12] that is,

$$x^e = \pi^e - \pi^e_w$$

Substituting this relation in the previous one, we obtain the uncovered real interest parity:

$$x = (r_w - \pi^e_w) - (r - \pi^e). \tag{2.11}$$

2.1.4 The policy makers

In order to focus on the stabilization capacity of the EMU, let us assume that all the policy makers, both central and national, pursue *pure stabilization*. This is what Dixit and Lambertini (2001) call 'monetary-fiscal symbiosis': that is to say, (i) all policy makers share the same model of the economy and the same targets of inflation and potential output, (ii) they wish to minimize deviations from target values of inflation and output with no 'inflation bias' in their objective functions (they abstain from using macroeconomic policies intended to manipulate the long-run equilibrium levels of inflation, output and unemployment). Therefore, we can simply assume that the target of each FA is $z_i = 0$, $\pi_i = 0$, and that the target of the ECB is $z = 0$, $\pi = 0$.

2.1.5 A characterization of shocks

Empirical as well as theoretical studies of the EMU pay close attention to the nature, magnitude and correlation of macroeconomic fluctuations across countries. In fact, these features significantly affect the optimum choice of stabilization policies. It is now customary to distinguish between symmetric shocks (which affect all countries to the same extent) and asymmetric shocks (which affect one single country). Yet if fluctuations are modelled as linear stochastic shocks, it seems more accurate to consider the correlation of shocks across countries. In fact, in countries with close interrelations, macroeconomic fluctuations generally arise in distributed form, with *different degrees of intensity*. Recent works by De Grauwe (2000), Cooper and Kempf (2000), Dixit (2001) and Dixit and Lambertini (2001), make use of the correlation coefficient of shocks in the various countries. This permits compact treatment of various hypotheses on the correlation of fluctuations which are more general than the two extreme cases. In particular, this formalization permits treatment of a case that may be of importance in Europe but has not received adequate attention: bilateral shocks due to intra-EMU trade (a shift of demand from one country to another).[13]

Here we consider demand shocks only, for the reasons explained in the Introduction. A related analytical advantage is that, in the presence of demand shocks such that fluctuations in output are positively correlated with those in prices, we need not specify the policy-makers' preferences because stabilization of output and prices are always mutually compatible and no policy dilemma arises.[14]

If $\text{var}(\delta_i)$ is the variance of demand shocks in country i, and $\text{cov}(\delta_i\delta_j)$ is the covariance of shocks in two countries, then

$$\rho_{ji} = \frac{\text{cov}(\delta_i\delta_j)}{\sqrt{\text{var}(\delta_i)\text{var}(\delta_j)}}$$

is the correlation coefficient of the shocks. Therefore, in the case of two countries, we may say that if we observe δ_1, we may expect, up to some random error,

$$\delta_2 = \rho\delta_1 \tag{2.12}$$

We may thus characterize three cases in terms of correlation:

- $\rho = 1$, *symmetric shocks* (e.g. fall in world demand), $\delta_1 = \delta_2 = \delta$
- $\rho = 0$, *unilateral shocks* (e.g. fall in domestic consumption), $\delta_1 \neq 0$, $\delta_2 = 0$
- $\rho = -1$, *bilateral shocks* (e.g. redistribution of intra-EMU trade), $\delta_2 = -\delta_1$

Note that I use the generic term 'asymmetric shocks' for any $\rho < 1$, i.e. shocks that hit all countries but with unequal intensity.

2.2 A first general view

To explore the model's properties, let us begin with the solutions of the endogenous variables (π_i, z_i) for a single country i, with all the other variables taken as given. Assuming rational inflation expectations, which can be shown to be $\pi^e = \text{E}(\pi) = 0$,[15] we obtain:

$$z_i = [-g_i + \alpha(\gamma_q\pi_j + \gamma_z z_j) - \gamma_{rq}r + \pi_i][1 + \gamma_q]^{-1} \tag{2.13}$$

$$\pi_i = z_i \tag{2.14}$$

with

$$r = \pi/m_r + [m_z z - \Sigma g_i - m]/2m_r \tag{2.15}$$

$$x = -r \tag{2.16}$$

$$\gamma_{rq} \equiv \gamma_r + \gamma_q(1 - \alpha)$$

Domestic fluctuations of inflation and output in each country (π_i, z_i) depend on three channels of influence by macroeconomic variables (the signs of the effects of the relevant variables are obvious and do not require particular explanation):

- the *domestic channel* represented by the fiscal component g_i and exogenous shocks, δ_i
- the *trade channel* activated by the other country's inflation and output, π_j, z_j, via intra-EMU trade as measured by the weight α
- the *financial channel* related to the common real interest rate; the real interest rate produces a compound effect on aggregate demand, $y_{rq} \equiv y_r + y_q(1-\alpha)$, where y_r measures the effect on the interest-sensitive domestic demand, and $y_q(1-\alpha)$ measures that on the euro-sensitive foreign demand via the uncovered interest-parity linkage of the euro rate with the real exchange rate.[16]

Therefore, the crucial aspect of the economic system represented by equations (2.13)–(2.15) is the *interdependence between countries* created by the trade and financial channels. The trade channel is the best known and most thoroughly studied form of macroeconomic interdependence among open economies, its prototype being the Keynesian international trade multiplier. Consequently, although trade interdependence is a phenomenon of great importance for the European economies, it is not specific to membership in the EMU – except for the fact that it now hinges on irrevocably fixed exchange rates among member countries. The distinctive feature of the move into an inter-regional monetary regime is exposure to the financial channel of interdependence. The primary reason for this is the creation of a single money market and of a single MA, which centralizes the determination of the interest and exchange rates. The single money market collects the impulses from individual countries and transmits them back in the form of changes in the common interest and exchange rates.[17]

Now let us examine the two countries simultaneously. By means of equations (2.14)–(2.15), and the measure of correlation given by (2.12), taking a shock δ_1 to country 1 as benchmark, we obtain the following reduced-form equations for output gaps and inflation rates:

$$z_1 = \Delta_1 g_1 + \Delta_2 g_2 + \Delta_3 m + (\Delta_4 + \Delta_5 \rho)\delta_1 \tag{2.17}$$

$$\pi_1 = z_1 \tag{2.18}$$

$$\pi_2 = \Delta_2 g_1 + \Delta_1 g_2 + \Delta_3 m + (\Delta_4 \rho + \Delta_5)\delta_1 \tag{2.19}$$

$$\pi_2 = z_2 \tag{2.20}$$

$$z = z_1 + z_2 \tag{2.21}$$

$$\pi = (\pi_1 + \pi_2)/2 \tag{2.22}$$

$\Delta_1?, \Delta_2?, \Delta_3 > 0, \Delta_4 > 0, \Delta_5 > 0$ (these coefficients are not given explicitly since their complete expressions are inessential).

These equations highlight two main issues.

2.2.1 *The diffusion of shocks*

Fluctuations (nominal and real) in each country depend on local shocks as well as on their degree of correlation ρ with concomitant shocks in the other country. Interdependence channels spread local shocks throughout the EMU. The domestic impact of domestic shocks is measured by Δ_4, whereas Δ_5 measures the imported impact of shocks abroad. If a country is hit by a unilateral shock, e.g. country 1 (with $\rho = 0$), the other country is also affected via the various interdependence channels discussed above. In the event of asymmetric shocks ($\rho < 1$), both countries are hit to different extents, and both import some of the shock of the other. Finally, if the shock is symmetric ($\rho = 1$), both countries are hit to the same extent, measured by Δ_4, with full reciprocal 'export' of the shock, measured by Δ_5, so that they eventually undergo the same overall impact given by $\Delta_4 + \Delta_5$. Thus the model captures one of the most important features of interdependent economies, namely that interdependence triggers shock-amplifying mechanisms.

2.2.2 *The anatomy of fiscal spillovers*

Economic activity in each country may also be influenced by domestic as well as foreign budget variations (g_1, g_2) for any given monetary policy choice m by the ECB. The coefficient Δ_3 measures the impact of changes in money supply on each economy and on the EMU inflation rate: it is positive as expected. The coefficients Δ_1 and Δ_2 measure the domestic impact of, respectively, domestic and foreign budget variations – the latter are generally known as 'fiscal spillovers' in EMU jargon. Both fiscal coefficients have ambiguous signs. Hence, we cannot establish a priori whether, say, a fiscal expansion $g_i < 0$ in one country stimulates or depresses economic activity domestically as well as abroad. The internal and external effects of fiscal policies are a crucial issue for stabilization in a currency union.[18] The present model can shed some light on some controversial points.

As explained above, any budgetary variation in one country ($g_i \neq 0$), activates domestic as well as union-wide macroeconomic effects through three channels: the domestic channel (the direct impact of the budget on domestic demand); the trade channel (via the relationship between domestic economic activity and intra-EMU trade); and the financial channel (via the relationship between the budget imbalance, the common interest and euro rates and their feedback onto aggregate demand). The coefficients Δ_1 and Δ_2 reflect the balance of strength among these channels: $\Delta_1 < 0$ means that the domestic channel is stronger than the financial channel, so that budget variations have domestic 'Keynesian' effects; they have 'non-Keynesian' effects in the opposite case. A value $\Delta_2 < 0$ means that the trade channel is stronger than the financial channel, so that budget variations abroad exert a positive fiscal

Table 3.1 Regimes of fiscal effects

$(y_{rq}/m_r) < (y_{rq}/m_r)_2$	$(y_{rq}/m_r)_2 < (y_{rq}/m_r) < (y_{rq}/m_r)_1$	$(y_{rq}/m_r) > (y_{rq}/m_r)_1$
$\Delta_1 < 0, \Delta_2 < 0$ EMU Keynesian effects	$\Delta_1 < 0, \Delta_2 > 0$ SGP hypothesis	$\Delta_1 > 0, \Delta_2 > 0$ EMU non-Keynesian effects

spillover with 'Keynesian' effects domestically; they produce a negative fiscal spillover with 'non-Keynesian' effects in the opposite case.[19]

Inspection of the coefficients Δ_1 and Δ_2 reveals that their sign depends on the relative weight of the parameters y_{rq}, measuring the aggregate-demand effect in each country of changes in the common interest rate, and m_r, determining money-bond substitutability and hence the impact of national budget imbalances on the common interest rate.[20] These two parameters rule the financial channel of interdependence, which is stronger the larger is y_{rq} and the smaller is m_r.

There exist two critical values of the y_{rq}/m_r ratio beyond which Δ_1 and Δ_2 turn out to be positive, i.e. determine non-Keynesian effects of budget variations. The critical value beyond which $\Delta_1 > 0$, say $(y_{rq}/m_r)_1$, is greater than the one beyond which $\Delta_2 > 0$, say $(y_{rq}/m_r)_2$. Note in particular that $(y_{rq}/m_r)_1 > 1$, $(y_{rq}/m_r)_2 < 1$. Consequently, there emerge three different regimes determining the macroeconomic effects, internal and external, of budget variations. They are summarized in Table 3.1.

In the first regime (first column) and in the third, budget variations in one country exert, respectively, Keynesian or non-Keynesian effects both domestically and abroad. The mid-regime combines a Keynesian effect in the originating country with a non-Keynesian one in the other. I call this the 'SGP hypothesis' since it figures prominently among the arguments in favour of binding fiscal rules for national FAs (see e.g. Buiter, Corsetti and Roubini (1993), Eichengreen and Wyplosz (1998), and Artis and Winkler (1999)). On the one hand, the argument runs, each government has an incentive to seize the domestic positive effects of budget deficits. On the other, if the financial effects of fiscal imbalances are large, a net negative fiscal spillover may emerge abroad, with a budget deficit in one country exporting a recession to the others. Hence, unfettered budget policies of individual member countries may hurt other members. Table 3.1 shows that this peculiar SGP hypothesis is possible within a limited range of parameter values.[21] Clearly, in the other regimes the problem underlying the SGP vanishes: in the first regime a budget deficit in one country may also stimulate economic activity in the others, whereas in the third regime no government would ever be tempted to run excessive budget deficits.

The model also points out two factors that may limit the strength of the financial channel of interdependence and hence the extent of negative fiscal spillovers in a currency union. The first concerns the parameter y_{rq} itself.

Since $y_{rq} \equiv y_r + y_q(1-\alpha)$, where $(1-\alpha)$ is the share of flexible-rate extra-EMU trade, y_{rq} is smaller the larger is α, and it is well-known that intra-EMU trade in fact takes a large share of almost all members' international exchanges.

The second factor relates to interest rate determination. As shown by equation (2.15), where the *summation* of g_i's appears, the impact of a single government's borrowing requirement on the interest rate in a currency union is diluted thanks to the increased market dimension. Moreover, completion of financial integration and participation in a single money market may enhance money-bond substitutability, raise the value of m_r and lower that of the y_{rq}/m_r ratio. To be sure, these same factors are often mentioned as possible incentives toward budget laxity for individual countries joining the EMU, but it is also true that the lower the y_{rq}/m_r ratio in each country, the less likely becomes the danger of negative fiscal spillovers for the EMU as a whole.

I do not conclude that negative fiscal spillovers will be a minor problem in the EMU and that fears about this problem are groundless. I contend instead that, though critical for fiscal policy conduct in a currency union, this issue is largely empirical in nature, that it deserves further accurate investigation, and that it can hardly be settled for all countries and in all circumstances.[22] As the model shows, this specific aspect of interdependence in a currency union should be framed within an extended analysis of aspects concerning the transmission mechanism of macroeconomic variables across the EMU, institutional and operational relations between the ECB and the national FAs, and in particular the reciprocal repercussions of their economic policies. These aspects are dealt with in the subsequent parts of this chapter.

3 Efficiency of stabilization policies in the EMU

To sum up the preliminary results established in the previous section, when the EMU economies are hit by domestic shocks with a certain degree of correlation, these have effects on domestic output and prices, and therefore on EMU output and prices. Consequently, also involved are the common money market, the EMU interest rate and the euro rate. I now examine the stabilization problem faced by the policy makers. As we show below, even in the ideal pure stabilization regime where all policy makers are disciplined and face no policy dilemmas, the stabilization problem still has a few pitfalls that have not been examined carefully in the literature. In particular, I reach more problematic conclusions than Dixit and Lambertini (2001), depending on three factors highlighted by equations (2.17)–(2.22): (i) the interdependence between countries, (ii) the degree of correlation of shocks ρ, and (iii) the 'division of labour' among the national fiscal instruments g_i and the central monetary one m.

The first question that naturally arises in the face of a shock is: who should stabilize? First, note immediately that since z_i and π_i (z and π) are perfectly correlated after a demand shock, policy makers need to choose just one target variable, say $\pi_i(\pi)$, the other being stabilized too. Second, only two of the inflation equations π_1, π_2, π are linearly independent; since there are three policy instruments in the system (m, g_1, g_2), one instrument is redundant. Hence there can only be two alternative answers to the previous question: *either* the ECB *or* the two national FAs.[23]

Let us first examine the ECB. It has one instrument, the money supply m, and one target, the EMU inflation rate π, whereas the national targets are two. By setting $\pi = 0$, $g_i = 0$, and solving for m we obtain:

$$m^* = -[m_r(1+\rho)/2y_{rq}]\delta_1 \tag{3.1}$$

$$\pi_1 = (1-\rho)[2(1+2y_q+y_z)]^{-1}\delta_1 \tag{3.2}$$

$$\pi_2 = -(1-\rho)[2(1+2y_q+y_z)]^{-1}\delta_1 \tag{3.3}$$

Clearly, $\pi_i \neq 0$ for $\rho \neq 1$, i.e. national economies are under-stabilized, and their degree of stabilization is an increasing function of the correlation of shocks ρ. The basic reason is that the ECB gears money supply to stabilization of the EMU aggregates, not necessarily of their country components. Therefore, our first conclusion is summarized in the following proposition:

Proposition 1 *Stabilization assigned to centralized monetary policy is always effective for the EMU as a whole, but it cannot be effective for all countries unless a symmetric shock occurs* ($\rho = 1$).

This result replicates those of De Grauwe (2000) and Cooper and Kempf (2000) who obtain it for supply-side shocks. De Grauwe relates this result to the interplay between asymmetric shocks and a 'representative' ECB's reaction function interpreted as the weighted average of national preferences. Cooper and Kempf obtain it in a traditional context of conflicting targets among policy makers. As is clarified above, the reason behind (P1) is more basic: the lack of instruments *vis-à-vis* objectives when asymmetric shocks occur. By contrast, Dixit and Labertini (2001) conclude that in a pure stabilization regime centralized monetary policy is always fully stabilizing for both the EMU as a whole and for each country for any kind of shock. The main reason is that in their model all countries always have the same EMU inflation rate; hence no problem of incomplete stabilization can ever arise no matter what stabilization policy is chosen. Yet continuous inflation alignment across EMU members is a strong (counterfactual) assumption as far as cyclical fluctuations are concerned. By contrast, proposition (P1) makes it necessary to distinguish the two scenarios of symmetric and asymmetric shocks.

3.1 Symmetric shocks

As far as symmetric shocks are concerned, P1 seems to be in line with the conventional wisdom: symmetric shocks should be stabilized by the ECB, and the centralized monetary policy may fit all. Yet the alternative assignment to decentralized fiscal stabilization is equally possible. In fact, the national FAs have one instrument, the budget adjustments g_i, and one target, the national inflation rate π_i, each. Consequently, there always exists a vector of fiscal instruments that completely stabilizes all the economies and the EMU. By setting $\pi_i = 0$, $m = 0$, in equations (2.17)–(2.22) with $\rho = 1$ and solving for g_i, we obtain

$$g_1^* = g_2^* = [m_r/(m_r - y_{rq})]\delta_1 \tag{3.4}$$

Should we conclude that in the case of symmetric shocks we are indifferent between monetary and fiscal stabilization? Probably not, as the principle of optimal assignment suggests. Notably, most current analyses of stabilization policies in the EMU do not address this issue.

Let us compare the fiscal full-stabilization solution (3.4) with the monetary one provided by equation (3.1) under a symmetric shock

$$m^* = -[m_r/y_{rq}]\delta_1 \tag{3.5}$$

As is well known, in the early Tinbergen-Meade approach, efficient assignment requires that, for any target variation dy, the instrument x_i that has to be assigned to y should satisfy

$$\min(|\partial x_i/\partial y|, |\partial x_j/\partial y|, \ldots)$$

Implicit in this assignment principle are considerations on the 'cost of the instrument'. Friedman's famous warning against the 'long and variable lags' of policy interventions were of similar nature. More up-to-date considerations, more relevant to stochastic environments, focus on how much of the variability of shocks is transmitted to policy variables. For example, recent studies on the conduct of monetary policy in industrialized countries (e.g. Clarida, Galì and Gertler, 1999) highlight the preference of central bankers for smooth changes in interest rates. Commitment to 'price stability' may be extended to asset prices and the exchange rate. In the present model, both monetary and fiscal instruments have repercussions on the EMU interest rate and the euro rate. Using equation (2.15) we can compute how much variability is transmitted to the interest rate by the two alternative policies. Denoting with σ_δ^2 the variance of the shocks, and with $\sigma_r^2|\bullet$ the variance of the interest rate conditional on one policy instrument, we obtain

$$\sigma_r^2|g_i^* = \sigma_\delta^2/(m_r - y_{rq})^2$$
$$\sigma_r^2|m^* = \sigma_\delta^2/y_{rq}^2$$

On this view, the choice of the stabilization instrument should follow from a minimum variance criterion.[24] Hence, the following second proposition holds:

Proposition 2 *Under symmetric shocks either central monetary stabilization or decentralized fiscal stabilization are effective. According to the minimum variance criterion, central monetary stabilization is more efficient if* $\sigma_r^2|m^* < \sigma_r^2|g_i^*$, *or* $y_{rq}/m_r > 1/2$.

The condition identified in P2 is, unsurprisingly, dependent on the y_{rq}/m_r ratio discussed in Section 2 in relation to the financial effects of budget imbalances. For the same reason, it is also akin to the well-known Mundell-Fleming assignment solution in an open economy with flexible exchange rate. In fact, under symmetric shocks (in a pure stabilization regime) all national FAs behave identically as if there were a single centralized FA, and the y_{rq}/m_r ratio operates as the Mundell-Fleming open-economy crowding-out parameter (reduced by the share of fixed-rate intra-EMU trade). Consider a negative shock. By raising the EMU interest rate and appreciating the euro rate, an equal fiscal expansion by all governments feeds some crowding-out effect *into all the economies*. If this effect is large, the overall extent of fiscal stabilization should also be larger, and hence the variability of the interest rate turns out to be greater than in the case of monetary stabilization. It also follows that the argument that national fiscal restraints are necessary because negative fiscal spillovers in the EMU are large is consistent with efficient assignment of stabilization to centralized monetary policy in the event of symmetric shocks.

3.2 Asymmetric shocks

We have seen that in case of asymmetric shocks full stabilization for every country cannot be achieved by centralized monetary policy. Consequently, a third proposition follows:

Proposition 3 *In the event of asymmetric shocks* ($\rho < 1$), *decentralized fiscal stabilization is the only assignment consistent with full stabilization.*

Referring back to the inflation equations (2.17)–(2.22), in consideration of the fiscal spillovers between the two countries discussed in Section 2, the decentralized stabilization problem can generally be treated in game-theoretic form. A large body of literature has been produced on comparing co-ordinated with unco-ordinated fiscal stabilization policies among interdependent economies. Generally, unco-ordinated policies in the presence of asymmetric shocks and fiscal spillovers are viewed as being inferior to co-ordinated policies, with positive fiscal spillovers inducing under-stabilization and negative fiscal spillovers inducing excess deficits (e.g. van der Ploeg, 1991; Goodhart and Smith, 1993). Hence those who foresee the former type of fiscal spillover in the EMU warn that decentralized fiscal stabilization may be insufficient, whereas those who are concerned with the latter type have urged the introduction of budget constraints (see e.g. Artis and Winkler, 1999). Yet the majority of recent analyses start from the existence of conflicting interests among national FAs or with the central bank, and/or of some 'cost of the instrument' in the use of budget adjustments (see e.g. Buti, Roeger and Veld, 2001). Here the problem can be re-examined in a disciplined system, where policy makers have no conflicting objectives and the cost of budget adjustments may be considered zero up to the SGP deficit ceiling. In this same framework, Dixit and Lambertini (2001) argue that national FAs can always

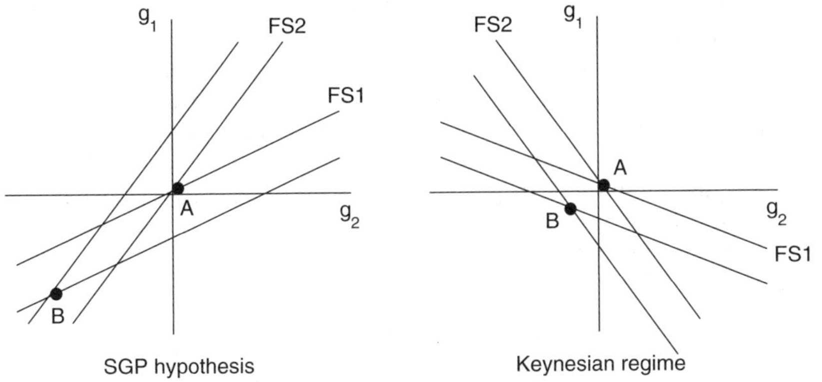

Figure 3.1 Fiscal reaction functions and unco-ordinated (Nash) equilibria

achieve full stabilization whether they co-ordinate or not; however, as noted above, their model does not examine decentralized fiscal stabilization from the efficiency point of view.

In the first place, let us study the unco-ordinated (Nash) equilibrium of the game, where each FA chooses g_i in relation to its own national target, taking the other FA's choice as given. Under the assumption that $\pi_i = 0$ is the target for all FAs, given $\rho < 1$ and $m = 0$, the two FAs' reaction functions are reproduced in Figure 3.1. The two functions have symmetric slopes $(-\Delta_2/\Delta_1)$ and $(-\Delta_1/\Delta_2)$, whose sign depends on the prevailing regime of fiscal effects among those in Table 3.1. Figure 3.1 reproduces the two most representative regimes: the one with EMU Keynesian effects, which implies $-\Delta_2/\Delta_1 < 0$, and the SGP hypothesis, which implies $-\Delta_2/\Delta_1 > 0$.

After a shock $(\delta_1, \rho\delta_1)$ in the two countries, the unco-ordinated optimal budget adjustments are, respectively,

$$g_1^* = [2m_r - y_{rq}(1-\rho)][2(m_r - y_{rq})]^{-1}\delta_1 \quad (3.6)$$

$$g_2^* = [2m_r\rho + y_{rq}(1-\rho)][2(m_r - y_{rq})]^{-1}\delta_1 \quad (3.7)$$

This outcome prompts some important considerations related to the discussion of fiscal spillovers in Section 2.

(1) The signs of the optimal budget adjustments are ambiguous in both countries. Once again, we have to examine the y_{rq}/m_r ratio, and we see that, as long as $\rho \geq 0$, $y_{rq}/m_r < 1$ is a sufficient condition for (g_1^*, g_2^*) to have the same sign as δ_1, i.e. for optimal budget adjustments to be anti-cyclical as traditionally expected. Under these conditions no difference is to be expected from moving from unco-ordinated to co-ordinated policy choices, the reason being that all governments share the same objective function.[25]

(2) Two particular cases are worth noting. The first is a unilateral shock, e.g. in country 1, $\delta_1 < 0$, $\rho = 0$: the result is $(g_1^*, g_2^*) < 0$. Note that country 2 should also run a budget deficit just in order to compensate for the imported shock, thereby itself contributing to the overall pressure on the interest rate. The second case is a bilateral trade shift from country 1 to country 2, $\delta_1 < 0$, $\rho = -1$: the result is $g_1^* = \delta_1$, $g_2^* = -\delta_1$, i.e. the two countries should exactly offset the change in aggregate demand with an equal budgetary compensation of opposite sign. Consequently, the aggregate borrowing requirement is balanced, and hence no negative financial spillover arises.

We can therefore put forward the following fourth proposition.

Proposition 4 *In the event of asymmeteric shocks of any degree, and for any sign of fiscal spillovers, if all national FAs consistently pursue the same objective of full stabilization, the unco-ordinated (Nash) equilibrium of their budget choices always achieves both domestic and EMU stabilization.*

This conclusion is in line with Dixit and Lambertini's; however, it should be qualified in consideration of the loss of efficiency of decentralized fiscal policies in the presence of negative fiscal spillovers. The condition $y_{rq}/m_r < 1$, as established in Section 2, admits of both fiscal regimes in Figure 3.1. What is the main difference between the two? It is the *extent* of budget adjustments. Figure 3.1 depicts a unilateral negative shock to country 1 ($\delta_1 < 0, \rho = 0$): in both fiscal regimes, the full-stabilization reaction function of government 1 (FS1) shifts downwards in the budget deficit region, while that of government 2 (FS2) also shifts leftwards in the deficit region by the amount of the imported shock. Consistently with equations (3.6) and (3.7), the Nash equilibrium shifts from point A to point B where $(g_1^*, g_2^*) < 0$ in both fiscal regimes. Yet the *absolute value* of (g_1^*, g_2^*) is different. It increases with ρ and with the y_{rq}/m_r ratio. In fact, the former parameter determines the diffusion of the negative shock in the EMU; the latter determines the extent of the crowding-out effect of budget deficits that should be overcome. Therefore, the larger the y_{rq}/m_r ratio, i.e. the more likely the SGP hypothesis, the larger (more volatile) the optimal budget responses should be in all countries, as a consequence of the fact that decentralized fiscal stabilization loses efficiency *also locally*.

3.3 A note on the deficit ceiling in the Stability and Growth Pact

From the previous conclusion it follows that the SGP hypothesis, the assignment of asymmetric shocks to decentralized fiscal stabilization and the imposition of budget constraints do not seem mutually consistent. Under the SGP hypothesis, national FAs forced to cope with their own domestic shocks with an inefficient instrument should be granted wider, not narrower, room for anti-cyclical fiscal manoeuvre.[26] To see this more formally, let $g_i^- < 0$ be the maximum budget deficit compatible with the SGP ceiling for the given observed GDP;[27] consequently, imposing $g_i^* \geq g_i^-$ and $m = 0$, then

$$|\delta_i| \leq |g_i^-| \frac{2(m_r - y_{rq})}{2m_r - y_{rq}(1 - \rho_{ij})} \tag{3.8}$$

is the amplitude of the shock that each individual economy can 'afford' to accommodate locally without violating the SGP constraint. In particular, (3.8) confirms that if the ECB does not intervene, and if all governments stabilize locally, then $|\delta_i|$ decreases (the deficit ceiling is more binding) as the y_{rq}/m_r ratio grows larger.

A number of exercises and simulations have recently been produced in order to assess the stringency of the SGP constraint (e.g. Buti, Franco and Ogena, 1997, Buti and Sapir, 1998, chaps 8–9, and Eichengreen and Wyplosz, 1998). These exercises have generally been run on the basis of country-by-country historical data on cyclical slumps and budget responses, and they point to the conclusion that the SGP deficit ceiling will probably not be a major impediment to stabilization. However, the institutional regime shift represented by the EMU should be taken into account. Condition (3.8) points out that, in a currency union such as the EMU, calculation of the margin of stabilization provided by the SGP cannot be performed by taking the country concerned in isolation. Instead, such calculation must take account of: (i) the contemporaneous fiscal position of the other countries in the union, (ii) the concomitant monetary stance of the central MA and (iii) the correlation of the domestic shock with those in the other member countries. Moreover, little attention has been paid to the consequences of constrained fiscal stabilization.

The SGP deficit ceiling can be seen as a special case of 'cost of the instrument' in policy choice-theoretic models. The general result in these models is that when the marginal benefit of stabilization is equated with the marginal cost of the instrument, the latter is used more parsimoniously and hence under-stabilization is the outcome (see e.g. Goodhart and Smith, 1993, and Buti, Roeger and Veld, 2001). Suppose for simplicity that each government, in the case of negative shock, chooses[28]

$$\max(g_i^*, g_i^-)$$

Suppose also that after a shock the optimal deficit for one government exceeds the ceiling, $g_i^* < g_i^-$, while for the other it does not. Then, the former government is constrained to the g_i^- deficit. In the light of equations (2.17)–(2.22), there are three main consequences: (i) the constrained government under-stabilizes, (ii) the unconstrained government can still stabilize domestically by changing its optimal budget choice and (iii) the EMU as a whole is under-stabilized.

These three consequences arise in both the fiscal regimes in Figure 3.1. There is however a major difference as regards the unconstrained government. Under the SGP hypothesis, the unconstrained government will stabilize domestically by choosing a *smaller* deficit (because the smaller deficit of the constrained government exerts a smaller *negative* fiscal spillover), whereas in the Keynesian regime the optimal deficit should be *larger* (because the smaller deficit of the constrained government exerts a smaller *positive* fiscal spillover).[29] Therefore, if the SGP hypothesis is true, the deficit ceiling, when it is binding, enforces the minimization of aggregate deficits (which may be reckoned as a collective benefit) *vis-à-vis* under-stabilization of the constrained country (which may be reckoned as a private cost). If instead the SGP hypothesis turns out to be untrue, when the deficit ceiling is binding there will still be under-stabilization of the constrained country but no, or negligible, reduction in aggregate deficits. The welfare implications of both outcomes are unclear, but neither of them is a Pareto improvement with respect to the Nash equilibrium of unconstrained stabilization.

4 Conclusions

Will policy makers within the institutional framework of the EMU designed by the Maastricht Treaty and the SGP be able to shelter member countries from undesirable macroeconomic fluctuations? This question, which has accompanied the EMU since its conception, is still unsettled. So far, theoretical research has mostly focused on the assumption that policy makers are undisciplined, in the sense that they pursue short-term goals that are inconsistent with long-run stability, and/or that national FAs pursue goals that conflict with those of the central MA. More recently, research has started investigating how the EMU may perform if, say as a long-run evolution of preferences induced by the existing rules themselves, policy makers will eventually be disciplined. I have examined the stabilization problem by means of a macroeconomic model with stochastic demand disturbances hitting two representative member countries of the EMU. In the absence of any inflation bias or policy dilemma, both decentralized fiscal policies and centralized monetary policy may in principle be used as stabilizers, but a traditional assignment problem arises. The model allows the following main conclusions to be drawn.

(1) Under symmetric shocks either central monetary policy or decentralized fiscal policies can fully stabilize each country and the EMU as a whole. However, in general the two assignments are not equally efficient. The efficiency (e.g. minimum variance) of monetary policy increases as the parameter governing the negative spillover of fiscal imbalances (y_{rq}/m_r) grows.
(2) In the event of asymmetric shocks ($\rho < 1$), centralized monetary policy can fully stabilize the EMU as a whole (its average inflation rate) but not each country. Therefore, decentralized fiscal policies are the only assignment consistent with full stabilization.

(3) In the event of asymmetric shocks of any degree, and for any sign of fiscal spillovers, the unco-ordinated (Nash) equilibrium of national budget choices always achieves both domestic and EMU stabilization. However, the efficiency of decentralized fiscal policies decreases to the extent that negative fiscal spillovers are larger.
(4) If negative fiscal spillovers are substantial, *ceteris paribus* larger budget imbalances are necessary. Therefore, an FA may find its optimal budget choice constrained by the SGP deficit ceiling. Constrained stabilization is never superior to the Nash equilibrium of unconstrained budget choices.

These conclusions highlight that the popular idea of an efficient 'division of labour' between one 'monetary giant' pursuing union-wide stabilization and many 'fiscal dwarfs' coping with their own domestic stabilization may turn out to be overly simplistic, even in the most favourable case in which policy makers face no policy dilemmas. First, in a world where shocks are generally correlated and unevenly distributed across countries, rather than being neatly symmetric or unilateral, the informational basis of the assignment choice may be flimsy. Secondly, and more importantly, we have seen that the assignment choice between centralized monetary stabilization and decentralized fiscal stabilization is not unconditional but depends on the net effect of the spillovers triggered by national budget imbalances. The architects of the EMU argue that *negative* fiscal spillovers may be such a serious problem that the adoption of the budget constraint in the SGP is justified. If this presumption is true, then centralized monetary policy is the right choice *in the event of symmetric shocks*, but by the same token decentralized fiscal policies are not the most efficient choice *in the event of asymmetric shocks*. Remarkably, this assignment would give rise to larger swings in fiscal budgets, in the interest rate and in the euro rate as the by-product of a system intended to limit fiscal activism. If national FAs are then bound to use the fiscal instrument although it is inefficient, they should be granted more, not less, room for fiscal manoeuvre, whereas the SGP budget constraint may induce under-stabilization in the system. Finally, to the extent that FAs consistently pursue pure stabilization, co-ordination or unco-ordination of fiscal policies is a matter of indifference as far as the efficiency loss of stabilization is concerned.

Whether the flaws in the EMU stabilization mechanisms will materialize, and how seriously, remain open questions essentially dependent on empirical factors. However, downgrading the stabilization problem in the EMU may be dangerous because excess instability and the perception of a lack of protection against adverse conditions may in the long run undermine people's confidence in this crucial new institution of the European Union, and political pressure may arise against the central bank's independence. In so far as the rules of disciplined policy conduct embedded in the EMU are successful in shaping all actors' preferences and behaviours, in the long run the instruments introduced to enforce those rules will probably hinder stabilization.

If such enforcing instruments are deemed necessary in the transition from undisciplined to disciplined policy-making, their progressive removal may be advisable as the transition proceeds.

Notes

1. For an overview of these arguments see Buti, Franco and Ogena (1998), Buti and Sapir (1998), Artis and Winkler (1999).
2. Dixit (2001), and Dixit and Lambertini (2001) provide one of the most up-to-date treatments of the consequences of various combinations of preferences/targets conflicts among policy makers in the EMU.
3. Recent empirical studies on the so-called 'monetary-fiscal policy mix' in Europe over recent decades also suggest that the theoretical concentration on targets/preferences conflicts between MAs and FAs may be due to the particular historical experience in the late 1970s and early 1980s. The evidence examined by Mélitz (1997), Wyplosz (1999), von Hagen and Strauch (2001), and von Hagen, Hughes Hallet and Strauch (2002) supports the view that the two policy arms have mostly been used as 'strategic substitutes'. That is to say, both have contributed to the same counter-cyclical goals, with one instrument being relaxed while the other was being tightened (see also Buti, Roeger and Veld, 2001, for a discussion of these works). Farina and Tamborini (2002) compute a measure of structural changes in the fiscal stance of the EU countries and show that a conflict of policy stance with the MAs probably arose between the second oil shock and the advent of the EMS, whereas the FAs returned to fiscal discipline as early as the mid-1980s. According to Farina and Tamborini (but see also De Grauwe, 1999), in general, the monetary stance in the EU countries failed to recognize the change in the fiscal stance, creating severe or prohibitive conditions for fiscal consolidation. As confirmed in a study by the European Commission (2000), the relaxation of monetary conditions took place only at the beginning of the 1990s.
4. It may also be added that demand shocks are in practice just as important as supply shocks and, according to various studies, more significant and frequent.
5. This class of models has been widely used by current research on stabilization policies in exchange-rate systems and currency unions. See in particular Eichengreen and Wyplosz (1993), Allsopp and Vines (1996, 1998), Allsopp, McKibbin and Vines (1999), De Grauwe (2000), and Dixit and Lambertini (2001) to mention only a few. Earlier versions of the present model have appeared in Tamborini (2001), and Farina and Tamborini (2002).
6. For details on this technique see also Allsopp and Vines (1996, 1998).
7. It is therefore also assumed that, in long-period equilibrium conditions, there is a uniform inflation rate, zero or otherwise, in the EMU countries. This condition does not conflict with the productive specialization of the countries (for which the equilibrium price *level* is not the same), in that it implies that relative prices remain constant.
8. Strictly speaking, each country also has the channel of the extra-EMU balance of payments. In order to make the model more compact and manageable, we assume that reserves of extra-EMU currencies are entirely centralized at the ECB, so that imbalances in a country's extra-EMU payments do not have effects on the domestic money stock.

9. A third channel could be net intra-EMU capital movements as a function of the interest differential on domestic bonds. However this is ruled by the assumption of intra-EMU perfect capital mobility so that domestic interest rates are continuously aligned with the EMU interest rate.
10. I consider g_i to be a net addition to both domestic demand and financial wealth. To the extent that g_i is strictly understood as a temporary deviation from the balanced budget, this is also consistent with the Barro-Ricardo approach.
11. Note that the EMU money market equilibrium, $\Sigma m_i^d = m$, and domestic money market equilibria, $m_i^d = m_i$, in their turn entail the condition $\Sigma m_i = m$, i.e. that the aggregate change in domestic money stocks must coincide with change in the EMU money supply. But, as explained above, Σm_i is given by the sum of intra-EMU balances of payments and by the sum of banks' borrowing from the ECB, μ_i. The sum of intra-EMU balances must be nil by construction, which entails $\Sigma \mu_i = m$, i.e. additional money is injected into the economies through their bank channels.
12. This assumption, of course, does not necessarily entail purchasing power parity, which in this model would conflict with the productive specialization attributed to each country. However, if the relative price between the EMU 'good' (the basket of goods produced by each EMU country) and that of the ROW is also included among the long-period equilibrium conditions, *deviations* from this equilibrium due to the inflation differential should be offset by the exchange rate.
13. For a model focused on bilateral demand shocks, and for discussion of their importance in the EMU, see Tamborini (2001).
14. Supply shocks and policy makers' preferences are introduced in a similar model by Farina and Tamborini (2003).
15. As explained above, we are considering a pure stabilization regime, that is, one in which the only objective of each national FA and the ECB is to stabilize inflation and output gaps after shocks with no alteration of long-run equilibrium values (no 'inflation' or 'deficit' biases). Accordingly, any policy maker's objective can be represented by minimization of a standard additive quadratic loss function defined over logarithmic inflation and output gaps, π_i and z_i, where targets coincide with long-run equilibrium values that are normalized to 0. As is well-known, in this class of models, when policy targets are credible they provide the anchor for the private sector's rational expectations.
16. The aggregate-demand effect measured by y_{rq} is clearly analogous to the one present in the traditional Mundell-Fleming open economy analysis. The main difference here is that whereas the traditional Mundell-Fleming open economy operates either in a fixed exchange-rate regime ($\alpha = 1$) or in a flexible exchange-rate regime ($\alpha = 0$), our EMU economies operate in a mixed regime which is of the first type by the amount of intra-EMU trade $0 < \alpha < 1$, and of the second type by the amount of extra-EMU trade $(1 - \alpha)$. The magnitude of y_{rq} is modified accordingly.
17. It might be objected that financial interdependence may also exist in an international regime with fixed exchange rates and complete financial integration, and that it was already in force among the EMS member-countries. This objection is correct; nonetheless, moving into an inter-regional regime entails a difference of degree, albeit not of substance, in financial interdependence. In the light of the EMS experience, it should be borne in mind that an international regime has two major differences from an inter-regional one. The first is the presence of formally independent MAs, which means that compensatory domestic monetary policies

might be implemented; the second is that bilateral exchange-rate realignments are possible.

18. Thorough analyses can be found in Van der Ploeg (1991), Goodhart and Smith (1993), Masson and Taylor (1993), Buiter, Corsetti and Roubini (1993), Kenen (1995, chap. 4), Bayoumi and Eichengreen (1995) and Eichengreen and Wyplosz (1998).
19. After the works by Alesina and Perotti (1995, 1997), and the ensuing literature on short-term and long-term macroeconomic effects of fiscal policies, it is now customary to call the expansionary or contractionary effects of budget deficits 'Keynesian' or 'non-Keynesian' (and vice versa for surpluses). These works and the related literature often employ different models with explicit microfoundations, and focus more on structural budget policies than on cyclical ones. On the other hand, more sophistication at the microeconomic level often comes at the expense of oversimplification of the macroeconomic frameworks: the most significant among these works consider individual countries in isolation, or ignore the concomitant monetary stance (see e.g. De Grauwe (1999) and Eichengreen (1998) for these observations). In any case, I borrow the terminology of this literature just for its emphasis on the reversal of the effects of fiscal policies.
20. In fact,

$$\text{sign}(\Delta_1) = \text{sign}(y_{rq}(2y_q + y_z - m_z) - 2m_r(1 + y_q))$$
$$\text{sign}(\Delta_2) = \text{sign}(y_{rq}(2(1 + y_q) + y_z + m_z) - 2m_r(y_z + y_q))$$

where 2 is the number of countries in the system.

21. A (perhaps more realistic) alternative is that the y_{rq}/m_r ratio may differ in different countries (being small in deficit-prone countries and large in the others). But in this case the problem with the SGP is that setting equal rules for different countries is not efficient (see e.g. Eichengreen and Wyplosz, 1998). The relationship between the y_{rq}/m_r ratio and the deficit rules in the SGP is also clarified in the next section.
22. The empirical literature has hitherto been inconclusive, not to mention that genuine data on the EMU are still lacking and that past experiences cannot be translated mechanically into the new institutional and market environment of the EMU. Masson and Taylor (1993) report that estimations run with the IMF world model MULTIMOD support earlier Mundell-Fleming conclusions that fiscal expansions in one country have positive effects on economic activity abroad under a flexible exchange rate (e.g. the US-EEC case in the 1980s) whereas they have negative effects abroad under a fixed exchange rate (e.g. the Germany-EEC case in the 1990s). Using the same model, Hughes Hallet and McAdam (1999) have simulated the process of convergence to balanced budgets in the EMU, finding that domestic fiscal restrictions do not stimulate partners' economic activity, and that a key variable in determining the overall effect on economic activity is the concomitant monetary stance. Allsopp, McKibbin and Vines (1999), using the McKibbin-Sachs Global Economic Model (MSG2), by contrast argue that collective fiscal consolidation forced by the SGP is *less costly* than if individually undertaken, because of the larger positive financial effect of lower interest rate and euro rate depreciation. However, this finding does not necessarily imply 'non-Keynesian' fiscal spillovers across countries. Eichengreen and Wyplosz (1998) present econometric estimations of a model for OECD countries from 1955 to 1996, showing that domestic fiscal coefficients are 'Keynesian', whereas external effects are negligible.

23. The case of the ECB and one FA can be excluded because it would give rise to a problem of 'country specificity' against the ECB intervention.
24. Of course, this criterion is only one among many others and is adopted here just for expository purposes. It can easily be checked from equations (3.4) and (3.5) that the early criterion of the 'minimum use' of the instrument would yield the same result.
25. In fact, as recalled by van der Ploeg, 'international cooperation occurs, first, through the international exchange of information, secondly, through international harmonization of rules, and thirdly, through international coordination of discretionary policies' (1991, p. 140). Each government pursuing the same objective function independently corresponds to the second requisite and is a substitute for the third.
26. The advice often offered to governments that they may keep their budget slightly positive if they wish to insure themselves against unexpected need for large deficits is extravagant, since aiming at a structurally positive fiscal budget may have distortionary effects which depress the level of potential output.
27. The SGP ceiling may exceed the normal value of 3 per cent of GDP under certified conditions of mild or severe recession: see Buti, Franco and Ogena (1998) for detailed treatment of these provisions.
28. In this case the fiscal cost function is zero up to g_i^- and infinite elsewhere. More precisely, under this interpretation g_i^- may be the maximal contingent deficit below which no ECOFIN procedure is activated.
29. The analogous result that stabilization in only one country is less efficient than if pursued in all countries has frequently been pointed out in the literature on fiscal policy coordination problems (see e.g. Van der Ploeg (1991), Goodhart and Smith (1993), and Abraham, Heremans and Van Rampuy (1991)). As we have seen, this principle only holds in so far as fiscal spillovers are positive.

References

Abraham P., D. Heremans and P. Van Rampuy (1991) 'Economic Federalism and the EMU, *European Economy*, vol. 56, pp. 109–35.

Alesina A. and R. Perotti (1995) 'Fiscal Expansions and Adjustments in OECD Countries', *Economic Policy*, vol. 21, pp. 205–47.

Alesina A. and R. Perotti (1997) 'Fiscal Adjustment in OECD Countries: Composition and Macroeconomic Effects', *IMF Staff Papers*, vol. 44, pp. 210–48.

Allsopp C., W. McKibbin and D. Vines (1999) 'Fiscal Consolidation in Europe: Some Empirical Issues', in A.J. Hughes Hallett, M.M. Hutchinson and S.E. Hougaard Jensen (eds), *Fiscal Aspects of European Monetary Integration* (Cambridge: Cambridge University Press), pp. 288–319.

Allsopp C. and D. Vines (1996) 'Fiscal Policy and EMU', *National Institute Economic Review*, no. 158, pp. 91–107.

Allsopp C. and D. Vines (1998) 'The Assessment: Macroeconomic Policy after EMU', *Oxford Review of Economic Policy*, vol. 14, pp. 1–23.

Artis M.J. and B. Winkler (1999) 'The Stability and Growth Pact: Trading off Flexibility for Credibility', in A.J. Hughes Hallett, M.M. Hutchinson and S.E. Hougaard Jensen (eds), *Fiscal Aspects of European Monetary Integration* (Cambridge: Cambridge University Press), pp. 157–88.

Bayoumi T. and B. Eichengreen (1995) 'Restraining Yourself: The Implications of Fiscal Rules for Economic Stabilization', *IMF Staff Papers*, vol. 42, pp. 33–48.

Buiter W., G. Corsetti and N. Roubini (1993) 'Excessive Deficits: Sense and Nonsense in the Treaty of Maastricht', *Economic Policy*, vol. 16, pp. 58–87.

Buti M., D. Franco and H. Ongena (1997) 'Budgetary Policies during Recessions. Retrospective Application of the Stability and Growth Pact to the Post-War Period', *Recherches économiques de Louvain*, vol. 64, pp. 321–66.

Buti M., D. Franco and Ongena H. (1998) 'Fiscal Discipline and Flexibility in EMU: The Implementation of the Stability and Growth Pact', *Oxford Review of Economic Policy*, vol. 14, pp. 81–97.

Buti M., W. Roeger and Jan in't Veld (2001) 'Stabilizing Output and Inflation in the EMU: Policy Conflicts and Co-operation under the Stability Pact', *Journal of Common Market Studies*, vol. 39, pp. 801–28.

Buti M. and A. Sapir (1998) *Economic Policy in EMU. A Study by the European Commission Services* (Oxford: Oxford University Press).

Clarida C., J. Gali and M. Gertler (1999) 'The Science of Monetary Policy', *Journal of Economic Literature*, vol. 37, pp. 1307–41.

Cooper R. and H. Kempf (2000) 'Designing Stabilization Policy in a Monetary Union', *NBER Working Paper*, no. 7607.

De Grauwe P. (1999) 'Discussion' of 'Asymmetric Business Cycles and Fiscal Linkages in Europe', in A.J. Hughes Hallett, M.M. Hutchinson S.E. and Hougaard Jensen (eds) *Fiscal Aspects of European Monetary Integration* (Cambridge: Cambridge University Press), pp. 234–45.

De Grauwe P. (2000) 'Monetary Policy in the Presence of Asymmetries', CEPR Discussion Paper, no. 2393.

Dixit A. (2001) 'Games of Monetary and Fiscal Interactions in the EMU', Papers and Proceedings of the European Economic Association, *European Economic Review*, vol. 45, pp. 589–613.

Dixit A. and L. Lambertini (2001) 'Monetary-Fiscal Interaction and Commitment versus Discretion in a Monetary Union', Papers and Proceedings of the European Economic Association, *European Economic Review*, vol. 45, pp. 977–87.

Eichengreen B. (1998) 'Comment' on 'The Political Economy of Fiscal Adjustments', *Brookings Papers on Economic Activity*, no. 1, pp. 255–62.

Eichengreen B. and C. Wyplosz (1993) 'The Unstable EMS', *Brookings Papers on Economic Activity*, no. 1, pp. 52–124.

Eichengreen B. and C. Wyplosz (1998) 'Stability Pact: More than a Minor Nuisance?', *Economic Policy*, vol. 19, pp. 67–112.

European Commission (2000) 'Public Finances in EMU 2000', *European Economy, Reports and Studies*, no. 3.

Farina F. and R. Tamborini (2002) 'Le politiche macroeconomiche di stabilizzazione in Europa nel nuovo regime di unione monetaria', in F. Farina and R. Tamborini (eds), *Da nazioni a regioni. Mutamenti strutturali e istituzionali dopo l'ingresso nella Unione Monetaria Europea*, Società Italiana degli Economisti, XLI Riunione Scientifica Annuale (Bologna: Il Mulino).

Farina F. and R. Tamborini (2003) 'Set a Sufficiently Ambitious Budget Target and Let the Automatic Stabilizers Work. Will it Really Work in the European Monetary Union?', *Open Economies Review* vol. 15, pp. 143–68.

Feldstein M. (1997) 'The Political Economy of the European Economic and Monetary Union: Political Sources of an Economic Liability', *Journal of Economic Perspectives*, vol. 11, pp. 23–42.

Goodhart C.A.E. and S. Smith (1993) 'Stabilization', *European Economy*, Reports and Studies, no. 5, pp. 417–56.

von Hagen J. and R. Strauch (2001) 'Fiscal Consolidations: Quality, Economic Conditions and Success', *Public Choice*, vol. 109(3–4), pp. 327–46.

von Hagen J., A. Hughes Hallett and R. Strauch (2002) 'Budgetary Consolidation in Europe: Quality, Economic Conditions and Persistence', *Journal of the Japanese and International Economies*, vol. 16(4), pp. 512–35.

Hughes Hallett A.J. and P. McAdam (1999) 'Implications of the Stability and Growth Pact: Why the "Growth" Element is Important', in A.J. Hughes Hallett, M.M. Hutchinson and S.E. Hougaard Jensen (eds), *Fiscal Aspects of European Monetary Integration* (Cambridge: Cambridge University Press), pp. 216–53.

Kenen P.B. (1995) *Economic and Monetary Union in Europe. Moving Beyond Maastricht* (Cambridge: Cambridge University Press).

Masson P. and M.P. Taylor (1993) 'Fiscal Policy within Common Currency Areas', *Journal of Common Market Studies*, vol. 31, pp. 29–44.

Mélitz J. (1997) 'Some Cross-Country Evidence about Debt, Deficits, and the Behaviour of Monetary and Fiscal Authorities', CEPR Discussion Papers, no. 1653.

Tamborini R. (2001) 'Living in the EMU: Prices, Interest Rates and the Adjustment of Payments in a Monetary Union', *Journal of Common Market Studies*, vol. 39, pp. 123–46.

van der Ploeg F. (1991) 'Macroeconomic Policy Coordination Issues during Various Phases of Economic and Monetary Integration in Europe', *European Economy*, no. 56, pp. 136–63.

Wyplosz C. (1999) 'Economic Policy Coordination in EMU: Strategies and Institutions', Zentrum für Europäische Integrationforschung Policy Papers, no. B11.

4

Price Convergence under EMU? First Estimates*

Matthias Lutz
Institute of Economics, University of St. Gallen, Switzerland

1 Introduction

Does a common currency lead to greater market integration? Certainly European policy-makers seemed to be convinced that it does, when they set out on the Maastricht agenda to create the economic and monetary union (EMU). Despite considerable scepticism throughout the first two stages, the third and final stage of monetary union started successfully in 1999, when the exchange rates of the participating countries were permanently fixed against the euro. This chapter examines to what extent price differences in the euro-zone narrowed as a result of the introduction of the single currency: has 'one money' really supported the creation of 'one market'?

The empirical analysis is based on four different sets of final goods prices: (i) Big Mac prices; (ii) the cover prices of *The Economist*; (iii) the prices of cars; and (iv) the prices of a range of goods and services from a publication by the Union des Banques Suisses (UBS). Estimating the single currency effect on price dispersion suffers from a problem afflicting most studies that attempt to evaluate the effects of economic policies – we do not have an observable counterfactual. A number of methodologies have been suggested in the literature. The estimates of the single-currency effect reported in this paper employ the difference-in-differences (DD) approach.

The results suggest that the common currency has had little impact on price convergence so far. Altogether, the paper reports 178 DD estimates of the single currency effect, which differ in terms of price series, estimator and control group. Even though 41 of them provide statistically significant evidence that the single currency has reduced the degree of price dispersion

* For comments and suggestions I would like to thank Lars Feld, Jacques Mélitz, Sarah Müller and seminar participants at the University of Magdeburg, the Technical University of Darmstadt, the 2002 Annual Conference of the Money, Macro and Finance Research Group at Warwick University and the 13th World Congress of the International Economic Association in Lisbon.

among the member countries, there are another 40 test results with a statistically significant positive effect on price dispersion. There are some differences across data sets and specifications. While the evidence favours a downward euro effect for 14 of the price series considered in this paper, there are nine others where the evidence shows just the opposite.

Several interpretations are offered. The preferred explanation is that there are many other influences on price dispersion, such as a lack of competition between firms, transaction costs and informational asymmetries. Even if a single currency could lower transaction costs in principle, this effect may be too small or too slow to show up in the estimates, given these other impediments to price convergence.

The structure of the chapter is as follows. The next section provides an overview of the issues related to common currencies and market integration, followed in Section 3 by a discussion of the methodology and estimation method. The fourth section describes the four data sets on prices in more detail. The estimates of the single currency effect on price differences are presented in Section 5 and Section 6 concludes the chapter.

2 Common currencies and market integration: the issues

During the past four decades, the member countries of the EU have adopted a range of measures to raise the level of economic integration, culminating in the creation of the European single market in 1993. Nevertheless, prices for identical goods have stubbornly refused to converge between member countries. This has been highlighted repeatedly by the popular press, in academic work and in Commission reports. Table 4.1 provides evidence on price differences within the EU around the time the single currency was introduced. Even though various sources were used, all entries in the table relate to identical, branded items and can thus justifiably be used for price comparisons. Some also feature in the analysis of this chapter.

The differences are substantial, ranging from 18 per cent (Monopoly game) to 74 per cent (Swatch watch). Although not necessarily representative of all products sold in the EU, the comparisons in Table 4.1 illustrate that European consumers frequently pay very different prices for identical products. Since the entries in the table mark the extreme values reported in each survey, they do not represent *average* price differences. However, they highlight the extent to which prices *can* differ. Part of the observed price dispersion may be due to variations in national sales taxes, but the percentage differences are much too big for them to play a dominant role. A further interesting feature of the table is that several countries feature in both the 'low' and 'high' price columns. This indicates that domestic relative prices of different goods also frequently differ across countries.

The question taken up in this chapter is whether the introduction of the single currency has led to a narrowing of price differences. That a

Table 4.1 Price differences in the European Union, some examples

	Item	*Price difference (%)*	*Low*	*High*	*Date*
(1)	*The Economist*	58	Greece	Denmark	Dec. 1998
(2)	Big Mac	41	Spain	Denmark	Apr. 1998
(3)	Canon Prima Super 135 camera	73	Germany	UK	Jun. 1998
(4)	Lacoste polo shirt	27	Spain	Austria	Jun. 1998
(5)	Swatch 'The Classics'	74	Italy	UK	Jun. 1998
(6)	Chanel No 5 (perfume)	59	Belgium	UK	Jun. 1998
(7)	Levi's 501 (jeans)	34	Italy	Germany	Jun. 1998
(8)	Kellogg's cornflakes	28	UK	Germany	Nov. 1999
(9)	Top 5 DVD	29	Germany	France	Nov. 1999
(10)	Duracell batteries, 4-pack	36	France	UK	Nov. 1999
(11)	Monopoly (game)	18	France	Germany	Nov. 1999
(12)	Sega Dreamcast	25	Germany	UK	Nov. 1999
(13)	Ford Mondeo	54	Spain	Portugal	Nov. 1998
(14)	VW Golf	30	Luxembourg	Ireland	Nov. 1998
(15)	Peugeot 406	28	Luxembourg	Portugal	Nov. 1998
(16)	BMW 3-series	41	Sweden	Ireland	Nov. 1998
(17)	Fiat Punto	33	France	Ireland	Nov. 1998

Notes: The cover prices of *The Economist* and Big Macs are taken from the 19 December 1998 and 6 April 1998 issues, respectively. Data for items (3)–(7) comes from 'A Single Price for a Single Currency?', a BEUC Press Release dated 21 December 1998. This reports prices from a survey covering major cities in 10 EU countries, which was undertaken in June 1998. Data for items (8)–(12) are taken from 'A Report into International Price Comparisons', prepared for the UK Department of Trade and Industry by ACNielsen and released on 13 February 2000. The report covers prices in France, Germany, UK and US surveyed in November and December 1999. The car price data (items (13)–(17)) come from *Car Prices in the European Union on 1 November 1998* (European Commission) which covers 12 EU countries.

single currency would have such an effect was first argued by the European Commission in its influential *One Market, One Money* (1990) publication:

> Without a completely transparent and sure rule of the law of one price for tradable goods and services, *which only a single currency can provide*, the single market cannot be expected to yield its full benefits – static and dynamic. (p. 19, *italics* added)

According to the Commission, a single currency deepens economic integration in a number of ways. First, the costs of doing business in other member countries would be reduced due to the reduction in exchange-rate premia (payable, for instance, on forward contracts). Second, lower uncertainty would make cross-border business more profitable, since lower risks would translate into higher risk-adjusted rates of return. Third, international transactions would become cheaper due to the elimination of currency exchange costs and reduced delays. The direct costs of foreign transactions in the EU were estimated by the Commission at between one-half and one per cent of its gross domestic product.

In a background paper to its 1996 single-market review the European Commission (1996) added a fourth potential benefit of the single currency. As a result of 'one money'

> ... increased price transparency will enhance competition and whet consumer appetites for foreign goods; price discrimination between different national markets will be reduced.... .(p. 74)

And, when the euro was finally introduced in 1999, the European Commission (1999, p. 2) repeated its conviction that it would 'squeeze price dispersion in EU markets'.[1]

Recent theoretical work has provided some additional insights. A common theme is that currency unions may alter the way firms set prices. Devereux, Engel and Tille (2003), for instance, argue that, when the euro develops into a vehicle currency for international trade, firms outside the euro area will tend to set common prices for the entire euro area. Friberg (2001) shows that firms that price-discriminate internationally will adopt different pricing strategies under a common currency, compared to a regime of fixed exchange rates. However, greater price convergence as a result of a common currency is not a forgone conclusion. Firms may respond to an exogenous lowering of arbitrage costs – e.g. via a common currency – by endogenously introducing greater arbitrage barriers to raise the degree of market segmentation, e.g. through vertical restraints, bundling with non-tradables or technical differentiation. Friberg and Martensen (2001) show that in this case lower transaction costs could lead to greater price differences.

Empirically, the potential effects of currency unions on economic integration have received a considerable amount of attention following the publication of a study by Andrew Rose (2000). He found that currency unions are associated with a large increase in trade between participating countries, even after controlling for a variety of other characteristics shared between such countries. While a number of subsequent papers (e.g. Persson, 2001; Mélitz, 2001) have questioned his results, in particular the magnitude of the effect, there is little doubt that trade flows tend to be higher for countries in a currency union.[2] This suggests that the widely discussed home-bias in international trade (McCallum, 1995; Helliwell, 1998) and border effect on prices (Engel and Rogers, 1996) could in part be due to the use of different currencies across countries.

There are some other recent studies that shed light on price convergence in the EU and the potential role of the common currency. Several have employed the city price data from the Economist Intelligence Unit. On the basis of this data set, Rogers, Hofbauer and Wada (2001) and Rogers (2001) report that price dispersion fell during the 1990s, but that most of this reduction occurred between 1990 and 1995. Parsley and Wei (2001) find a significant reduction in price dispersion due to the introduction of the euro for the EMU member countries in their econometric analysis of the city price data. However, when they simultaneously control for EU membership, the EMU effect is no longer significant.[3] In contrast, Isgut (2002) finds a significant euro effect for the 2001 cross-section of the city price data, even when controlling for EU membership.

Other studies have used the monetary union between Belgium and Luxembourg as a case study to inform on the likely euro effects. Lutz (2004) examines price differences in the European car market during 1993–98 and reports that between Luxembourg and Belgium they were significantly smaller than for other country pairs, even after controlling for a variety of additional determinants of economic integration. Mathä (2003) examines differences in individual product prices between Luxembourg and four surrounding regions in Belgium, France and Germany in 2001/02. He also finds that price differences for Luxembourg–Belgium comparisons were significantly lower than those for other bilateral comparisons.

3 Methodology and estimation strategy

The issue addressed in this paper is a classic policy evaluation question. There is a substantial literature on the evaluation of economic policies, particularly in labour economics (e.g. Angrist and Krueger, 1999), which provides the basis for the empirical strategy employed here. This section follows Frondel and Schmidt (2001) who discuss the application of these tools to the evaluation of environmental policies. The discussion of the different estimators will be kept in general terms, referring to 'policy' or 'treatment' to denote the introduction of the single currency. Accordingly, the term 'treatment group' refers to the euro-zone countries. Of course, since the observations in this study are at a national level, potential data sets tend to be much smaller than those commonly used in labour studies where they relate to individuals or households.

Let the variable of interest that may be affected by the policy (in our case the degree of price dispersion among a group of countries) be denoted by X_r^j where $j \in (Y, N)$ and $r \in (T, T')$. Y identifies the group undergoing the treatment (here the 11 original EMU countries), N the group(s) not affected by the treatment; T denotes the treatment period (here the EMU period, i.e. 1999 and after) and T' non-treatment periods. We want to estimate the effect of a policy, i.e. the 'treatment effect'. Ideally this would be estimated as the difference between the outcome for the treatment group after receiving the treatment (i.e. price dispersion among EMU member countries after the introduction of the euro), X_T^Y, and the hypothetical outcome the same group would have experienced had it not undergone the treatment, $\tilde{X}_T^Y$,

$$S^* = X_T^Y - \tilde{X}_T^Y \tag{3.1}$$

Thus S^* is the ideal estimator of the treatment effect. The fundamental difficulty is that we cannot observe the counterfactual $\tilde{X}_T^Y$ with non-experimental data. It needs to be replaced by an observable variable that serves as proxy (instrument). Two simple possibilities are the *before-after approach*,

$$S_1 = X_T^Y - X_{T'}^Y \tag{3.2}$$

where the unobservable $\tilde{X}_T^Y$ in (3.1) is replaced by $X_{T'}^Y$, the outcome for the treatment group before the treatment period, and the *cross-section approach*,

$$S_2 = X_T^Y - X_T^N \tag{3.3}$$

where $\tilde{X}_T^Y$ is proxied by X_T^N, the outcome for a control group not undergoing the treatment.

However, S_1 and S_2 only yield unbiased estimates under certain assumptions. The before-after approach requires the identifying assumption $E(\tilde{X}_T^Y) = E(X_{T'}^Y)$, which implies in our case that price dispersion would not have changed over time had these countries not joined the EMU. The cross-section approach requires that $E(\tilde{X}_T^Y) = E(X_T^N)$ and will therefore only be unbiased if selection into the treatment is independent of the outcome without the treatment.[4]

Both sets of requirements are unlikely to hold in our context. There are other factors which may have changed the degree of price dispersion over time irrespective of currency union – one only needs to think of improvements in transport and transaction technologies such as the internet. In this case the before-after estimate S_1 would overstate the EMU effect. The cross-section approach requires that the EMU and non-EMU countries are completely alike apart from participation in the monetary union. This, too, is an unrealistic assumption since, as the theory of optimal currency areas explains, the greater the prior degree of economic integration, the stronger the incentive to form a currency union. Countries forming a currency union are thus likely to be more integrated to start off with. In this case, the cross-section approach will also overstate the impact of monetary union on lower price dispersion.

The estimator employed to test the EMU effect in this study is based on the difference-in-differences (DD) approach, which can be viewed as a combination of the before-after and cross-section approaches. This estimator is denoted by S_3 and given by

$$S_3 = (X_T^Y - X_{T'}^Y) - (X_T^N - X_{T'}^N) \tag{3.4}$$

By comparing the changes in outcomes for treatment and control groups, S_3 avoids the drawbacks of (i) the cross-sectional approach by netting out fundamental differences between the two groups and (ii) the before-after approach by netting out changes in the outcome variable affecting all groups. The assumption necessary to identify the treatment effect this way is $E(\tilde{X}_T^Y - X_{T'}^Y) = E(X_T^N - X_{T'}^N)$. This requires that there are no other factors during the treatment period which affect the treatment and control groups differently. An interesting application of the DD approach in a macroeconomic context can be found in Slaughter (2001).[5]

The DD approach will be implemented in a linear regression framework,

$$s_{rt}^j = \alpha_1 + \alpha_2 D_T + \alpha_3 D^Y + \alpha_4 D_T^Y + \sum_{k=1}^{K} \gamma_k Z_{krt}^j + \varepsilon_{rt}^j \tag{3.5}$$

where the dependent variable is the estimated standard deviation of the logarithm of common-currency prices for a given group, and (i) D_T, (ii) D^Y and (iii) D_T^Y are dummy variables equal to one when (i) $r = T$, (ii) $j = Y$ and (iii) $r = T$ and $j = Y$ simultaneously, zero otherwise. The residual ε_{rt}^j is assumed to have the usual desirable characteristics.

The dummy variables capture influences that are not directly measured but specific to the treatment and control groups and/or specific to periods before and during the treatment. Empirical studies on the determinants of economic integration, for instance, often control for geographical factors such as distance and common borders, or whether countries share a common language. If there are differences in average distances, language patterns or other time-invariant characteristics across groups, their influence will be captured by α_3 in the DD regression equation (3.5).[6] In addition, changes in general influences that are likely to affect all groups (such as lower transportation costs etc.), will be captured by α_2. Thus, all terms in (3.5) can be given a distinct interpretation, since there is a direct mapping between the dummy effects and the terms used in the DD estimator in equation (3.4):

$$\begin{aligned} \alpha_1 &\rightarrow X_{T'}^N \\ \alpha_1 + \alpha_2 &\rightarrow X_T^N \\ \alpha_1 + \alpha_3 &\rightarrow X_{T'}^Y \\ \alpha_1 + \alpha_2 + \alpha_3 + \alpha_4 &\rightarrow X_T^Y \end{aligned}$$

Most importantly, the DD effect in (3.4) thus corresponds to the estimate of α_4 and its statistical significance is easily tested by considering the corresponding t-statistic. However, α_4 only identifies the treatment effect if all factors with a differential effect on treatment and control groups during the treatment period are controlled for. Thus the Z_{krt}^j $(k = 1, 2, ...K)$ terms in equation (3.5) are additional control variables that are thought to influence price dispersion and vary over time and across groups.

Modelling the euro effect as a structural break in form of a simple shift in the standard deviation, as in equation (3.5), is the most straightforward way to implement the DD approach. However, we do not have any a priori knowledge of the shape the potential narrowing of price dispersion could take. Thus, in addition to the specification shown in (3.5), results will also be presented for a specification where the dummies are interacted with time trends to allow for group- and period-specific changes in price dispersion over time, and one where both the dummies and differential time trends are included. These two additional specifications are given by

$$s_{rt}^{j} = \alpha_1 + \beta_1 t + \beta_2 tD_T + \beta_3 tD^Y + \beta_4 tD_T^Y + \sum_{k=1}^{K} \gamma_k Z_{krt}^{j} + \varepsilon_{rt}^{j} \quad (3.6)$$

where the DD estimate is given by β_4, and

$$\begin{aligned} s_{rt}^{j} &= \alpha_1 + \alpha_2 D_T + \alpha_3 D^Y + \alpha_4 D_T^Y \\ &\quad + \beta_1 t + \beta_2 tD_T + \beta_3 tD^Y + \beta_4 tD_T^Y + \sum_{k=1}^{K} \gamma_k Z_{krt}^{j} + \varepsilon_{rt}^{j} \end{aligned} \quad (3.7)$$

which contains both a DD shift (α_4) and a DD change in trend (β_4) estimate. To examine the sensitivity of results, all versions are estimated with and without additional control variables.

4 Data description

The analysis uses four different data sets on final goods prices:

- the prices of Big Macs that are published annually in *The Economist*;
- the cover prices of *The Economist*;
- pre-tax car prices from *Car Prices in the European Union*, a survey of car prices regularly released by the European Commission;
- data on the costs of various goods and services from *Prices and Earnings around the Globe*, a publication by the Swiss bank UBS.

All four data sets have in one form or another been used in previous work, usually to study issues related to the law of one price and market integration. Big Mac prices, for instance, were used in Cumby (1996), Ong (1997) and Pakko and Pollard (1996). *The Economist* cover prices were employed, amongst others, in studies by Ghosh and Wolf (1994), Knetter (1997) and Knetter and Slaughter (1999). Lutz (1999), Gaulier and Haller (2000) and Goldberg and Verboven (2001) have utilised the European Commission's data on car prices and Lutz (2001) the UBS data set.

Table 4.2 describes the basic characteristics of the four data sets. They differ in various respects, such as the frequency which ranges from monthly (*Economist*) to three-year intervals (UBS data). They also cover different time

Table 4.2 Description of the four data sets

	Big Mac[a]	*The Economist*[b]	*Cars*[c]	*UBS*[d]
Source	The Economist Newspapers Limited	The Economist Newspapers Limited	European Commission	UBS
Period	1987–2001	1995–2001	1995–2001	1970–2000
Frequency	annual (usually April)	monthly (last issue each month)	bi-annual (1 May; 1 November)	every three years (usually second quarter)
Number of series	1	1	17	13
EMU countries	France, Germany, Italy, Spain	Austria, Belgium, Finland, France, Germany, Ireland, Italy, Luxembourg, Netherlands, Portugal, Spain	Austria, Belgium, France, Germany, Ireland, Italy, Luxembourg, Netherlands, Portugal, Spain	Austria (Vienna), Belgium (Brussels), Finland (Helsinki), France (Paris), Italy (Milan), Luxembourg (Luxembourg), Netherlands (Amsterdam), Portugal (Lisbon), Spain (Madrid)
Other EU countries	Denmark, Sweden, UK	Denmark, Greece, Sweden, UK	Sweden, UK	Denmark (Copenhagen), Greece (Athens), Sweden (Stockholm), UK (London)
Other OECD countries	Australia, Canada, Japan, USA	Iceland, Norway, Switzerland, USA		Australia (Sydney), Canada (Montreal), Japan (Tokyo), Norway (Oslo), Switzerland (Zurich), USA (New York)

[a] Since the first two Big Mac price surveys were in September 1986 and January data for 1987, these were merged by using 1996 observations for 1997 where the latter were missing. Survey dates: 17/1/1987 (or 1/9/1986), 28/3/1988, 11/4/1989, 30/4/1990, 9/4/1991, 10/4/1992, 13/4/1993, 5/4/1994, 7/4/1995, 22/4/1996, 7/4/1997, 6/4/1998, 30/3/1999, 25/4/2000, 17/4/2001.

[b] *Economist* prices for December in the UK and US are based on the issue preceding the higher-priced Christmas issue. Local currency prices were converted into US dollars using end-of-period exchange rates (code..AE.ZF) from the IMF's *International Financial Statistics* database.

[c] Pre-tax prices. Data up to the 1998 surveys were converted into ecus and those from 1999 onward into euros using the exchange rates given in each volume.

[d] Data collection periods: July 1970, July/Aug 1973, May/June 1976, June/July 1979, March/April 1982, Spring 1988 and 1991, and the second quarter in 1994, 1997 and 2000.

Source: *The Economist*, European edition (for Big Mac and *Economist* cover prices); *Car Prices in the European Union* (European Commission); *Prices and Earnings around the Globe* (UBS).

spans and, as a result of the particular countries included, vary with respect to the composition of treatment and control groups. Moreover, the UBS data refer to specific cities while the other three data sets apply at the national level. Lastly, the car price data are unique here in being available before tax.

Ideally, the treatment group should contain all eleven starting EMU member countries. The most natural control group would then contain the four remaining EU countries. Alternatively, one might consider a broader control group including both the remaining EU members and other OECD countries. One would then like to cover the 1995–2001 period, since Austria, Finland and Sweden were not formal EU members before then. In practice, however, several concessions have to be made due to specific limitations in each of the four data sets. As a result, in most cases either the selection of group members or time periods deviates in some dimension from the 'ideal' data set.

The following selection criteria were used to set up the data. First, there had to be a sufficient number of observations over time. For Big Mac prices and UBS data this meant going further back than 1995 (in both cases the entire available period was used). Second, only countries are included where observations on prices are available without gaps, since changes in the composition of groups might otherwise bias the results. For Big Macs, the treatment group thus only consists of four countries; for the UBS data, the treatment group omits Ireland (since Dublin featured only intermittently) and Germany (since there is no German city with data throughout all surveys). The analysis of car prices omits Denmark, Finland and Greece, since the European Commission reports did not include them prior to 1999.

The UBS and car price data sets are somewhat different since each contains more than one good or model. To make the tests strictly comparable across goods/models, only those are included where data are available for the entire set of countries in treatment and control groups. In addition, there had to be a sufficient number of consecutive observations over time (at least ten for each car model and nine in the case of the UBS data). As a result, of more than 90 models covered at one point or another in the car price reports, only 17 had sufficient data.[7] Similarly, of more than 30 individual price series featured at some point in the UBS price reports, only 13 had a sufficient number of observations to be included.[8]

The resulting observations are plotted in Figure 4.1. The four diagrams show the standard deviations of the logarithm of prices for both treatment and control groups in each data set, and for the periods selected for this study. The diagrams for the car and UBS price series depict the means across models/series. Looking at the treatment group – i.e. the EMU countries – there is little visual evidence that price dispersion decreased after 1999 except for the prices of *The Economist*. However, in this case the prices for the control groups appear to have converged too. The diagrams also reveal that, during the sample periods covered here, price dispersion was often considerably lower for the treatment group compared to the two control groups. There are

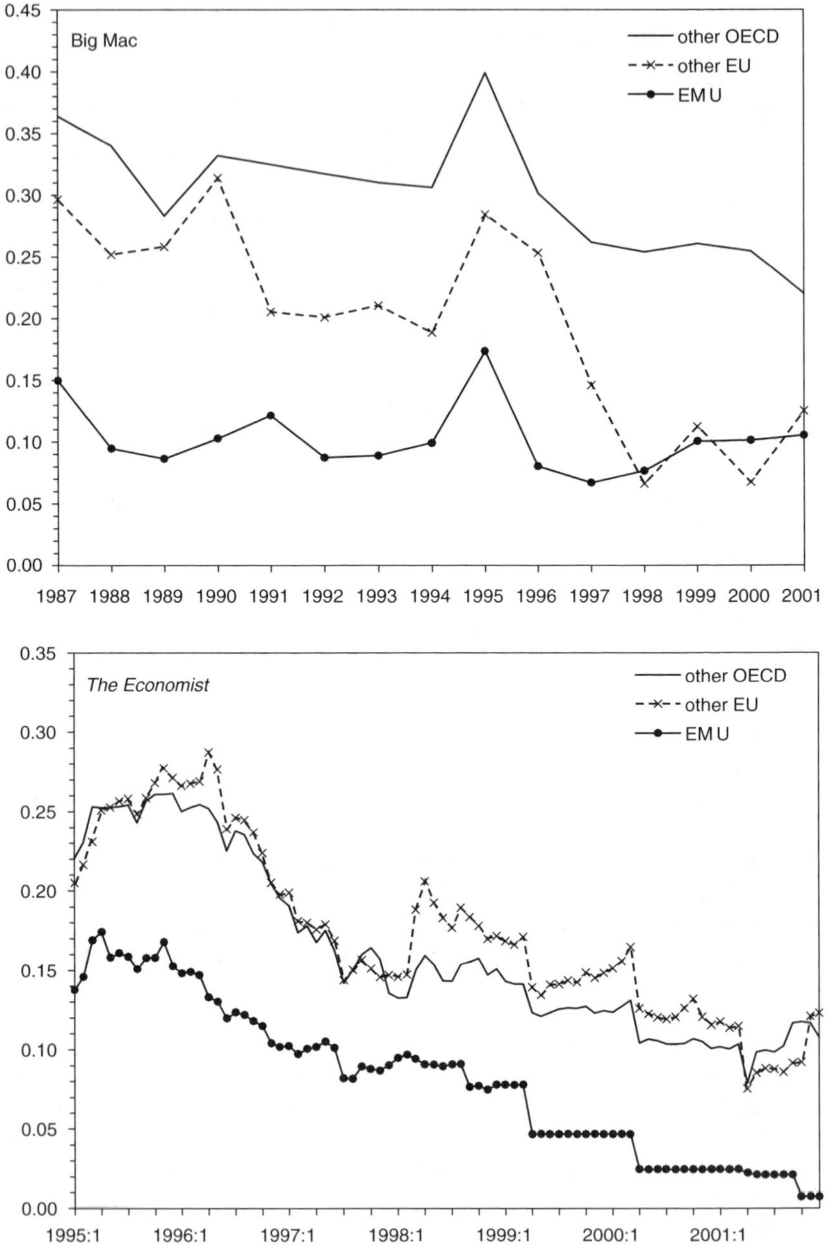

Figure 4.1 Standard deviations over time

Note: The panel containing the car price data shows the mean standard deviation across 17 models and that for the UBS data the mean standard deviation across 13 series.

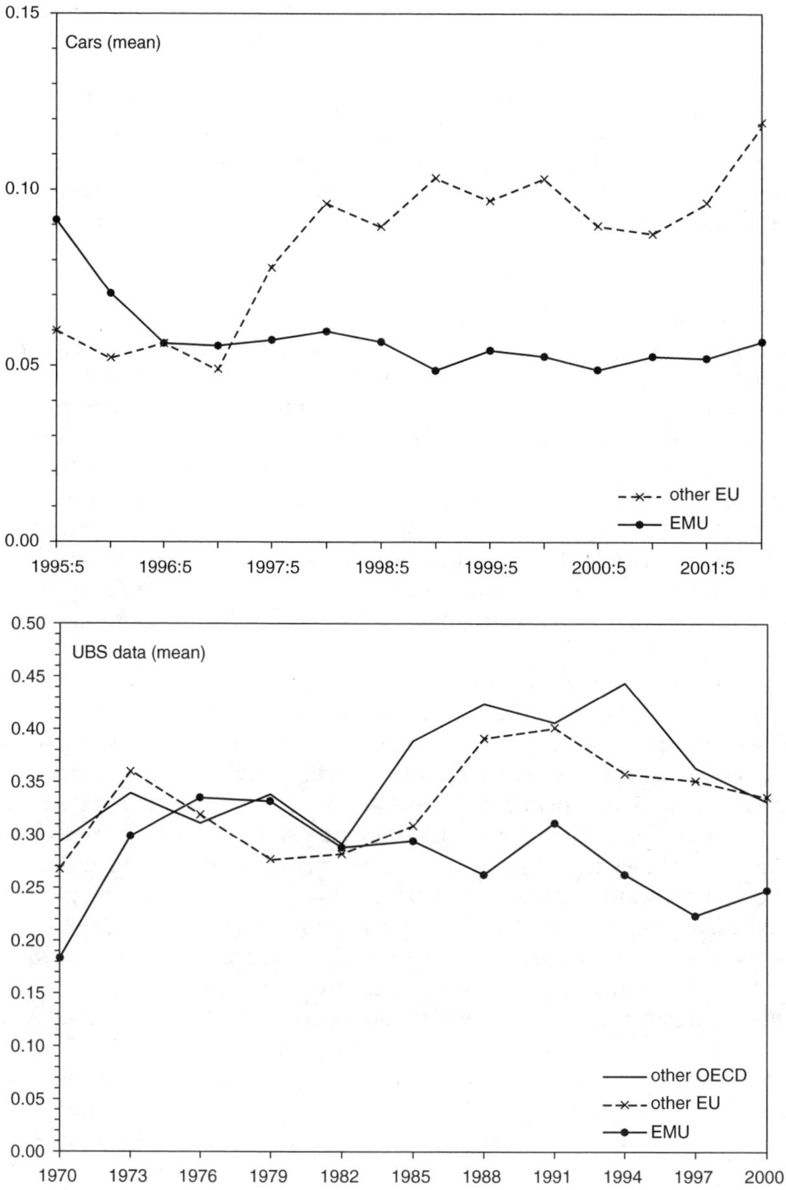

Figure 4.1 Continued

some exceptions to this, such as the earlier observations of the UBS and car price data, and Big Mac prices during the later periods where price dispersion in the euro zone and EU control group were very similar.

Table 4.3 reports before-after and cross-section comparisons of standard deviations. Each entry in the table shows the ratio of two standard deviations, either for different periods or for different country groups. A lower degree of price dispersion during the EMU period compared to previous periods, or for the treatment group relative to a control group, is indicated by a ratio smaller than one. Due to the multitude of car price and UBS series, the table also reports the median relative standard deviation as a summary measure for these two data sets. Entries marked by an asterisk (*) indicate that a standard F-test, given by $s_1/s_2 \sim F(n_1 - 1, n_2 - 1)$, results in a statistically significant difference (at a 10% level or lower) between the two respective variances.

The relative standard deviations in the table confirm the visual impression from Figure 4.1. Looking at the standard deviation of log prices before and after the introduction of the euro, there is little indication of a downward shift. This is irrespective of whether one compares the entire first three EMU years (1999–2001) to the three years before (1996–98), or whether one takes a longer view by comparing the third euro year (2001) to the third year before its introduction (1996). As already noted, the prices of *The Economist* are the exception here, and the reduction in price dispersion is also statistically significant in this case.

There are some cars with lower price dispersion after 1999 (e.g. the Audi A4, the Mercedes S-Class and the Ford models), but this has to be offset against several where price dispersion rose (e.g. three of the Opel models). The overall evidence for cars, as summarized by the median, reveals little overall trend, since it is either just below or a little above one, depending on whether three-year periods or just 2001 and 1996 are compared. This mixed picture on car prices does not change when one considers only those differences that are statistically significant. There are five that are significantly smaller but also five that are significantly larger. A similar picture emerges across the various UBS price series. For some, price dispersion declined during 2000, but this depends on whether one draws a comparison with 1997 or 1994. The median is again close to one, slightly above for the 2000/1997 comparison and slightly below for the 2000/1994 comparison.

The cross-section comparisons of relative standard deviations in Table 4.3 send out a clearer message. For the periods examined, the entries in the table show that, with few exceptions, price dispersion was in general lower among euro-zone countries than among either of the two control groups. This applies to all data sets, including Big Mac prices, where the difference to the OECD control group is statistically significant when three-year periods are used for comparison. The evidence on large differences between treatment and control groups is particularly strong for *The Economist* and across the various car models. The median estimates for cars are now 0.61 and 0.46, and

Table 4.3 Before-after and cross-section comparisons of standard deviations

Item	*Before-after*		*Cross-section*			
Period:	*1999–01*	*2001*	*1999–01*	*2001*	*1999–01*	*2001*
Relative to:	*1996–98*	*1996*	*EU*	*EU*	*OECD*	*OECD*
Big Mac	1.37	1.31	1.01	0.84	0.42*	0.48
The Economist	0.31*	0.17*	0.27*	0.24*	0.28*	0.21*
Audi A4	0.77*	0.65	0.24*	0.17*		
Ford Fiesta	0.71*	0.74	0.64*	0.40*		
Ford Focus	0.77*	0.84	0.48*	0.46*		
Ford Mondeo	0.96	0.87	0.68	0.46*		
Mercedes S-Class	0.51*	0.34*	0.29*	0.15*		
Opel Corsa	1.30*	1.66*	0.84	1.02		
Opel Astra	1.40*	1.42	0.50*	0.52*		
Opel Vectra	1.34*	1.32	1.13	1.27		
Opel Omega	0.84	0.89	0.33*	0.38*		
Peugeot 307	0.98	1.16	0.27*	0.23*		
Renault Laguna	1.00	1.05	0.34*	0.23*		
Seat Ibiza	1.19	1.35	1.20	1.18		
Seat Toledo	0.93	1.07	0.33*	0.38*		
Toyota Avensis	1.05	1.25	0.75	0.66		
VW Golf	1.36*	1.32	0.61*	0.65		
VW Passat	1.09	0.87	0.90	1.31		
Volvo S40	0.90	0.86	0.90	2.70		
Median (cars)	*0.98*	*1.05*	*0.61*	*0.46*		
Period:	*2000*	*2000*	*2000*	*2000*		
Relative to:	*1997*	*1994*	*EU*	*OECD*		
Food	0.97	0.95	0.50*	0.48*		
Women's clothing	0.97	0.86	0.63	0.42*		
Men's clothing	1.50	0.97	1.23	0.85		
Rent	1.08	0.64	2.59*	0.76		
Household appliances	1.33	0.86	0.31*	0.33*		
Automobile	0.60*	0.70	0.99	0.97		
Public transport	0.91	0.94	0.63	0.96		
Taxi ride	1.10	1.22	0.91	1.05		
Automobile service	1.16	0.86	0.85	1.01		
Restaurant meal	1.22	1.09	1.05	0.71		
Hotel stay	1.34	0.97	0.66	0.64		
Basket of services	1.08	1.12	0.83	0.90		
Basket of goods and services	1.45	1.12	0.58*	0.80		
Median (UBS)	*1.10*	*0.95*	*0.83*	*0.80*		

Notes: Each entry in the table is the ratio of the two standard deviations indicated in the column header. *The Economist* cover price data refer to July and the car price data to November of each year. For the UBS series the number of comparisons is restricted by the low sampling frequency. The standard deviations across multiple time periods (1999–01; 1996–98) were calculated using period-specific means. An asterisk (*) denotes that an *F*-test for the equality of the two variances is statistically significant at the 10% significance level or lower.

most ratios are significantly different from one. The median relative standard deviations across the UBS price series are now also clearly below one, as are most of those that are statistically significant.

Altogether, these comparisons provide a mixed picture. The before-after comparisons, on the one hand, indicate that price dispersion did not fall during the first three years of the euro. The cross-section comparisons, on the other hand, reveal that price dispersion during 1999–2001 was considerably lower among euro-zone countries than among either of the two control groups. While these comparisons are useful descriptions of the basic properties of the data, they have their limitations, since they cannot be used to isolate the effect of the introduction of the euro on price dispersion (see section 3). In the next section the DD approach is used to test the euro hypothesis per se.

5 Difference-in-differences estimates of the single-currency effect

The results of the DD estimates of the single-currency effect are presented in Tables 4.4 to 4.6. As discussed in Section 3, the DD approach controls for both additional influences during the treatment period and differences between treatment and control groups. Tables 4.4 and 4.5 (Big Mac, *Economist* and cars) contain estimates for all three DD specifications: the first relates to DD estimates of the differences in the level of price dispersion (denoted by 'shift' in the column header) and based on equation (3.5), the second to differences in the trend in price dispersion (denoted by 'change in trend' in the column header) and based on equation (3.6), and the third allows for both simultaneously as in equation (3.7). The corresponding *t*-ratios are shown in parentheses. Estimates that are statistically significant at the 10 per cent level or below are marked by an asterisk (*). To save space, only the estimates of the single currency effect are reported in the tables, i.e. the estimates of α_4 and β_4. All regressions were estimated individually by ordinary least squares.[9] Due to the inherent limitation of the car price (only EU countries) and UBS data sets (only one EMU observation), Table 4.5 only features the EU control group and Table 4.6 only includes specification (3.5). Each specification was estimated with and without the following additional control variables:

- the standard deviation of inflation rates to capture (i) differences in the extent of local-currency pricing across groups and (ii) the extent to which monetary conditions (i.e. relative movements in money supply and demand) are similar;
- the standard deviation of the growth rates of the nominal dollar exchange rate to allow for different price movements as a result of import price changes and the degree to which incomplete exchange rate pass-through matters;

Table 4.4 Difference-in-differences estimates: Big Mac and *Economist* prices

Item	*n*	*Control group*	Z^j_{krt}	1 *Shift*	2 *Change in trend*	3*a* *Shift*	3*b* *Change in trend*
Big Mac	30	EU	no	0.121*(4.32)	0.068*(2.37)	0.073 (0.95)	−0.014 (0.47)
		OECD	no	0.071*(3.62)	0.091*(4.79)	0.012 (0.33)	0.020*(2.22)
		EU	yes	0.122*(3.86)	0.071*(2.65)	0.074 (0.98)	−0.010 (0.33)
		OECD	yes	0.084*(3.95)	0.101*(3.40)	0.012 (0.36)	0.026*(2.43)
Economist	168	EU	no	0.001 (0.15)	0.001*(4.71)	−0.016 (1.53)	0.000 (0.10)
		OECD	no	0.003 (0.31)	0.001*(3.26)	−0.010 (1.24)	−0.002*(4.36)
		EU	yes	−0.082*(9.61)	−0.001 (1.51)	−0.042*(4.39)	0.000 (0.71)
		OECD	yes	−0.031*(3.07)	0.000 (0.30)	−0.030*(3.80)	−0.001*(3.70)

Notes: The estimates are based on equations (3.5)–(3.7) in the text. Robust *t*-ratios are shown in parentheses. In column 1 the DD estimate relates to differences in the level of price dispersion, in column 2 to differences in its trend and column 3 allows for both. Only the estimates of the single-currency effect are reported in the table. The Z^j_{krt} column indicates whether the additional control variables are included or not. Significant estimates (at the 10% significance level or lower) are marked with an asterisk (*).

Table 4.5 Difference-in-differences estimates: car prices

Item	*n*	Z^j_{krt}	1 *Shift*	2 *Change in trend*	3*a* *Shift*	3*b* *Change in trend*
Audi A4	28	no	−0.085* (4.51)	−0.019* (4.64)	0.013 (0.50)	−0.007 (0.92)
		yes	−0.095* (4.44)	−0.009 (1.34)	0.002 (0.07)	−0.009 (1.14)
Ford Fiesta	28	no	−0.067* (3.75)	−0.020* (3.70)	−0.014 (0.34)	−0.007 (0.76)
		yes	−0.074* (3.88)	−0.010 (1.16)	−0.022 (0.52)	−0.009 (0.89)
Ford Focus	28	no	−0.058* (3.01)	−0.011 (1.69)	−0.024 (0.51)	0.000 (0.02)
		yes	−0.062* (2.48)	0.000 (0.03)	−0.014 (0.23)	0.002 (0.13)
Ford Mondeo	28	no	−0.028 (1.06)	−0.001 (0.09)	−0.001 (0.02)	0.016 (0.97)
		yes	−0.026 (0.88)	0.017 (1.35)	−0.002 (0.05)	0.016 (1.01)
Mercedes S-Class	28	no	−0.012 (0.79)	−0.001 (0.11)	0.010 (0.44)	−0.007 (0.80)
		yes	−0.007 (0.35)	−0.007 (0.70)	0.004 (0.17)	−0.007 (0.92)
Opel Corsa	28	no	−0.006 (0.19)	−0.010 (1.31)	0.032 (0.81)	−0.029* (2.14)
		yes	0.006 (0.15)	−0.028* (2.28)	0.025 (0.70)	−0.029* (2.10)
Opel Astra	28	no	−0.002 (0.16)	0.004 (0.95)	0.010 (0.30)	−0.011 (1.44)
		yes	0.010 (0.64)	−0.008 (1.30)	0.019 (0.56)	−0.009 (1.07)
Opel Vectra	28	no	−0.046* (3.94)	−0.013* (2.56)	−0.029 (1.41)	0.007 (1.33)
		yes	−0.048* (3.47)	0.004 (0.61)	−0.028 (1.26)	0.007 (1.28)
Opel Omega	28	no	−0.108* (6.43)	−0.017* (2.72)	−0.048 (1.25)	0.012 (1.29)
		yes	−0.126* (7.57)	0.006 (0.68)	−0.056 (1.58)	0.010 (1.14)
Peugeot 307	28	no	−0.099* (3.16)	−0.013 (1.68)	0.056 (1.60)	0.008 (0.76)
		yes	−0.125* (3.70)	0.011 (0.96)	0.049* (1.77)	0.006 (0.66)
Renault Laguna	22	no	−0.082* (2.51)	−0.018* (2.48)	0.065 (1.31)	0.010 (0.76)
		yes	−0.069 (1.63)	0.017 (0.97)	0.056 (1.12)	0.009 (0.68)
Seat Ibiza	24	no	0.089* (3.03)	0.025* (2.58)	0.158* (3.29)	0.030* (2.56)
		yes	0.080* (2.04)	0.040* (1.82)	0.151* (3.29)	0.030* (3.01)
Seat Toledo	24	no	−0.043 (1.21)	0.001 (0.12)	0.091* (3.19)	0.037* (4.39)
		yes	−0.036 (0.76)	0.049* (3.23)	0.092* (3.09)	0.037* (4.22)
Toyota Avensis	28	no	0.016 (0.74)	0.010 (1.48)	0.016 (0.36)	0.010 (0.94)
		yes	0.011 (0.51)	0.010 (1.08)	0.010 (0.23)	0.009 (0.82)
VW Golf	28	no	0.005 (0.14)	0.022* (2.88)	0.053* (1.87)	0.049* (4.92)
		yes	−0.021 (0.58)	0.052* (4.80)	0.049* (1.88)	0.048* (4.71)
VW Passat	28	no	0.008 (0.28)	0.019* (3.21)	0.016 (0.70)	0.048* (5.85)
		yes	−0.009 (0.29)	0.049* (6.78)	0.013 (0.60)	0.048* (5.56)
Volvo S40	28	no	−0.016 (0.50)	0.013* (1.91)	−0.113* (2.52)	0.038* (3.23)
		yes	−0.018 (0.51)	0.030* (2.39)	−0.119* (2.56)	0.038* (3.26)
Median		no	*−0.028*	*−0.001*	*0.013*	*0.010*
		yes	*−0.026*	*0.010*	*0.010*	*0.009*

Note: The results in this table only feature the EU control group. See Table 4.4 for further details.

- the standard deviation of output growth rates to capture the degree to which business cycle movements are correlated.

The data on exchange rates, growth and inflation were taken from the August 2002 CD-ROM edition of the International Monetary Fund's *International Financial Statistics*.[10] The three variables vary between groups and over time, thus

Table 4.6 Difference-in-differences estimates: UBS price series

Item	*n*	*Versus EU*		*Versus OECD*	
		without Z^j_{krt}	*with* Z^j_{krt}	*without* Z^j_{krt}	*with* Z^j_{krt}
Food	22	−0.015 (0.51)	−0.071*(2.17)	−0.034 (0.97)	−0.071*(1.80)
Women's clothing	22	0.081*(2.97)	0.004 (0.12)	0.048 (1.71)	0.023 (0.48)
Men's clothing	22	0.125*(3.68)	−0.010 (0.31)	0.115*(3.19)	−0.003 (0.05)
Rent	20	−0.376*(6.16)	−0.011 (0.25)	−0.361*(5.29)	−0.001 (0.01)
Household appliances	22	0.031 (1.15)	0.017 (0.71)	0.003 (0.12)	−0.002 (0.07)
Automobile	22	−0.140*(2.86)	0.074 (1.50)	−0.164*(3.17)	0.065 (1.01)
Public transport	20	0.157 (1.58)	0.068 (1.10)	0.139 (1.45)	0.076 (1.20)
Taxi ride	20	0.172*(3.47)	0.072 (1.68)	0.155*(2.51)	0.080*(1.84)
Automobile service	18	−0.207*(2.51)	0.036 (0.46)	−0.185 (1.69)	−0.030 (0.33)
Restaurant meal	22	−0.077 (1.61)	0.017 (0.39)	−0.133*(2.98)	−0.027 (0.48)
Hotel stay	22	−0.106*(2.56)	−0.164*(5.09)	−0.142*(3.56)	−0.161*(6.11)
Basket of services	20	−0.003 (0.09)	−0.001 (0.02)	−0.048 (1.68)	−0.029 (1.18)
Basket of goods and services	18	−0.103*(3.79)	−0.060*(2.27)	−0.133*(6.17)	−0.061 (1.58)
Median		*−0.015*	*0.004*	*−0.048*	*−0.003*

Note: The estimates are all based on the 'shift' specification shown in DD equation (3.5); see Table 4.4 for further explanations.

not only capturing exogenous influences specific to treatment and control groups, but also specific to each period. The dispersion of exchange rate movements, for instance, is zero for EMU countries from 1999 onwards, but not for the other groups and periods. Similarly, including the dispersion of inflation rates helps to control for the fact that monetary policies were already becoming increasingly harmonized across prospective euro zone members in the run up to the introduction of the euro, but not necessarily for other countries.

First consider Table 4.4 which contains the estimates for Big Mac and *Economist* prices. Almost all DD estimates for Big Mac prices are positive, irrespective of control group and whether the other control variables are included or not. The two estimates that are negative – the 'change in trend' coefficient in specification 3 with the other EU countries as control group – are statistically insignificant. In contrast, all those that are significant are positive. Big Mac prices, therefore, do not provide any evidence in favour of the price-equalizing effects of the euro. On the contrary, the results in this case suggest that, if anything, price dispersion rose as a result of the introduction of the euro.

The estimates for the prices of *The Economist* are a lot more supportive of the European Commission's euro hypothesis. The majority of estimates are negative, in particular when the additional control variables are included.

The exceptions are the estimates of specification 2 without additional controls, where both estimates are positive and significant. However, this result does not extend to the corresponding estimate of specification 3 where both level shift and trend change are allowed for. In those cases where the additional controls are added the evidence is unambiguous: the majority are significant, and all of those are negative. Thus, in contrast to Big Mac prices, the evidence based on the cover prices of *The Economist* is more supportive of significant euro effects on lower price dispersion between member countries.

Moving to the car price data, there are now seventeen further 'goods' to consider. Consider first the point estimates in Table 4.5. While the majority of 'shift' estimates are negative (26 out of 34 with and without additional controls), the opposite is the case in specifications 2 and 3 (15 out of 32 and 22 out of 64, respectively). Hence the point estimates themselves do not lend any clear-cut evidence either way. Looking only at those estimates that are statistically significant provides similarly mixed evidence. Whenever trends are allowed for – as in specifications 2 and 3 – the evidence is more supportive of a rise than of a fall in price dispersion after the introduction of the euro. The inclusion of additional control variables does not alter the results by much. The point estimates are fairly similar, as indicated by the median point estimates (shown in the last two rows of the table), except for specification 2 where there is a slight increase when controls are added. In terms of significance, there are 27 estimates without controls versus 24 with controls that are significantly different from zero.

As an alternative to a summary by test specification, one can also evaluate the evidence by car model. For instance, consider those DD estimates that are statistically significant and then examine whether, for a given model, they point in the same direction. On the basis of this approach there are seven models (Audi A4, Ford Fiesta, Ford Focus, Opel Corsa, Opel Vectra, Opel Omega and Renault Laguna) where there is some statistically significant evidence of a downward movement in price dispersion due to EMU but none against. Yet, there are also five models (Seat Ibiza, Seat Toledo, VW Golf, VW Passat and Volvo S40[11]) where the evidence points in the opposite direction: for each of these five models, there is at least one statistically significant DD estimate with a positive sign and none with a negative sign. For the remaining models, the DD tests are either all insignificant (Ford Mondeo, Mercedes S-Class, Opel Astra and Toyota Avensis) or provide contradictory evidence (Peugeot 307).

The results for the UBS price series are presented in Table 4.6. As indicated earlier, they relate to specification 1 ('shift') only. The majority of point estimates carry a negative sign (31 versus 21). This also applies to the majority of those DD estimates that are statistically significant (15 versus 6). The inclusion of the three additional control variables weakens the evidence somewhat in comparison to the tests without – the median point estimate is larger and fewer of the estimates are significant. However, it makes little difference whether the EU or OECD control groups are employed. Considering the individual price series, seven (food, rent, automobile, automobile service, restaurant meal, hotel stay and basket of goods and services) provide evidence of a statistically significant narrowing of price dispersion in one or more cases (and no evidence against), while three show the opposite (women's clothing, men's clothing and taxi ride).

A summary of the results across data sets and test specifications is provided in Table 4.7. This last table lists for each data set and DD specification (i) the overall number of single currency estimates, (ii) how many are negative and statistically significant, (iii) how many are positive and significant and (iv) what is called the 'net %' and defined as the difference between (ii) and (iii) as a percentage of (i). This last measure can theoretically range from 100 per cent in the case where all estimates are significant and indicative of a downward single currency effect on price dispersion, and −100 per cent when all estimates are significant but point exactly the other way. While the 'net %' number does not constitute a statistical test, it is a useful way to represent the overall balance of DD results.

In total, there are 178 DD tests of the single currency effect, differing in terms of price series, data set, specification and control group.[12] Of these, 41 provide statistically significant evidence that the single currency has reduced the degree of price dispersion among EMU countries. However, there are also 40 tests where the results are statistically significant but point in the opposite direction, i.e. an upward effect on price dispersion due to the single currency. If one weighs up the statistically negative and positive estimates against each other, the net effect across all DD tests is practically zero. Considering the aggregate results across specifications, the DD approach thus lends no support to the European Commission's claims.[13]

There are some differences across data sets. The evidence based on Big Mac prices, for instance, provides no support for the European Commission's claims. The results on car price and *Economist* cover prices are somewhat sensitive to the inclusion of additional controls. Considered across all tests, car prices do not support a single-currency effect in either direction. The strongest evidence of a downward single-currency effect on price differences comes from the cover prices of *The Economist.* Some support for the Commission's claims can also be found among the UBS price series.

Alternatively, the DD test results can be summarised by price series. There are 14 price series (seven each in the car and UBS data sets) where the evidence points to a significant negative euro-effect on price dispersion, and nine price series (Big Macs, five car models, three UBS series) where the evidence points in the other direction. While this perspective lends a little more support for the claim that the European single currency would reduce the degree of price dispersion, it is also far from overwhelming.

Table 4.7 Summary of difference-in-differences results

Item		*Versus EU*		*Versus OECD*		
		without Z^j_{krt}	*with* Z^j_{krt}	*without* Z^j_{krt}	*with* Z^j_{krt}	*Total*
Big Mac	*Total*	3	3	3	3	12
	signif. <	0	0	0	0	0
	signif. >	2	2	3	3	10
	net %	−66.7	−66.7	−100.0	−100.0	−83.3
The Economist	*Total*	3	3	3	3	12
	signif. <	0	2	1	2	5
	signif. >	1	0	1	0	2
	net %	−33.3	66.7	0.0	66.7	25.0
Cars	*Total*	51	51			102
	signif. <	13	8			21
	signif. >	10	12			22
	net %	5.9	−7.8			−1.0
UBS	*Total*	13	13	13	13	52
	signif. <	5	5	3	2	15
	signif. >	3	2	0	1	6
	net %	15.4	23.1	23.1	7.7	17.3
Total	*Total*	70	70	19	19	178
	signif. <	18	15	4	4	41
	signif. >	16	16	4	4	40
	net %	2.9	−1.4	0.0	0.0	0.6

Notes: The first three rows for each data-set report (i) the total number of tests, (ii) the number of tests resulting in a significantly smaller degree of price dispersion and (iii) the number of tests resulting in a significantly larger degree of price dispersion (at a ten per cent significance level). The row labelled 'net %' is the difference between (ii) and (iii) expressed as a percentage of (i), for each test category and data-set.

6 Conclusion

The results in this chapter suggest that EMU has not led to a widespread narrowing of price differences during the first three years, at least for the goods prices studied here. Taken at face value, this suggests that the use of different currencies has not exerted a significant influence on the degree of market segmentation across the European Union. This may not only come as a surprise given the statements made by the European Commission and other commentators in the run-up to EMU, but also when one considers the recent evidence on the effect of common currencies on trade. It is therefore natural to ask whether the evidence provided in this paper is truly indicative of a general pattern. Could it be unrepresentative – possibly even biased – as a result of the particular data and method employed?

The first question that arises relates to the goods covered in this study. Is the small selection of goods covered in this paper indicative of more general price trends? A thorough answer could be provided by considering a larger set of goods, but there is currently only a very limited number of data sets on prices of individual goods. As reported earlier, the study by Parsley and Wei (2001) uses a larger set of goods but also fails to find a significant euro-effect once EU membership is controlled for. At least, the evidence provided in this study is based on four independent data sets and a fairly wide range of goods and services. There is no a priori reason to suspect that the results presented here are inherently biased against finding a significant single market effect.

A second potential limitation may be that only the first three years of EMU are covered here. It may be that the integrating effects of the euro take longer to materialize. However, while the relatively low convergence speeds – half-life estimates of three to five years – typically estimated in research on purchasing-power parity may be a 'puzzle' (Rogoff, 1996), there is some evidence of faster convergence in Taylor (2002) and recent research with disaggregated and micro-level price data comes up with half-life estimates of less than two years, some even below one year.[14] It thus appears that prices do converge rapidly enough to expect some evidence of lower price dispersion in our three-year period, *if* the single currency really has such an effect.

A third question is whether one should draw a distinction between the first three years of EMU and the period from 2002 onwards. Could it matter whether people have actual notes and coins in their pockets? The standard answer is no, if agents are rational and therefore capable of telling the difference between nominal (i.e. prices in different currencies) and real variables (i.e. relative prices between countries). If not, we would be dealing with some form of money illusion. The evidence in Fehr and Tyran (2001) suggests that money illusion may be a realistic phenomenon.[15] There is also strong evidence of 'framing effects' in the experimental literature and perhaps a particular currency serves as a reference frame to agents.

It will therefore be interesting to see whether the introduction of actual euro notes and coins has a separate effect on price convergence, but systematic evidence on this will only be available in a few years' time. The casual evidence is mixed. A survey reported in *The Times* (5 September 2002), for instance, indicated that price differences in the euro zone were still substantial in 2002. In contrast, *The Economist* started charging a common price in euro countries (except for Greece) in 2002. Two recent studies that examine price differences before and after the euro changeover in January 2002 provide more systematic, though still preliminary, evidence. Mathä (2003), comparing prices in Luxembourg and surrounding regions in Belgium, France and Germany, reports no reduction in price differences between October 2001 and April 2002. Baye et al. (2002) compare online prices for a range of goods between October 2001 and May 2002 and report no convergence after the changeover.

Altogether, the results of these studies and those presented in this chapter suggest that the use of different currencies was probably not the major barrier to further economic integration in the EU it was often made out to be. Instead, the focus should shift to other influences on the degree of product market integration in the EU. Clearly, some goods and services are non-tradable by nature. Others, however, are rendered non-tradable in practice due to lack of competition between producers and/or distributors, transport and transaction costs and informational asymmetries between local and foreign consumers about local prices. It is also possible that, precisely because of these additional constraints on market integration, the single currency has so far had such a negligible effect on price dispersion in the EMU.

Notes

1. Similar views were voiced by European consumer organizations. Jim Murray, director of the Bureau Européen des Unions de Consommateurs (BEUC), for instance, argued that 'the euro should help to reduce these price differences', but also conceded that it would 'not in itself bring full price convergence' (BEUC, 1998).
2. There are many studies related to Andrew Rose's work, including his own subsequent work. A useful list can be found on Rose's homepage under http://faculty.haas.berkeley.edu/arose/RecRes.htm.
3. Note that their study uses the standard deviation of the common currency price differential across different goods for each bilateral country comparison. This is a measure of the dispersion of relative rather than absolute prices. The current study, in contrast, looks at the standard deviation of prices for a given good across countries. These two measures could give different results, since the dispersion of relative prices can be low even if prices for individual goods differ substantially across countries.
4. In other words, there should be no fundamental differences between treatment group and control group which simultaneously affect (i) the likelihood of undergoing the treatment and (ii) the outcome without the treatment.
5. A fourth method discussed in Frondel and Schmidt (2001) is the matching approach. This entails finding for each entity (individual, household, etc.) undergoing treatment a 'similar' or 'matching' entity (in terms of their general characteristics) not undergoing treatment to identify the treatment effect. This approach cannot be applied here due to the large data requirements.
6. This will also include measurement issues, such as differences in group size.
7. These are: Audi A4, Ford Fiesta/Focus/Mondeo, Mercedes S-Class, Opel Corsa/Astra/Vectra/Omega, Peugeot 307, Renault Laguna, Seat Ibiza/Toledo, Toyota Avensis, VW Golf/Passat and Volvo S40.
8. Only those price series are included that have appeared in at least nine consecutive surveys. These are: cost of a weighted basket of goods and services (1976–2000; 1976 value excl. rent); cost of a food basket (1970–2000); costs of a set of men's and a set of women's clothing (1970–2000); rent for a 4-room furnished apartment (1973–2000); cost of purchasing a set of household appliances (1970–2000); price of a one-way ride on public transport (bus, tram or subway) of about 10 km (6 miles) or at least 10 stops (1973–2000); price of a taxi ride, 5km (3miles) during

daytime within city limits (1973–2000); average labour costs (not including price of spare parts and oil change) for a 15 000 km car service (1976–2000); price of a dinner for one (1970–2000); cost of a double room with bath and breakfast for two, incl. service, in a first class hotel (1970–2000); cost of a basket of services (1970–2000); price of a medium-sized automobile (1970–2000; models vary).

9. System estimation such as seemingly unrelated regression, which might be considered for the car and UBS price series, would not lead to efficiency gains here, since each regression contains identical right-hand side variables.
10. The data used in the estimation were as precisely as possible matched to the respective periods of observation and sample intervals of each data set. Inflation rates are based on the consumer price index (code..64..ZF..). The exchange-rate data are end-of-period observations (code..AE.ZF..). Output growth is based on real gross domestic product (code..99BV..), except for Greece (manufacturing production up to 2000), Ireland (industrial production) and Luxembourg (industrial production up to 2000:6).
11. In specification 3 the two DD estimates for the Volvo S40 point in opposite directions. Since a change in trend will always dominate a shift over a sufficiently long time interval, the 'change in trend' estimate is considered to dominate in this case and thus the results for specification 3 are taken as evidence of a positive effect on price dispersion.
12. Note that, as explained in note 11 estimates of the third specification (equation 3.7) are counted as a single test here. In cases where both α_4 and β_4 are statistically significant but of opposite sign, the β_4 estimate is used for Table 4.7.
13. These results also demonstrate that the lower euro-zone price dispersion found in cross-section comparisons is not related to the single currency, but merely reflects the fact that euro countries were already more integrated than others before they joined the single currency.
14. See, for instance, Cumby (1996), Lutz (2001, 2004) and Goldberg and Verboven (2001).
15. However, their experimental set-up – where 'money illusion' is driven by strategic complementarities between price-setters – may not be strictly applicable to the single currency issue.

References

Angrist, J. and A. Krueger (1999) 'Empirical Strategies in Labor Economics', in O. Ashenfelter and D. Card (eds), *Handbook of Labor Economics*, vol. 3a (Amsterdam: Elsevier), pp. 1277–366.

Baye, M., R. Gatti, P. Kattuman and J. Morgan (2002) 'Online Pricing and the Euro Changeover: Cross-country Comparisons', Working Paper 17/2002 (Cambridge, UK: Judge Institute of Management, University of Cambridge).

BEUC (1998) 'A Single Price for a Single Currency?', *BEUC Press Release*, 21 December 1998 (Brussels: Bureau Européen des Unions de Consommateurs).

Cumby, R. (1996) 'Forecasting Exchange Rates and Relative Prices with the Hamburger Standard: Is What You Want What You Get with McParity?', Working Paper no. 5675 (Cambridge, MA: NBER).

Devereux, M., C. Engel and C. Tille (2003) 'Exchange-rate Pass-through and the Welfare Effects of the Euro', *International Economic Review*, vol. 44(1), pp. 223–42.

Engel, C. and J. Rogers (1996) 'How Wide is the Border?', *American Economic Review*, vol. 86, pp. 1112–25.

European Commission (1990) 'One Market, One Money: An Evaluation of the Potential Benefits and Costs of Forming an Economic and Monetary Union', *European Economy*, no. 44, October.

European Commission (1996) 'The 1996 Single Market Review: Background Information for the Report to the Council and European Parliament', *Commission Staff Working Paper*, SEC (96) 2378 (Brussels), 16 December.

European Commission (1999) 'Report on Economic and Structural Reform in the EU', *European Economy* (Supplement A, *Economic Trends*), no. 1, January.

European Commission (various issues) *Car Prices in the European Union* (Brussels: Directorate-General IV-Competition).

Fehr, E. and J. Tyran (2001) 'Does Money Illusion Matter?', *American Economic Review*, vol. 91, pp. 1239–62.

Friberg, R. (2001) 'Two Monies, Two Markets? Variability and the Option Value to Segment', *Journal of International Economics*, vol. 55, pp. 317–27.

Friberg, R. and K. Martensen (2001) 'Endogenous Market Segmentation and the Law of One Price', Working Paper Series in Economics and Finance 471 (Stockholm: Stockholm School of Economics).

Frondel, M. and C. Schmidt (2001) 'Evaluating Environmental Programs: The Perspective of Modern Evaluation Research', Discussion Paper no. 397 (Bonn: Institute for the Study of Labor).

Gaulier, G. and S. Haller (2000) 'The Convergence of Automobile Prices in the European Union: An Empirical Analysis for the Period 1993–99', Working Paper 2000–14 (Paris: CEPII).

Ghosh, A. and H. Wolf (1994) 'Pricing in International Markets: Lessons from *The Economist*', Working Paper no. 4806 (Cambridge, MA: NBER).

Goldberg, P. and F. Verboven (2001) 'Market Integration and Convergence to the Law of One Price: Evidence from the Automobile Industry', Working Paper no. 8402 (Cambridge, MA: NBER).

Helliwell, J. (1998) *How Much Do National Borders Matter?* (Washington, DC: Brookings Institution Press).

Isgut, I. (2002) 'Common currencies and market integration across cities: How strong is the link?', mimeo (Middletown, CT: Department of Economics, Wesleyan College).

Knetter, M. (1997) 'The Segmentation of International Markets: Evidence from *The Economist*', Working Paper no. 5878 (Cambridge, MA: NBER).

Knetter, M. and M. Slaughter (1999) 'Measuring product market integration', Working Paper no. 6969 (Cambridge, MA: NBER).

Lutz, M. (1999) 'EU Commission versus Volkswagen: New Evidence on Price Differentiation in the European Car Market', *Review of Industrial Organization*, vol. 17, pp. 313–23.

Lutz, M. (2001) 'Beyond Burgernomics and MacParity: Exchange Rate Forecasts Based on the Law of One Price', mimeo (St. Gallen: University of St. Gallen).

Lutz, M. (2004) 'Pricing in Segmented Markets, Arbitrage Barriers and the Law of One Price: Evidence from the European Car Market', *Review of International Economics*, vol. 12(2).

Mathä, T. (2003) 'What to Expect of the Euro? Estimating Price Differences using Individual Products from the Surrounding Regions of Luxembourg', mimeo, Banque Centrale de Luxembourg.

McCallum, J. (1995) 'National Borders Matter: Canada–U.S. Regional Trade Patterns', *American Economic Review*, vol. 85, pp. 615–23.

Melitz, J. (2001) 'Geography, Trade and Currency Union', Discussion Paper no. 2987 (London: CEPR).

Ong, L. (1997) 'Burgernomics: The Economics of the Big Mac Standard', *Journal of International Money and Finance*, vol. 16, pp. 865–78.

Pakko, M. and P. Pollard (1996) 'For Here or to Go: Purchasing Power Parity and the Big Mac', *Federal Reserve Board of St. Louis Review*, vol. 78, pp. 3–21.

Parsley, D. and S. Wei (2001) 'Limiting Currency Volatility to Stimulate Goods Market Integration: A Price-Based Approach', Working Paper no. 8468 (Cambridge, MA: NBER).

Persson, T. (2001) 'Currency Unions and Trade: How Large is the Treatment Effect?', *Economic Policy*, vol. 33, pp. 434–48.

Rogers, J. (2001) 'Price Level Convergence, Relative Prices and Inflation in Europe', International Finance Discussion Paper no. 699 (Washington, DC: Board of Governors of the Federal Reserve System).

Rogers, J., G. Hufbauer and E. Wada (2001) 'Price Level Convergence and Inflation in Europe', Working Paper 01-1 (Washington, DC: Institute for International Economics).

Rogoff, K. (1996) 'The Purchasing Power Parity Puzzle', *Journal of Economic Literature*, vol. 34, pp. 647–68.

Rose, A. (2000) 'One Money, One Market: The Effect of Common Currencies on Trade', *Economic Policy*, vol. 30, pp. 7–45.

Slaughter, M. (2001) 'Trade Liberalisation and Per Capita Income Convergence: A Difference-in-difference Analysis', *Journal of International Economics*, vol. 55, pp. 203–28.

Taylor, A. (2002) 'A Century of Purchasing Power Parity', *Review of Economics and Statistics*, vol. 84(1), pp. 139–50.

The Economist Newspapers Limited (various issues) *The Economist*, European edition (London: The Economist Newspapers Limited).

UBS (various issues) *Prices and Earnings around the Globe* (Zurich: UBS).

5
EU Expansion and EU Growth*

Alan V. Deardorff and Robert M. Stern
University of Michigan, USA

1 Introduction

The exercise in economic integration that today is called the European Union (EU) began in the 1950s amid high hopes for the benefits that it would provide, both economically and politically. The political benefits, by eliminating the historic military conflict among the participating countries, have been unambiguous and very large. The economic benefits (in addition to avoidance of economic destruction caused by war) have also been fairly clear, but not so obviously large. The static welfare gains from economic integration have always been estimated to be comparatively small, while the 'dynamic gains' that many have hoped for have been both less well understood and difficult to identify in the data.

Meanwhile, a distinctive characteristic of the EU[1] has gone largely unremarked in discussions of its effects on the participating countries: the EU has expanded its list of member countries several times throughout its history, periodically adding new members and promising to continue to do so into the future. This raises the question of whether EU expansion has had an effect on the participating countries distinct from their participation *per se*. That is, can the effects of the EU on, say, the original six members be fully understood from just their participation in a customs union among themselves or even with a larger group of countries, or does a full understanding of these effects require that we take account of the fact that the EU was repeatedly expanding? This seems particularly relevant for the issue of the effects of the EU on the growth of participating countries, which is our primary focus here.

---

* We have benefited from guidance to the literature on European integration provided by David Greenaway and Alan Winters, as well as from comments by participants in seminars at Stockholm School of Economics, Stockholm University, and University of Copenhagen. Alan Deardorff is grateful to Tore Browaldh's Research Foundation for financial support while working on this paper at the Institute for International Economic Studies, Stockholm University.

Whatever may be the evidence and rationale for countries within a larger whatever may be the evidence for countries within a larger integrated trading bloc to grow permanently faster than non-members, one might expect an additional effect on GDP over time, and thus on growth in the intermediate run, if the trading bloc itself is expanding over time.

In this chapter we do two things. First, we review the empirical evidence on the long-term growth effects of the EU. As we will see, this evidence is not very strong, even though it has inevitably been collected from an era in which the EU was periodically expanding. We then turn to the theory of how such expansion might affect the rates of growth that are observed to accompany the expansion. Even a simple static model has implications for this, which we review. But we find more interesting implications from models with increasing returns to scale, in which the dynamic path of EU expansion plays a role in determining which countries are able to attract increasing-returns industries, and therefore in producing the resulting effects on per capita GDP. We spell this out in the simplest possible model of trade with increasing returns, and then sketch how the same results might arise in a more sophisticated model of economic geography.

The conclusion that we, as the authors of this chapter, have derived from our investigation is to seriously question the existence of the 'dynamic effects' of EU integration as they have commonly been understood. That is, we see little evidence for the belief that countries of the EU have realized a boost to their long-term rates of economic growth. This is partly because of the likelihood of a different kind of dynamic effect, one that increases some members' rates of growth, but only temporarily, during the process of expansion. Thus, whatever evidence exists for a growth effect of the EU may include an effect of expansion that cannot, by definition, continue indefinitely. Since the evidence itself is minimal, this further weakens the case for the EU as a long-run stimulus to growth.

If this sounds like a negative message, we do not mean it to be so. We already noted the overwhelming success of the EU in securing political stability in a historically turbulent part of the world, and that by itself would be enough to justify its existence. We also see the economic benefits as being clearly positive and important, even though we doubt that they extend to the point of increasing long-run rates of economic growth. If countries want to secure permanently higher rates of growth, the means are more likely to be found in conventional tools of increased investment, especially investment in research and development and human capital accumulation, than in the quick fix of economic integration.

2 Evidence

We first look directly at the available data on income and growth in the EU member countries. Then we review the empirical literature on how trade and integration in Europe may have affected these countries, especially in terms of growth.

2.1 The data

Figures 5.1a–5.1o show the ratio of real GDP per capita to the average of all OECD countries for each EU member country over the period 1951–97.[2] For each country, a vertical line shows the year in which it joined the EU, while a horizontal dashed line shows the ratio during the year before entry.[3] Relative to these two lines, benefits from joining are clearest if the graph passes from the lower left to the upper right quadrant. This is the case for Belgium, France, Germany, Ireland, and Italy. It is also roughly true of Finland, Portugal, and Spain, although each of these three countries also enjoyed a few years of relative prosperity just before entry. In contrast, the graphs pass into the lower right quadrant for Austria, Denmark, Greece, and the United Kingdom, each of which therefore only fell, relative to the OECD average, after entering. The remaining three countries – Luxembourg, Netherlands, and Sweden – show diverse behaviours, each of which is rather unlike the other countries. Of course, for more than half of these countries the data include only a few years either before or after entry, so that these patterns are hardly conclusive.

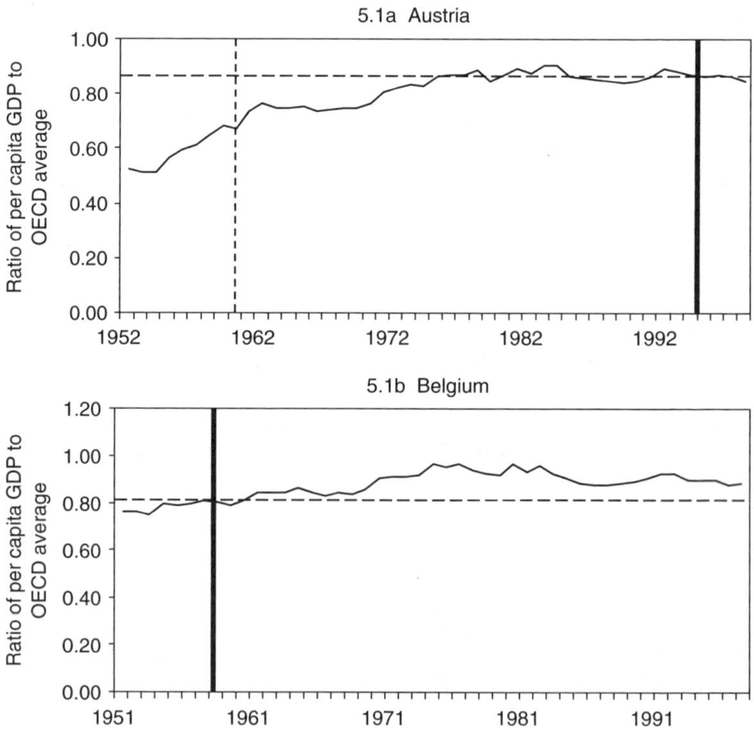

Figure 5.1 Per capita GDP relative to OECD

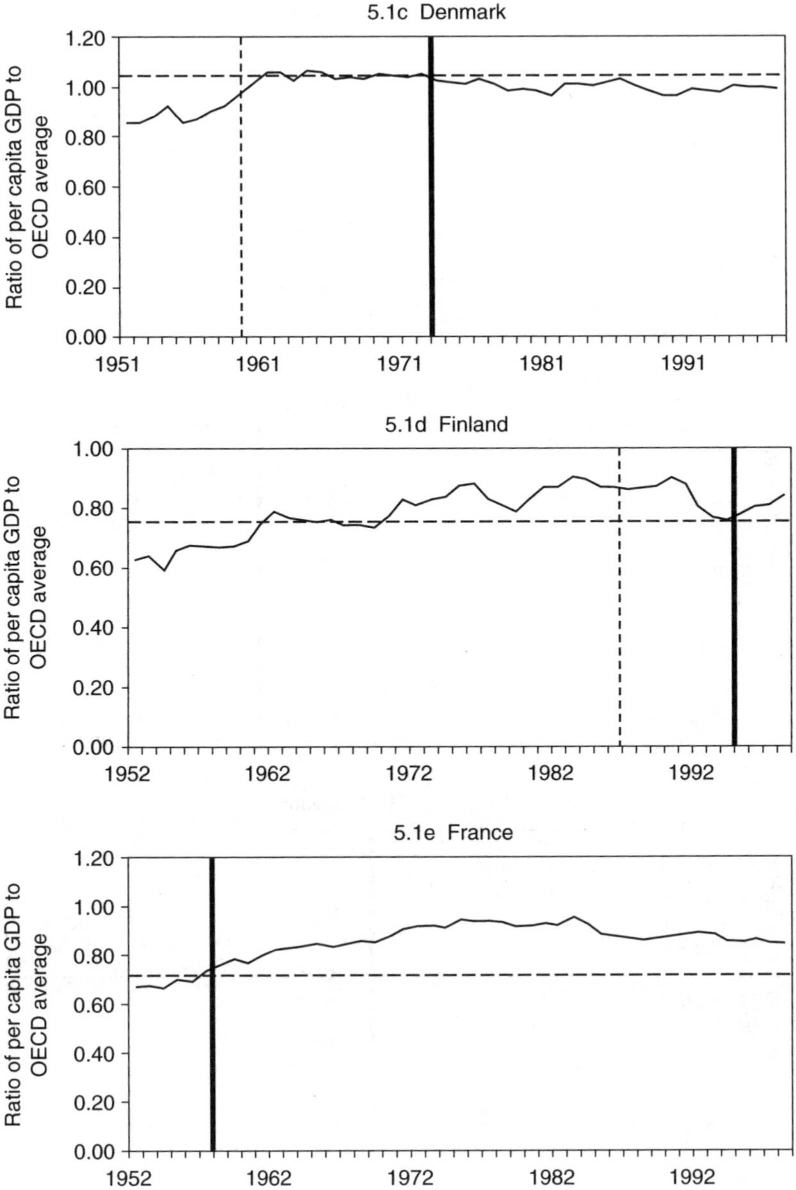

Figure 5.1 Continued

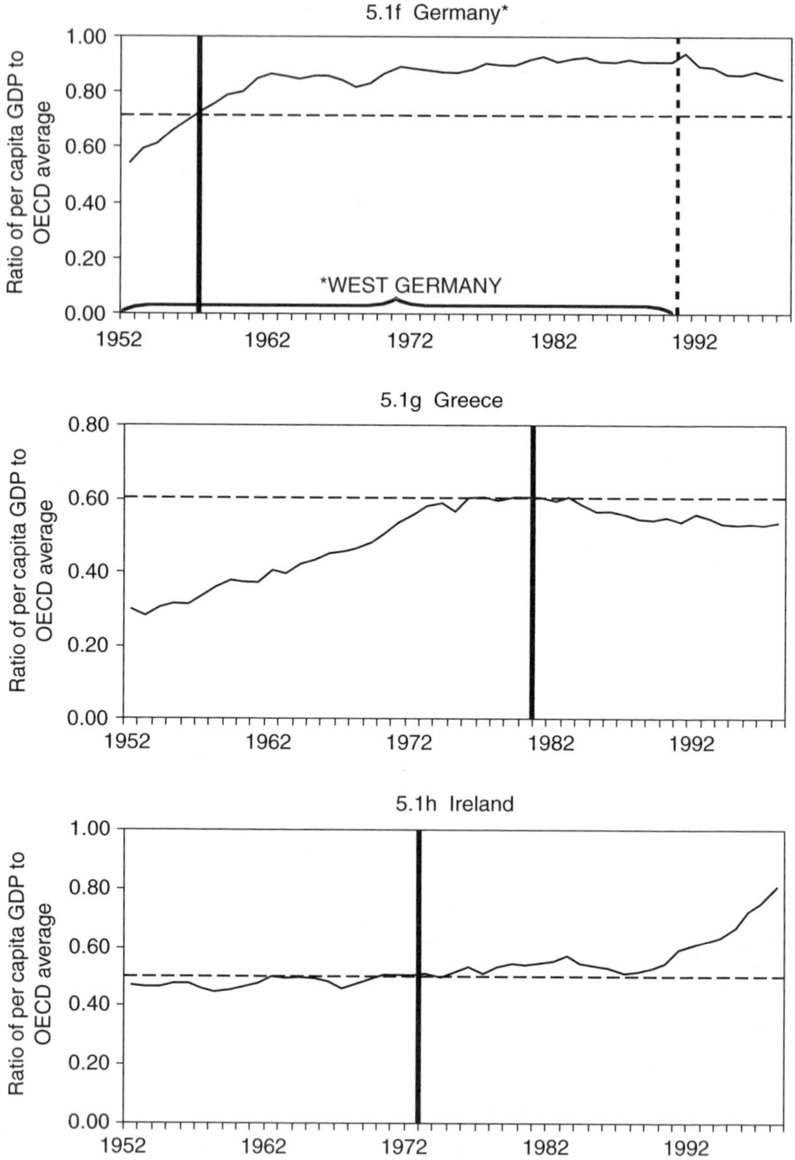

Figure 5.1 Continued

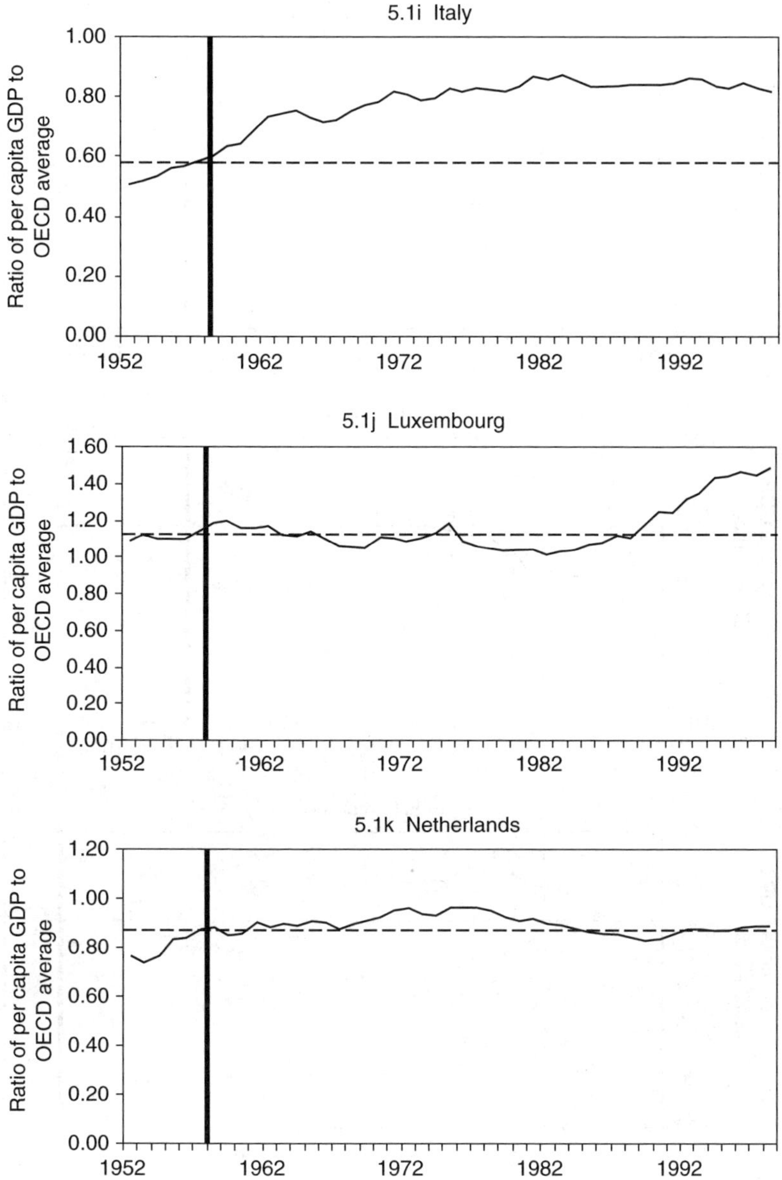

Figure 5.1 Continued

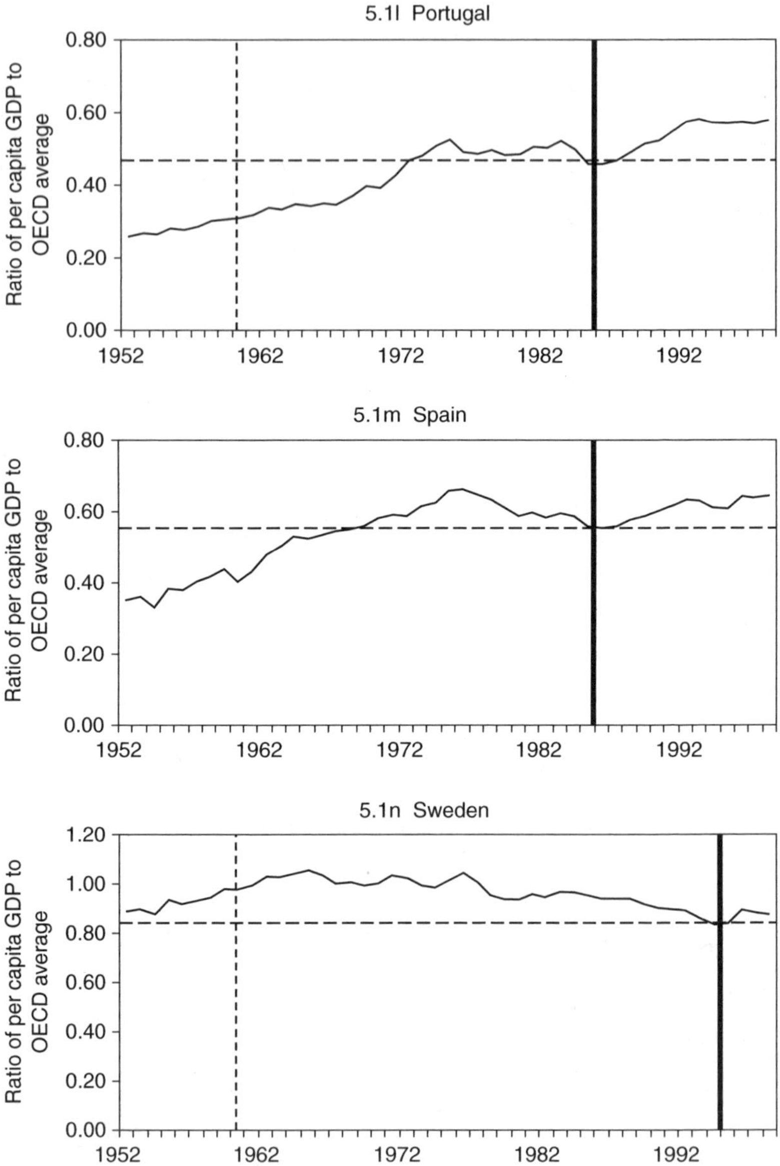

Figure 5.1 Continued

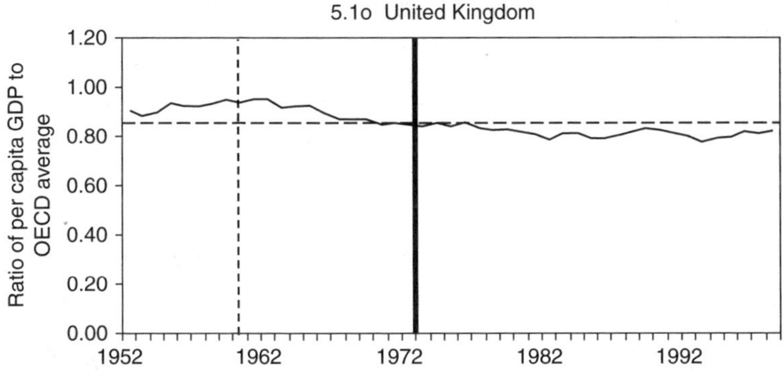

Figure 5.1 Continued

Based solely on inspection of these graphs, one certainly cannot say with any confidence that all countries have benefited economically from joining the EU. On the other hand, it does appear that the majority of the members, especially those who joined it initially and have been in the longest, are enjoying higher per capita GDP, relative to the OECD average, than they did before joining.

That, however, is not the same as a higher long-run rate of growth. With the exception of Ireland, all of the countries that most clearly gained after joining also reached a peak some years later and then declined relative to the OECD average, indicating that at best their levels of GDP increased, but not their rates of growth. Only three countries – Finland, Ireland, and Luxembourg – show distinct increases in the final years that could be the beginning of steeper growth paths, while two others – Portugal and Spain – reach higher levels a few years earlier that may augur well for their futures. But for the remaining countries, if EU membership has led to permanently higher growth rates, that fact is well disguised in these data.

What does seem plausible from these graphs, however, is that the larger of the original six countries of the EU may have gained substantially in their levels of GDP. France, Germany, and Italy all advanced steadily in per capita GDP relative to the OECD average during the two decades after the EU began as the European Economic Communities. After that they levelled off and declined a bit, but the improvement during those two decades was substantial and lasting, something like 10, 20 or even 30 percentage points. Of course, these countries started this process while still recovering from the Second World War, and it may be that much of this improvement would have happened even without the EU. Other countries' performance during the same period was mixed, with Austria showing similar improvement without membership in the EU, while the UK shows no such improvement at all, even after joining.

Of the smaller original members, Belgium performed similarly to its larger neighbours, but its gain was smaller and somewhat delayed. The Netherlands also gained a little, but then lost it completely. Meanwhile the smallest, Luxembourg, showed no sign at all of gaining from membership, and it might even have lost, until more than three decades after integration when it finally took off.

2.2 Studies of the growth effects of European integration

There has been no shortage of studies of European integration. Initially, and of necessity, such studies were prospective, using either extrapolation from the past or simple economic models to calculate what the effects of integration might be.[4] As time went on, the prospective studies became increasingly sophisticated in their use first of general equilibrium models and then their incorporation of imperfect competition,[5] and they also were supplemented by retrospective empirical analyses of the actual economic performance of the countries involved. However, until the 1990s, almost all of the attention of these studies was on the effects of integration on trade, not on income or economic growth. Perhaps influenced by the theoretical attention directed by Viner (1950) toward trade creation and trade diversion, and perhaps simply looking at what was easiest to observe, the few retrospective studies sought to determine whether the EU (or its predecessors) had increased trade, and if so with whom.

Srinivasan *et al.* (1993) surveyed the empirical literature on the effects of regionalism (not just the EU) up to that time, and they identified only three retrospective empirical studies, all of which dealt only with effects on trade. Although these trade effects are not our main interest in this chapter, these studies show clearly and unsurprisingly that European integration caused a large expansion of the countries' trade, especially with each other. Viner (1950) had shown that not all such trade within a trading bloc is welfare improving, so this does not itself assure that the EU had increased incomes. But the sense of this literature was also that trade creation had sufficiently exceeded trade diversion so that European integration had been beneficial, and most would agree that it had raised real incomes even if the increase had not been measured.

Throughout this period, however, the effects that integration might have on incomes through expansion of trade, when viewed through the lens of simple and therefore static economic models, was presumed to be rather small. Even when trade liberalization is non-discriminatory and thus not trade-diverting, the gains from trade consist of the removal of the deadweight losses due to distortion of producer and consumer behaviour, and these tend to be relatively small. For a large country that does not rely very heavily on trade, typical estimates of the gains from trade based on these models tend to be just a few per cent of GDP. It was customary, therefore, to speak of unspecified 'dynamic effects' that trade liberalization would also have, even though these were based more on hope than on analysis.

Possibly the first effort to measure such dynamic effects was by Brada and Mendez (1988), who reported panel regression estimates for two equations with investment shares and growth rates as dependent variables and with dummy variables for participation in six regional integration arrangements including the EU. They found a significant positive effect on investment due to membership in the EU, but no such effect separately on the growth rate.[6] This study predated the theoretical literature on the dynamics of integration and growth, as well as the huge empirical literature of cross-country growth regressions and the criticisms of that literature, many of which would undoubtedly apply to it.

In the 1990s, both the theory and the empirics of dynamic effects took off. This started with the theoretical contributions of Grossman and Helpman (1991), who built on the closed-economy, endogenous-growth models of Romer (1986) and Lucas (1988) to show several ways in which international trade could increase long-run rates of economic growth. Also noteworthy is the work by Baldwin (1989), who sought to quantify the dynamic effects of trade and to show that the prospective gains from the EU's single market programme ('Europe 1992') would be a multiple of, and perhaps even an order of magnitude larger than, the static gains estimated in the Cecchini Report (1988).

Empirical studies followed and are summarized in Table 5.1. In addition to the country coverage and time span of the data, which may help to place the results in the context of the country behaviour displayed in Figures 5.1a–5.1o, we also record how integration was captured: by dummy variables for membership in the EU or other trading arrangement; or by a variable based on amounts of trade. For each study, we state what we see as the major conclusion as related to our issue of the effects of European economic integration on growth. For those studies that found a significant effect and reported its size, we report the effect either on the rate of growth or on accumulated GDP over the time span of the data. The details are as follows:

- Coe and Moghadam (1993) applied cointegration analysis to quarterly data on French output, 1971:1–1991:4, so as to identify long-run relationships between capital accumulation, growth, and trade integration measured by intra-EC trade as a percentage of total EC output. They found a clear beneficial effect of European integration on French growth. However, they stressed that the relationship was between the level of integration and the level of output, and that it did not imply that integration had a long-run impact on the rate of growth.
- Italianer (1994) regressed GDP growth on capital, labour and trade-based proxies for integration among EC-6 and EC-12 countries for 1961–92. He found significant positive effects of integration on growth, suggesting

Table 5.1 Empirical studies of the effects of economic integration on growth

Study	*Countries*	*Years*	*Integration variable*	*Conclusions for Europe*	*Estimated effect of European integration on*	
					Level of GDP (%)	*Growth Rate of GDP (%pts)*
Brada and Mendez (1988)	Members of six integration schemes, including EEC	1951–77	Dummies for membership	Membership in EEC positively related to investment but not separately to growth.	+0.48	
Coe and Moghadam (1993)	France	1971–91	Intra-EC trade/output	Level of European integration positively related to French output.		+0.7
Italianer (1994)	EC-6	1961–92	Trade-based proxies	Proxies for integration and openness have significant impact on growth.	+10	+0.3
Landau (1995)	17 OECD countries	1950–90	Dummies for EU membership	No significant effect of integration on growth.		Not significant
Baldwin & Seghezza (1996)	n.a.	n.a.	Dummy for EU membership	EU membership has a positive effect on technology spillovers but not on investment.		n.a.
Henrekson *et al*. (1997)	All countries, also narrowed to OECD	1976–85	Dummy for EC/EFTA	EC and/or EFTA membership increase growth.		+0.6–0.8
Vamvakidis (1999)	All countries	1950–92	Dummies for type of liberalization	Dummies for broad liberalization are positive and significant, but not for regional liberalization.		Not significant
Vanhoudt (1999)	23 OECD countries	1950–90	Dummies for EU membership	EU membership did not have a significant effect on members' growth.		Not significant
Johansson (2001)	France, Germany, Italy, UK	1973–90	Imports from EU vs. non-EU	Industry TFP is positively related to intra-EU imports, not to imports from outside.		+

that growing trade had contributed to growing GDP. During the period of estimation, integration contributed on average 0.3 percentage points to economic growth, which accumulates to an additional output of 10 per cent by the end of the period.

- Landau (1995) took a slightly different approach to a larger sample of OECD country growth rates over the longer period, 1950–90. He used dummies for membership in the EU and added controls for time, initial per capita GDP and others. With one exception, the EU membership dummies were insignificant, the exception being a regression with no controls in which the dummy by itself had a significant positive coefficient and the dummy interacted with time had a significant negative coefficient. This suggested a positive effect that may have existed in the early years but disappeared in the 1970s.
- Baldwin and Seghezza (1996) also used dummies for EU membership, adding these both to the technology-spillover analysis of Coe and Helpman (1995), which we will discuss further below, and to their own previous analysis of determinants of investment. They found a positive effect on technology spillovers, but nothing significant for investment.
- Henrekson, Torstensson and Torstensson (1997) performed a variety of regressions on growth rates during 1976–85 across a large sample of both developed and developing countries, and included a dummy for membership in the EU or EFTA. They found a significant, positive effect that became smaller, but retained its significance, when the sample was restricted to developed OECD countries. The effect was as valid for membership in EFTA as in the EU, and it seemed to arise from technology, not investment.
- Vamvakidis (1999) sought to avoid the pitfalls of cross-country growth regressions by using fixed effects in a time series of five-year average growth rates for all available countries over 1950–92. In these he included dummies to indicate whether the countries participated in broad liberalization or in regional trade agreements. Only the former appeared to have a significant positive effect on growth. In Table 5.1 we therefore record as 'not significant' the effect of the EU on growth, although of course the study did not look at EU integration separately from the many other regional trade agreements.
- Vanhoudt (1999) also used a time series, but tailored it specifically to the issue of EU membership by defining his time periods between EU expansions. Within that context, and in several specifications using various controls, the coefficient on EU membership was consistently insignificant.
- Johansson (2001) narrowed attention to just four large EU countries and examined growth in total factor productivity (TFP) in 22 manufacturing industries in each country. Using imports from within the EU and imports from outside as explanatory variables, she found the former to be

significant, while the latter was not, suggesting a positive effect of intra-EU trade on growth of TFP.

One's first impression from Table 5.1 may be that the results are very mixed, some studies finding effects of integration on growth while others look for such effects but fail to find them. There is however one suggestion of a pattern in the results that might be worth noting: All of the studies that fail to find an effect of integration on growth use dummy variables to measure integration, while most (but not all) of the studies that do find an effect use a trade-based measure of integration. This could mean that the former studies simply use too crude a measure of integration, and we should believe the latter studies instead. Or it could mean that the trade-based measures are subject to the criticisms that Levine and Renelt (1992) levied against growth regressions more generally.[7]

We are not prepared to sort out these issues definitively here. We can only say that we remain unconvinced, based on the evidence we have seen, that European integration has increased the long-run growth rates of the countries involved. We do not doubt the static benefits of European integration. And we are prepared to believe that at least some of the EU member countries enjoyed increased rates of growth following integration that lasted for a number of years, perhaps benefiting from the 'medium term' growth effects that Baldwin (1989) extolled. But if the EU has caused its member countries to advance to permanently higher rates of economic growth, we have a hard time seeing it.

2.3 Other evidence

In addition to the studies mentioned in Table 5.1, there has been other empirical work that bears on the issue of how the EU may have affected growth in its member countries, even though these other studies did not address the question directly. This includes, for example, the work of Ben-David (1993, 1996), who has shown a tendency for per capita incomes to 'converge' as a result of economic integration and trade. This means a fall over time in the dispersion of per capita incomes across countries, particularly those that trade a lot such as the original six members of the EU. This result does not, of course, say anything about whether this convergence is achieved by the initially poorer countries growing faster or *vice versa*, and it therefore has no direct implications for the effects of integration on rates of growth.[8]

Another body of evidence that certainly deserves mention is the work on technology spillovers initiated by Coe and Helpman (1995). They regressed changes in TFP on import-weighted averages of other countries' expenditures on research and development (R&D) and found a significant positive effect. They concluded that the fruits of R&D spill over to other countries through trade, suggesting therefore that a country's growth can be stimulated by increasing its trade with other countries that are doing a lot of R&D.

Of course, this assumes that such trade does not adversely affect the country's own level of R&D, which continues to be important, but it certainly provides a plausible case for integration among, and with, high-R&D countries in order to stimulate growth. This, indeed, is one of the mechanisms developed theoretically by Grossman and Helpman (1991), and the Coe and Helpman results provide empirical support for it. This is so compelling, in fact, that one has to wonder why the more direct search for growth effects of European integration, reviewed above, has not been more successful.[9]

Which brings us to the broader literature on the effects of trade on growth. This extends back at least to the work of Michaely (1977) and includes contributions during the 1990s that are too numerous to list here. The point for us is that, if indeed trade contributes to growth, as many believe in spite of the many criticisms of this literature, then doesn't the fact that the EU has increased trade mean that it must also have increased growth? Unfortunately, no. In addition to the concerns that causation may run from growth to trade rather than the reverse, there is also the question of which, among the many causes of trade, may lead to trade that is beneficial for growth.

The point can be made quite simply in terms of Frankel and Romer's (1999) very clever demonstration that at least one sort of trade does indeed cause growth. By using economic geography variables as instruments for trade, they avoid the endogeneity problem of most trade and growth regressions and show conclusively that such trade as is caused by geographic factors, such as proximity and size, does indeed contribute to growth. But does it follow that such trade as may be stimulated by economic integration will cause growth? We don't know. For the trade that is caused by integration is inherently *not* the same trade that Frankel and Romer capture with their instruments. Until we know why the geography-based trade plays the role that it does in promoting growth, we have little basis for assuming that the same causation applies to trade that arises for other reasons, such as integration. Indeed, we know from the theory of trade creation and diversion that not all trade is the same in its effects, so we should not assume that here.

In short, we have a long way to go before empirical work will tell us all that we want to know about this issue.

3 Theory

In this section we use economic theory to address the question of EU expansion. Our concern is not just with the effects of economic integration, especially regional or preferential integration, although that is certainly part of the story. We are also concerned with the phenomenon of a growing trading bloc, one that, once formed among a few countries, repeatedly adds additional countries as the EU has done. The question is whether this process of expansion has implications that differ at all from the original formation of the trading bloc.

Traditional trade theory has not usually addressed this question, perhaps because it was not viewed as interesting. In a static model of trade creation and diversion, each new country added to a preferential arrangement causes the same kinds of things to happen, with new opportunities for trade creation and new ones also (unless the added country is that last outsider remaining) for trade diversion. Of course, some trade diversion that had occurred in an earlier expansion may be reversed by a later one, so the likelihood of expansion being beneficial may improve. But otherwise, further expansion of a trading bloc is just more of the same. If trade creation dominates trade diversion when a bloc is first formed, then it is likely to continue to do so as the bloc is expanded, and the welfare of participating countries as a group ought to expand fairly smoothly as the bloc gets larger. The gains may not be shared uniformly among them, however, as new members cause changes in relative prices within the bloc that benefit some members and harm others.[10] A new member that exports the same goods as an existing member will turn the terms of trade against that existing member.

The issue of expanding trading blocs was addressed a few years ago in a paper by Krugman (1991b), and also a bit later by us, in Deardorff and Stern (1994).[11] The focus of these papers was not so much on the expansion of a single trading bloc, but rather the effect on the world as countries group together into preferential arrangements that in turn combine to become larger and, therefore, fewer. Krugman used a monopolistic competition model of intra-industry trade in which the world is divided into some number, n, of trading blocs. He simulated the effects of expanding the blocs and thus reducing n. What he found was that world welfare first declines as blocs expand, reaching a minimum when there are just three blocs each comprising one third of the world. Beyond that, as the number of blocs falls to two and then one (free trade), welfare increases. Deardorff and Stern (1994) used a model based on comparative advantage, in which larger trading blocs are more likely to include, and thus to take advantage of, countries with diverse abilities. In their model, although a fall in welfare as blocs expand is possible, a lower bound on welfare rises monotonically with bloc size from autarky to free trade. This suggests a likelihood, though not a certainty, that bloc expansion will be beneficial.

All of these models treat countries symmetrically, so that whatever happens to the welfare of the group of countries in a trading bloc also is presumed to happen to each member. Yet one of the messages of the data displayed in Figures 5.1a–5.1o is that the countries of the EU seem to have performed quite differently from one another, both comparing large and small members of the original EC-6 (such as France vs. Netherlands) and comparing the original members with countries of comparable size that entered later (such as France vs. UK). To allow for such asymmetric performance across countries, either or both in terms of exogenous country characteristics or in terms of their positions in the resulting equilibrium, it seems useful to examine a model in which increasing returns plays a larger role.[12] Indeed, we have been motivated to do that by reading Puga and Venables (1997), in whose model increasing returns and related forces lead to agglomeration of industry in particular locations within a trading bloc, so that the benefits of integration are shared unequally. We will return to their model a little later, but first we explore the role that increasing returns can play in a much simpler model.

3.1 Increasing returns

The model we use is a variation of Ethier (1982), which also appears in various forms in textbooks on international trade. There are two sectors, both of which employ only labour. One sector – call it wheat – has constant returns to scale; the other – call it manufactures – has increasing returns to scale that are external to firms but internal to the country.[13] Both sectors, therefore, can be perfectly competitive, even though for a given wage, average cost in the manufactures sector will decline with industry output.

This model is routinely used to illustrate the effects of increasing returns on patterns of trade and the gains from trade, looking at a world of two countries that move from autarky to free trade. For our purpose of examining expansion of a trading bloc, we abstract from the realistic complications of trade that is subject to non-prohibitive barriers (and thus also from the possibility of trade diversion) and ask, in a world of many countries initially in autarky, identical except perhaps for size, what happens first when a group of them trade freely, and then when that group expands to include more countries.

In Ethier's (1982) model, costs of manufactures decline from infinite to zero as output expands from zero to infinite, giving rise to a greater multiplicity of equilibria than we care to confront here. We therefore depart from his model slightly by assuming that average cost in manufactures is finite and declines with rising output less rapidly than does the price that consumers are willing to pay. Multiple equilibria will still be possible, involving different patterns of specialization across countries, but the model with trade will be somewhat better behaved and more tractable.

Consider first, then, the standard problem of two (out of many) countries opening from autarky to free trade. Figure 5.2 shows the autarky equilibria. The larger country, A (with a larger labour force) has production possibilities given by the curve $T_A T'_A$. The smaller country, B, because it has the same technologies, has a transformation curve $T_B T'_B$ that is the same as $T_A T'_A$ but shifted vertically downward. In each country, zero profit in the autarky equilibrium requires that the price of manufactures equal its average cost and thus, wherever production takes place along the interior of TT', the price line must extend from the wheat intercept of TT' to the production point. That price line is then the budget line for aggregated consumers, who must in equilibrium choose to consume also at that same point.

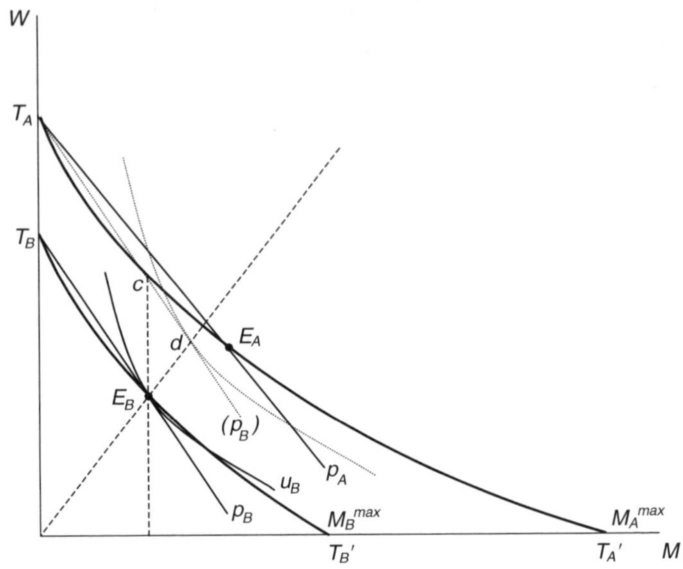

Figure 5.2 Autarky equilibria in two countries with increasing returns in sector *M*

Thus the autarky equilibrium in country *B* is at E_B with price line p_B (its slope is minus the relative price of manufactures) tangent to the indifference curve u_B, which therefore intersects T_BT_B' at E_B. The autarky equilibrium in the larger country, *A*, is at a point like E_A, with autarky price p_A.

The main purpose of putting both countries in the same figure is to show that $p_A < p_B$; that is, the increasing-returns good, manufactures, is cheaper in autarky in the larger country. This is shown by noting that, since T_AT_A' is identical to T_BT_B' but vertically above it, it must cross a price line parallel to p_B at point *c*, vertically above E_B. But with homothetic preferences that are identical in the two countries, at that price consumption would be at point *d*, where the ratio of wheat and manufactures is the same as in country *B*. The indifference curve through *d* also indicates that the market-clearing price at point *c* would be higher than p_B, providing the incentive for output of manufactures to increase. Thus autarky equilibrium is found at a higher output of manufactures, and thus at a lower average cost and price, as at E_A.

Now suppose that these two countries were to open to free international trade in goods but not in labour.[14] Although several equilibria may actually exist, this price difference will, under normal circumstances, tell us where we go. If initially outputs remain at their autarky levels, those outputs will be demanded at a single free-trade price that is somewhere between the autarky prices. Higher than p_A, it will provide the incentive for manufactures output

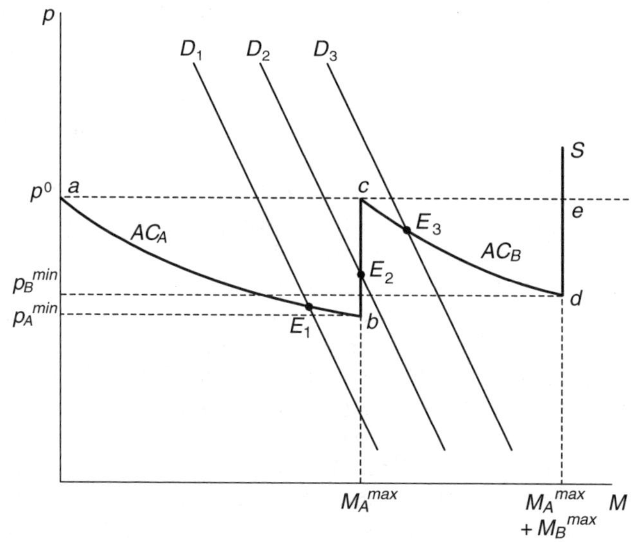

Figure 5.3 Free trade equilibria with three different levels of demand

to expand in the larger country, *A*; lower than p_B, it will cause manufactures in the smaller country *B* to contract.

Either or both countries may then completely specialize, though of course in different goods. Which of several possibilities occurs depends on the relative demands for manufactures and wheat, each with rather different implications for the well-being of the citizens of the two countries. The role of demand is shown in Figure 5.3, in which one should first look at the supply curve, *S*, that exists within these two markets now that they are integrated. Of necessity, this curve does not have the usual interpretation of describing quantity supplied at given prices. Rather, it should be read vertically as the supply price corresponding to each quantity. As such, it starts at point *a*, the price p^0 at which the smallest quantity of *M* would be produced in either country, which is equal to the slope of the transformation curves in Figure 5.2 at their vertical intercepts. As output rises from zero in the larger country *A* (since that is the country that we know, from the autarky prices, will increase its production of *M*), the average cost falls due to increasing returns and the supply price declines. This only continues, however, until country *A* reaches its maximum output of *M*, M_A^{max}. At this point the price must rise again to p^0 in order to induce any output of *M* in country *B*. From there the supply price again declines, this time reflecting average cost in country *B*, until its output too reaches its maximum. The supply curve therefore follows the crooked path, *abcdeS*.

This supply curve can then be combined with whatever demand curve characterizes incomes and preferences in this trade-integrated market, three different examples of which appear in Figure 5.3.[15] If demand for M is not too large, such as the curve D_1, then the whole market for M is served by the larger country, which also produces some wheat. The smaller country specializes in wheat in this case, and the price of manufactures is determined by average cost in the large country. For small shifts in the demand curve around D_1, note that an increase in demand for M will lower its price. If demand is larger, however, such as curve D_2, then the large country produces only M while the small country produces only W. The price is now above average cost in country A, in order to clear the market, but fails to increase output since country A is already producing all it can. And price is still too low, below p^0, to permit production of M to begin in country B. Finally, for even larger demand, such as curve D_3, the smaller country does produce some M, along with W, and price becomes the average cost of M in country B.

Now suppose that another country, C, is added to this trading bloc. What will happen depends on the autarky price in country C compared, not to the autarky prices of A and B, but rather to the price that prevailed with free trade between them. In spite of the large size of their combined market, as we've seen, that price could be quite high, if demand was such that the smaller country was producing M and not too much of it, as at E_3. If so, the small country's manufactures industry may be replaced by producers from country C. Alternatively, it is just as possible that country C will have a higher autarky price than that in the trading bloc, and that it will be the one to reduce manufactures production.

In this simple model, it is therefore difficult to say in what order the countries will enter the manufactures market, since the market price is so very sensitive to demand as was seen in Figure 5.3. Let us assume, however, that new entrants to the trading bloc typically have slightly higher costs of manufactures than do member countries, perhaps for reasons that are currently outside this model.[16] Then we can describe the process of bloc expansion in terms of a series of average cost curves, like Figure 5.3, but for multiple countries arranged in the order of their entry to the trading bloc. This is shown in Figure 5.4, where each average cost curve also has a short horizontal line crossing it at the level of its respective autarky price.

Here the complete world supply curve is composed of the average cost curves of six countries, $A, B, \ldots, F$. Demand curves are drawn for bloc sizes of 2 to 6: A and B together yielding D_2; A, B and C together yielding D_3; etc. Thus as the trading bloc expands through the addition of more countries, the demand for manufactures within the bloc expands as well. As drawn, the first expansion, adding the rather small country C, leaves patterns of specialization within the bloc unchanged and country A just increases output of M by a small amount, also reducing its price as cost falls. The next expansion, to include the rather large country D, shifts demand to D_4, causing country A to

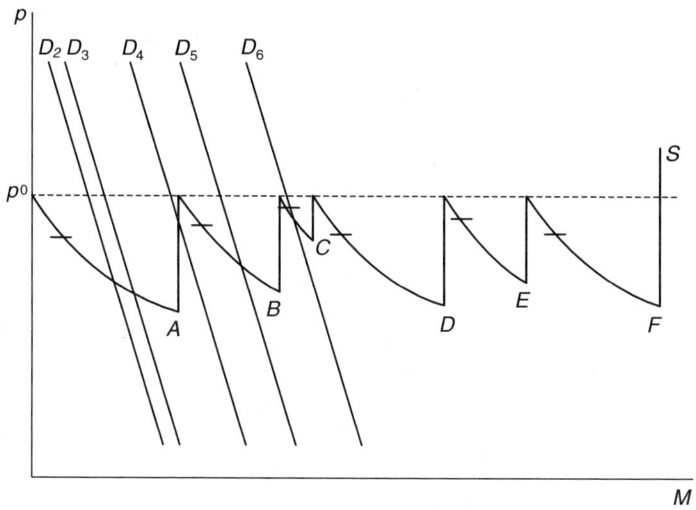

Figure 5.4 Expansion of a trading bloc from two up to six countries

increase output of *M* to its maximum so that price rises. Yet another expansion, adding country *E*, brings country *B* into production of manufactures as well as *A* and, as drawn, causes the price to fall again. Finally, expansion of the bloc to include the last country, *F*, increases demand so much that even the smallest country *C* begins to produce manufactures.[17]

This, then, is part of the story that this simple model is able to tell about expansion of a trading bloc. With an increasing-returns-to-scale sector, that sector will be pulled by integration into a single country until that country's capacity for its production is exhausted. With global free trade among many countries, one might expect that sector to expand in the largest country, whatever that may be. But by forming a trading bloc, a group of countries may be able to direct that production instead into one of their own. Then by expanding the bloc to include more countries and thus increasing the size of the internal market, they can induce that sector to grow beyond just one member country and into others.

Does this do them any good? The answer can be seen in Figures 5.5a and 5.5b, where the production possibilities for countries *A* and *B* are reproduced from Figure 5.2. In each, the equilibrium prices for each stage of bloc expansion from Figure 5.4 are drawn, anchored by the patterns of production in the two countries that are also indicated in Figure 5.4. In the top panel, for example, price p_2 reflects equilibrium in the two-country bloc of just *A* and *B*, and at this price country *A* produces both goods and exports *M*, reaching utility level u_2. When a third country, *C*, is added to the bloc, Figure 5.4 shows that price falls, to a level shown as p_3 in Figure 5.5. Country *A* expands

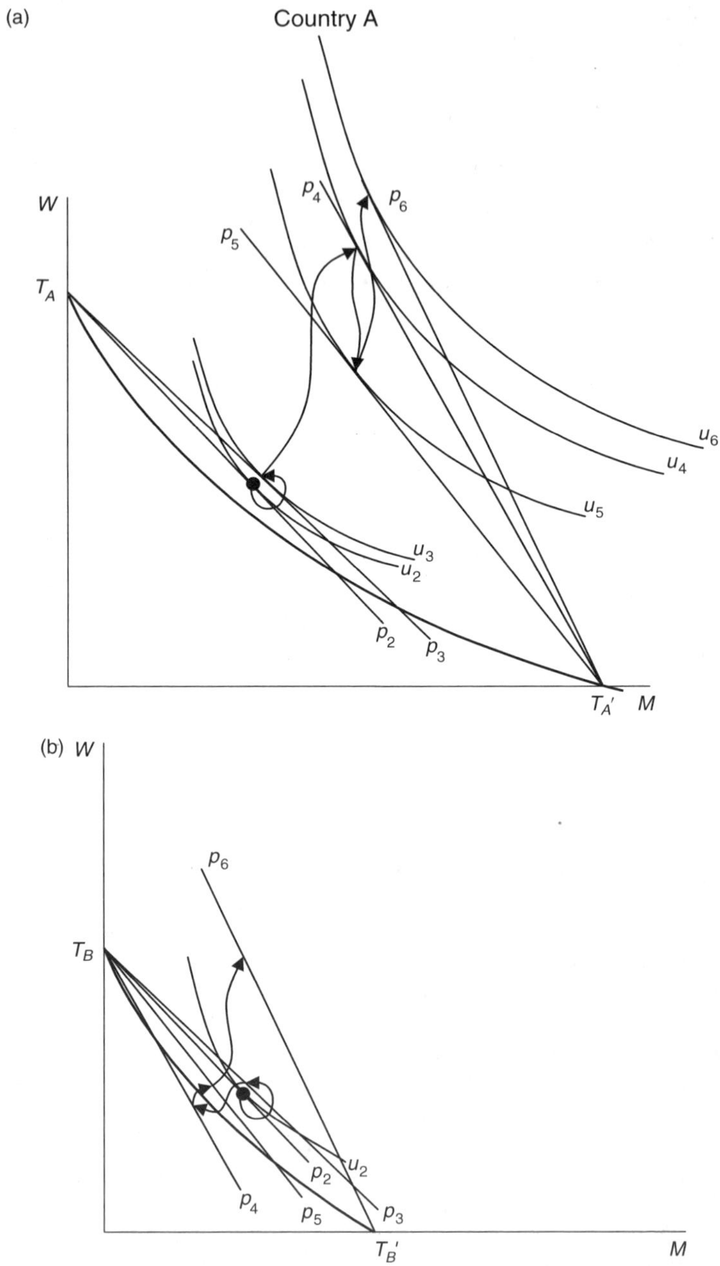

Figure 5.5 a and b Bloc expansion and trade of initial bloc members

its output of *M* and reaches a slightly higher utility, u_3. However, when the fourth country, *D*, is added to the bloc, then country *A* specializes in *M* and is also able to sell it for a higher price, p_4. This is where the country gets the biggest boost to its welfare, utility rising to u_4. From here on, further expansion of the bloc causes the price to rise and fall, changing country *A*'s utility in proportion to that price.

Figure 5.5b shows the situation in country *B*, though omitting all indifference curves except u_2 to reduce clutter. Following the same prices as appeared in Figure 5.5a but recognizing the different specialization of country *B*, one observes that it gains slightly from the first expansion from 2 to 3, loses considerably from the second, from 3 to 4, recovers somewhat with the addition of the fifth country, and then gains massively when expansion finally enables it to specialize completely in increasing-returns manufactures, at price p_6. Of course, it is not just the price that makes this possible, but the expansion of demand that occurred with the larger market, and the fact that country *B* was able to enter the manufacturing sector before other countries, *D* and *F*, that might have captured the market instead had they been part of the bloc from the start.

Figure 5.6 plots the levels of welfare reached by each country as a function of the number of countries in the trading bloc. Assuming that countries join the bloc at regular intervals, the horizontal axes of these graphs represent time, and these are therefore roughly comparable to the graphs of per capita income over time that we saw in Figure 5.1. Notice that, like France, Germany, and Italy, the larger of our two initial countries, A, gains steadily for some time after the bloc is formed, levelling off after it includes several additional countries. In contrast, the smaller of our countries, B, actually loses relative to autarky at one point after the bloc is formed, and only takes off to higher levels of welfare when the bloc is large, roughly like the performance of the smaller countries of the EC-6.

This, of course, is just an example of what might happen. Even with these same countries, other equilibria exist that might be reached if industries follow different paths of expansion and contraction. And with other configurations of country sizes and orders of admission to the trading bloc, it is difficult to imagine any robust predictions that could be sustained. But the example does draw attention to a few patterns that seem plausible and that resonate well with the data that we looked at earlier in the chapter.

1. Large countries gain more than small countries from the initial formation of a trading bloc.
2. Small countries may gain more from the subsequent expansion of the trading bloc than they gained from its initial formation.
3. Other countries that enter a trading bloc late may find it difficult to exploit a comparative advantage in increasing-returns industries, and they may therefore gain less from membership than earlier entrants.

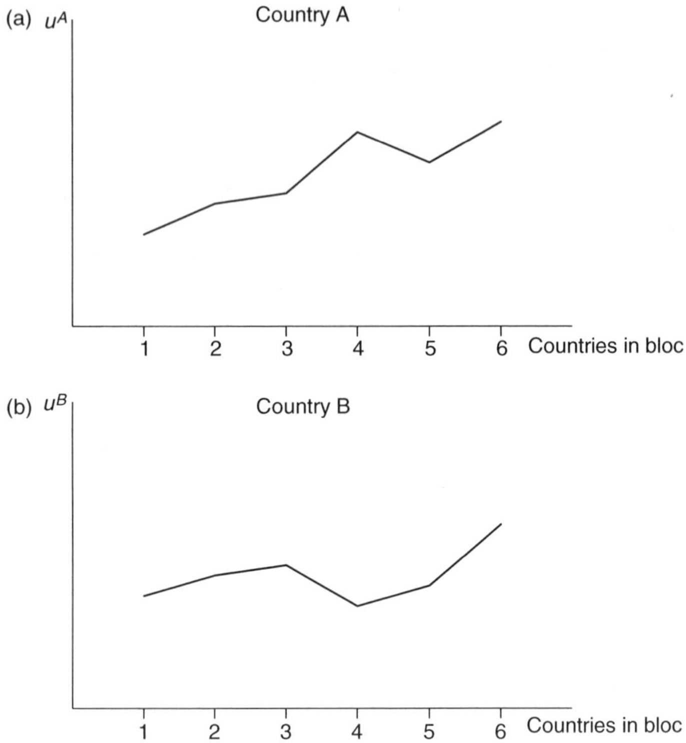

Figure 5.6 a and b Bloc size and welfare of initial bloc members

4. Growth of real income in a trading bloc, even that of the original members, may depend on the expansion of the bloc to include new members, thus expanding the market size and allowing them to further exploit the scale economies in the industries where their early participation secured a foothold.

Looking back at the data of Figures 5.1a–5.1o, it seems plausible to interpret the performance of France, Germany, and Italy as consistent with that of country *A* in our model. The somewhat delayed success of Belgium might be an example of country *B*, while Luxembourg and Ireland may be examples of country *C*. Meanwhile the UK, in spite of its size, seems never to have gained much, if at all, from the EU. In the context of the model, the UK may be like countries *D* or *F* that, in spite of their size, are put at a disadvantage by their late entry into the bloc.

Obviously, all of this is making far more of a simple model than is justified, and we are only suggesting this model as a possible and very partial explanation of what the experiences of countries in the EU have been. One lesson of this sort of model, in contrast to more traditional models with which we, at least, are more familiar and comfortable, is that the experiences of different countries may well be very diverse and complex, with effects that vary across countries in both their magnitude and their timing. It may therefore be expected that empirical efforts to relate performance to membership in a trading bloc will be fraught with difficulty.

3.2 Geography models

Our use of the simple increasing-returns model above was motivated by what we have learned from the literature on New Economic Geography. Starting with several papers by Krugman that built on his earlier work,[18] this literature stresses the forces that encourage and deter 'agglomeration', that is, the concentration of economic activity at a single location, due to benefits that derive from being close to other economic activity. The application of such models to regional integration was done most elegantly by Puga and Venables (1997), who noted that regional trading blocs are likely to create concentrations of increasing-returns industries into their member countries, attracted by their enlarged markets.[19]

Puga and Venables addressed primarily the differences between simple regional blocs and 'hub and spoke' arrangements in which a single country makes separate free trade agreements with two or more other countries. The former tends to centre agglomeration within the larger member country, while the latter tends to attract it to the country at the hub. Clearly, market size is all-important in these models.

The geography models are far more complex than the simple increasing-returns model that we have used here, but they share several common characteristics, including this importance of market size. Indeed, the Puga and Venables model produces very much the same patterns of specialization that we saw above as depending on the share in demand of the increasing-returns sector. That is, when two countries integrate, in their model as well as in ours, if demand for manufactures is relatively small, then the larger country will produce it along with the other good; if demand is somewhat larger, both countries will specialize; and if demand for manufactures is large, then the smaller country will produce both goods.

The geography model goes beyond our simple model in at least two important ways. First, it provides explicit underpinnings for the increasing returns that we simply assumed. In geography models, increasing returns arises from a combination of fixed costs in producing individual varieties of manufactures, and from the cost reductions that arise when more varieties of manufactures become available. The latter constitute an externality that produces a decreasing-cost industry within a country, but it also spills over, to some extent, across borders in a way that our simple model does not capture.

A second difference is that geography models include an essential role for transportation costs. If these are too high, then the forces of agglomeration are swamped by the need to produce close to geographically dispersed consumers. On the other hand, since the increasing returns arise primarily through access to varieties, if transportation costs are too low then the forces of agglomeration are also diminished, since the relevant market becomes the world. Only if transportation costs are of intermediate size does the model display its distinctive geographical properties.

These differences are of course important, and they provide a much richer understanding of the geographic patterns of production and specialization than is possible with our simpler model. However, although we have not succeeded in solving the Puga–Venables model ourselves to verify this, we feel confident that it would yield much the same conclusions as our simple model if it were applied to the problem of trading bloc expansion.

4 Conclusion

In this chapter we have asked whether, and in what sense, European integration has contributed to the economic growth of the participating countries. That is, have the traditional static gains from trade (assuming these even exist for this potentially trade-diverting preferential arrangement) been augmented by 'dynamic gains' that extended over time and produced larger benefits? And in particular, since many have argued that this could happen, has the EU made it possible for its members to enjoy increases in their long-run rates of economic growth? Finally, with or without such an increase, what is the pattern of these dynamic effects, both across countries (who gets them?) and across time (when?)?

We looked first at the data, then at the empirical literature that has attempted to answer the question of whether European integration has increased growth. We then examined a simple theoretical model of increasing returns to see what it could tell us about which countries are likely to gain from integration, and when, during a process in which an economic bloc expands over time by adding more members. Our main conclusions are as follows:

1. Based on the evidence, we are doubtful that European integration has produced increases in long-run growth rates.
2. What appears to have happened instead is that
    a. the large countries among the original membership grew faster than other OECD countries for a period of years and then settled into new higher levels of per capita income;
    b. the smaller original members gained little at first, but enjoyed similar movement to relatively higher levels of income some years later as the EU expanded to more countries;

   c. countries that were added later to the EU trading bloc have had diverse experiences, some gaining (though also with a delay), others not.
3. These patterns can be understood in the context of a model in which increasing returns to scale at the country level causes greater specialization and gains from trade in large members of a trading bloc than in small ones, and in early entrants than in late ones.

If these conclusions are correct, then they have implications not only for the countries that are already members of the EU, but also for the countries that may join in the future. To the extent that some current members have not yet been able to take advantage of the larger market by expanding into increasing-returns sectors, further expansion of the EU may provide that opportunity. On the other hand, new entrants – especially small ones – may find that their gains from participation will be limited, at least at first, as they specialize instead in sectors that do not have the potential for such economies of scale.

Notes

1. For convenience we will call it the EU even for the years when it was called, first, the European Economic Community and then, from 1967 to 1992, the European Communities. We will however use EC-6 to denote the six countries that originally formed the EEC, EC-9 for the membership after the first expansion in 1973, and so forth.
2. Data are from the Penn World Tables, version 6.0, real per capita GDP, chain method, 1996 prices, except for Germany prior to 1991, for which the per capita GDP of West Germany is adapted from version 5.6. The OECD figure is the real-GDP-weighted average of the 22 countries included in the OECD Development Assistance Committee: the OECD members as of 1990, but excluding Iceland and Turkey.
3. For those countries that were members of the European Free Trade Association (EFTA) before their entry into the EU, we also include a vertical dashed line when they joined EFTA.
4. See Balassa (1975).
5. See Smith and Venables (1988).
6. The growth rate equation had capital accumulation as an explanatory variable, so this is consistent with EU membership stimulating the growth rate, but only through investment, not through improved technology. Since the data for the study ended in 1977, this corresponds to the period of steady improvement in per capita GDP that we saw in Figures 5.1a–5.1o for the larger EU countries.
7. The main message of Levine and Renelt (1992) was that effects found in growth regressions were seldom robust to the inclusion of other control variables. See also Frankel and Romer (1999), who stressed that causation may be expected to go both directions between trade and growth.
8. Nor does it imply that per capita incomes converge *within* countries, across internal regions and/or across other economic groups.
9. The answer may be implicit in the paradoxical observation of Keller (1998), who showed that the Coe-Helpman results did not require that the R&D levels be weighted by trade. What Keller called random weights, as well as simple arithmetic

averages, would work as well. Coe and Hoffmaister (1999) argued that Keller's weights were not really random, but were centred on arithmetic averages. That is apparently true, but it leaves open the question of why these arithmetic averages work as well as import-weights. Until this is sorted out – and Keller does not provide an explanation, only the observation – it seems that there is still a mystery here.

10. We are grateful to Helene McCarren for pointing this out.
11. See also Baldwin (1996), Levy (1997), and Krishna (1998).
12. The model of Krugman (1991b), though it assumes increasing returns at the level of the firm in order to generate monopolistic competition, does not permit that feature to play much of a role in the resulting equilibrium. As is common (but not universal) in such models, assumptions about preferences, technology, and number of firms lead to a constant output per firm, with industries expanding and contracting only through entry and exit of identical firms, not through changes in firm size.
13. Ethier (1979) also explores the implications of internationally increasing returns, but these would not have anything like the implications that we are interested in here unless their effect declines with distance, as is true, in effect, in Puga and Venables (1997).
14. It is true of course that the EU came to include the free movement of labour, not just goods. However, even today, it is our understanding that labour is far less mobile even within European countries than would be needed for a unified labour market. We therefore view the assumption of immobile labour – which is essential to our results – as more appropriate than perfect mobility.
15. The demand curve is well defined, given first the incomes that consumers in both countries derive from the patterns of production reflected in the supply curve. It is then the relative price of manufactures that will induce these aggregated consumers, given those incomes, to demand the indicated quantity of M and the corresponding quantity of W that the remaining labour will produce. With identical homothetic preferences, there is no problem assuring that the demand curve is downward sloping. It is likely, however, to have a slight kink at M_A^{max}, although we do not attempt to show that.
16. For example, the increasing returns, which so far we have simply taken as given, may be the result of an externality among producers in close proximity or in the same market. Then contrary to the model here, that externality might spill across borders to some extent, reducing costs in other bloc members by a portion of what it reduces costs at home. This, in effect, is what happens in the economic geography model of Puga and Venables (1997) that we discuss below.
17. Reaching this equilibrium, with C producing M and the much larger countries D and F not producing M, may be problematic, since autarky prices, shown for each country in Figure 5.4 by short horizontal lines, are likely to be lower than C's. It is here that we may need the sorts of cross-border externalities mentioned in the preceding note. However, the situation with C producing M certainly *is* an equilibrium, since the price is below the cost, p^0, at which the other countries could begin production.
18. See Krugman (1991a, 1992).
19. These models also incorporate imperfect competition, a feature that is required by their assumption of increasing returns to scale that are internal to the firm. But imperfect competition does not seem to be otherwise important in generating their agglomeration effects.

References

Balassa, Bela (ed.) (1975) *European Economic Integration* (Amsterdam: North Holland).

Baldwin, Richard (1989) 'The Growth Effects of 1992', *Economic Policy*, October, pp. 247–81.

Baldwin, Richard (1996) 'A Domino Theory of Regionalism', in Richard Baldwin, P. Haaparanta, and J. Kiander (eds), *Expanding Membership of the EU* (Cambridge: Cambridge University Press), pp. 25–48.

Baldwin, Richard E. and Elena Seghezza (1996) 'Growth and European Integration: Towards an Empirical Assessment', CEPR Discussion paper no. 1393, May.

Ben-David, Dan (1993) 'Equalizing Exchange: Trade Liberalization and Income Convergence', *Quarterly Journal of Economics*, vol. 108(3), pp. 653–79.

Ben-David, Dan (1996) 'Trade and Convergence among Countries', *Journal of International Economics*, vol. 40, pp. 279–98.

Brada, Josef C. and Jose A. Mendez (1988) 'An Estimate of the Dynamic Effects of Economic Integration', *Review of Economics and Statistics*, vol. 70, pp. 163–8.

Cecchini Report (1988) *The European Challenge 1992* (London: Gower).

Coe, David T. and Elhanan Helpman (1995) 'International R&D Spillovers', *European Economic Review*, vol. 39, pp. 859–87.

Coe, David T. and Alexander W. Hoffmaister (1999) 'Are There International R&D Spillovers among Randomly Matched Trade Partners? A Response to Keller', IMF Working Paper WP/99/18, February.

Coe, David T. and Reza Moghadam (1993) 'Capital and Trade as Engines of Growth in France', *IMF Staff Papers*, vol. 40, pp. 542–66.

Deardorff, Alan V. and Robert M. Stern (1994) 'Multilateral Trade Negotiations and Preferential Trading Arrangements', in Alan V. Deardorff and Robert M. Stern (eds), *Analytical and Negotiating Issues in the Global Trading System* (Ann Arbor: University of Michigan Press), pp. 27–94.

Ethier, Wilfred J. (1979) 'Internationally Decreasing Costs and World Trade', *Journal of International Economics*, vol. 9, pp. 1–24.

Ethier, Wilfred J. (1982) 'Decreasing Costs in International Trade and Frank Graham's Argument for Protection', *Econometrica*, vol. 50, pp. 1243–68.

Frankel, Jeffrey A. and David Romer (1999) 'Does Trade Cause Growth?' *American Economic Review*, vol. 89, pp. 379–99.

Grossman, Gene M. and Elhanan Helpman (1991) *Innovation and Growth in the Global Economy* (Cambridge, MA: MIT Press).

Henrekson, Magnus, Johan Torstensson, and Rasha Torstensson (1997) 'Growth Effects of European Integration', *European Economic Review*, vol. 41, pp. 1537–57.

Italianer, Alexander (1994) 'Whither the Gains from European Economic Integration?' *Revue Économique*, vol. 45(3), pp. 689–702.

Johansson, Helena (2001) 'Regional Integration and Productivity Growth: The Case of EU', *Journal of Economic Integration*, vol. 16, pp. 1–20.

Keller, Wolfgang (1998) 'Are International R&D Spillovers Trade-Related? Analyzing Spillovers among Randomly Matched Trade Partners', *European Economic Review*, vol. 42, pp. 1469–81.

Krishna, Pravin (1998) 'Regionalism and Multilateralism: A Political Economy Approach', *Quarterly Journal of Economics*, vol. 113, pp. 227–51.

Krugman, Paul R. (1991a) 'Increasing Returns and Economic Geography', *Journal of Political Economy*, vol. 99, pp. 183–99.

Krugman, Paul R. (1991b) 'Is Bilateralism Bad?', in Elhanan Helpman and Assaf Razin (eds), *International Trade and Trade Policy* (Cambridge, MA: MIT Press), pp. 9–23.

Krugman, Paul R. (1992) *Geography and Trade (Gaston Eyskens Lecture)* (Cambridge, MA: MIT Press).

Landau, Daniel (1995) 'The Contribution of the European Common Market to the Growth of its Member Countries: An Empirical Test', *Weltwirtschaftliches Archiv*, vol. 131(4), pp. 774–82.

Levine, Ross and David Renelt (1992) 'A Sensitivity Analysis of Cross-Country Growth Regressions', *American Economic Review*, vol. 82, pp. 942–63.

Levy, Philip I. (1997) 'A Political-Economic Analysis of Free-Trade Agreements', *American Economic Review*, vol. 87, pp. 506–19.

Lucas, Robert E., Jr. (1988) 'On the Mechanics of Economic Development', *Journal of Monetary Economics*, vol. 22, pp. 3–42.

Michaely, Michael (1977) 'Exports and Growth: An Empirical Investigation', *Journal of Development Economics*, vol. 4, pp. 49–53.

Puga, Diego and Anthony J. Venables (1997) 'Preferential Trading Arrangements and Industrial Location', *Journal of International Economics*, vol. 43, pp. 347–68.

Romer, Paul M. (1986) 'Increasing Returns and Long-Run Growth', *Journal of Political Economy*, vol. 94, pp. 1002–37.

Smith, Alasdair and Anthony J. Venables (1988) 'Completing the Internal Market in the European Community', *European Economic Review*, vol. 32, pp. 1501–25.

Srinivasan, T.N., John Whalley, and Ian Wooton (1993) 'Measuring the Effects of Regionalism on Trade and Welfare', in Kym Anderson and Richard Blackhurst (eds), *Regional Integration and the Global Trading System* (New York: Harvester Wheatsheaf), pp. 52–79.

Vamvakidis, Athanasios (1999) 'Regional Trade Agreements or Broad Liberalization: Which Path Leads to Faster Growth?' *IMF Staff Papers*, vol. 46, pp. 42–68.

Vanhoudt, Patrick (1999) 'Did the European Unification Induce Economic Growth? In Search of Scale Effects and Persistent Changes', *Weltwirtschaftliches Archiv*, vol. 135(2), pp. 193–220.

Viner, Jacob (1950) *The Customs Union Issue* (New York: Carnegie Endowment for International Peace).

6

Regional Policies and Economic Growth in the EU*

Michele Boldrin
University of Minnesota, and Federal Reserve Bank of Minneapolis, USA

1 Introduction

The expression 'structural and regional policy' denotes, in the parlance of the European Union, industrial, fiscal, and labour policies aimed at supporting economic activity either in a territorial area or an economic sector deemed to be in need of public assistance. In the language of economics, structural and regional policies (I use the two terms as synonymous from now on), are transfers to a subset of protected firms and workers, aimed at either reducing their costs (often, the cost of capital) or supplementing their market revenues. Structural policies have been the hallmark of the European Union since its inception in the 1950s as a customs union for coal and steel. Indeed, during its fifty years of history, the EU has characterized itself for this double-edged approach: eliminating trade restrictions and other barriers to the free movement of labour and capital within the Union, while at the same time increasing its intervention in almost every sector of economic activity. In this chapter I look at both the theoretical underpinnings and the practical outcomes of the structural policies, as they have been implemented in the EU since the middle 1970s. I argue two points. First, that the empirical support for the class of economic models implying such policies is, to say the least, weak; in fact, most of the evidence of which I am aware argues against such models. Secondly, that in the data there is no detectable positive impact of EU subsidies on economic growth at the regional level; in fact, the evidence suggests that these policies may even be detrimental to the long-run development of the recipient regions. I conclude, therefore, that EU structural policies should be drastically reformed, and that the economic theories of growth and trade they are founded upon, should be dismissed.

Such theories claim that, when trading through competitive and unconstrained markets, countries starting at different levels of technological

* Financial support from the National Science Foundation, the Fundacion BBVA (Madrid) and the BEC2002-04294-C02-01 (Spain) is gratefully acknowledged.

development tend to move further and further apart. Although this is theoretically possible, there is no reason to believe that trade integration, per se, may lead economies to diverge. On the contrary, all past experiences of trade integration, especially those that took place in Europe since the 1950s, have led to sizeable improvements in the factor endowments of the poorest partners, and in the efficiency with which such factors are allocated to production. This has reduced income inequalities and enhanced production possibilities across the EU. Hence, as a principle, further trade integration should be pursued among European countries, and between the EU and the rest of the world. These recommendations, and the hard evidence upon which they are grounded, run against the received wisdom within the European Union and, in particular, within those sectors of the European Commission that are designing and managing European structural and regional policies. Since the Delors Report, the European Commission has adopted new growth and new trade theory as its theoretical reference point. These economic theories argue that growth and trade are driven by increasing returns, due to either fixed costs or some kind of externality.

In the presence of increasing returns, free trade and factor movements among differently endowed countries at different stages of economic development lead to economic divergence, with rich countries growing faster than poor ones, and with relative income differences increasing in the long-run. The empirical research I discuss in this chapter strongly contradicts such predictions. It suggests that, on the one hand, growth and trade are probably not driven by increasing returns, and that, on the other, the EU regional and structural policies are a naked emperor without scientific clothes. Even if they seem out of fashion in the international policy-making circles, free trade and free factor movements are good for growth, and for economic convergence among poor and rich regions as well.

2 Regional inequalities and EU policies

2.1 Regional inequalities

Regional economic inequalities within the European Union are more than twice those in the United States when measured by the standard deviation of regional (state) per capita income. According to current EU policies, regions with per-capita income equal to or lower than 75 per cent of the average, are admissible for receiving aid under the structural policies illustrated below. This corresponds to about a quarter of the total population of the EU-15. If the same criteria were applied to the United States of America, only two states, Mississippi and West Virginia would barely qualify, covering 2 per cent of the population. Similarly, the ratio of per-capita income between the poorest and the richest 10 regions of the EU is about 3.5, while the same ratio between states of the United States is of about 1.5. To get orders of magnitude comparable to those of the EU regions we need to look at the ratio between the per-capita income of the US and that of Mexico, which is slightly higher than 4. When the ten newly admitted members (starting in 2004 for Cyprus, Czech Republic, Estonia, Hungary, Latvia, Lithuania, Malta, Poland, Slovak Republic and Slovenia) are taken into account, even the USA-Mexico ratio gets dwarfed; the ratio between the top and bottom ten European regions may then reach a value close to 6. Part of this difference is real, part is due to the EU official definition of what is a 'region'. In setting criteria for its regional policies, the European Commission has adopted the 206 NUTS-2 regions of the EU-15 as the appropriate territorial units (in the 15 member states, there are 77 NUTS-1 regions, and 1031 NUTS-3 regions). This is a debatable choice, as NUTS-2 regions are extremely heterogeneous in size, population, and geographical conditions; even more so than the already heterogeneous 50 states of the United States. Some NUTS-2 regions (e.g. Andalusia and the two Castillas in Spain, Aquitaine and Midi-Pyrénée in France, Lombardia and Sicilia in Italy) are large and have populations on the order of seven or even ten million people. Others are remarkably small (Molise and Valle d'Aosta in Italy, Cantabria in Spain, Ionia Nisia and Voreio Aigaio in Greece, etc.) and with equally minuscule populations, often around 100 000 people. The average size is 12 900 square kilometres (with 1.86 million population), with the minimum at 300 km^2 (0.12 million) and the maximum at 94 200 km^2 (10.7 million). The choice of NUTS-2 regions as units of measurement seriously affects the evaluation of inequality. For example, the population-weighted standard deviation of per-capita GDP jumps from 17 to 28 per cent when one moves from countries to regions (1990 data). Excluding tiny and wealthy Luxembourg, the ratio between the per-capita income of the richest (Denmark) and of the poorest (Portugal) EU-15 country is about 1.7, which is half of the value we obtain using the top and bottom ten regions. These are very large differences, especially when it comes to policy evaluation.

Most of the poorest regions of the EU-15 are concentrated in the Mediterranean area, comprising all the regions of Greece and Portugal, more than half of those of Spain, and seven of the eight regions in the southern third of Italy. To this historic group, one should add the six Eastern Länder of Germany, and a few sparse and small provinces of Austria, Belgium, France and the UK. Ireland, which was well below the 75 per cent threshold in 1986, and which is still a recipient of EU regional funds, has now reached an income per-capita level above 115 per cent of the EU average.

Regional inequalities are not very large in the newly admitted countries and, to some extent, they are smaller or at most comparable to those already present in the EU-15. There are two reasons for this: most of the ten new countries are small, in size and population, and this fact limits heterogeneity among reasonably sized internal territorial units; the high level of inequality among countries (one to three in per-capita GDP) dwarfs the within country differences. In fact, nine of the ten accession countries can be treated in the same way as moderately large NUTS-2 units of the EU. For example, the size of the Lithuanian republic, which is the median among them, is only 65 300 square kilometres, and the population is less than 4 million people, smaller than Catalunia (Spain) and roughly equal to Veneto (Italy). The second largest is the Czech Republic, which is equal in population (10 million) to the Land of Bavaria (Germany) or the Regione of Lombardy (Italy), and smaller than North Rhein-Westphalia (Germany). Obviously, one can always find large differences within these countries by looking at smaller territorial units. Nevertheless, one needs to try hard to find differences larger than those characterizing Italian and Spanish provinces, for which both unemployment and per-capita GDP ratios between highest and lowest reach levels equal to four or even five. Poland is the only new large country, with 38.5 million people on land that is approximately the size of Italy. While regional disparities do exist in Poland, they are small relative to those present in several of the EU countries. For example, the unemployment rates in the voivodships (provinces) of Poland average at 16 per cent (on 2001 data), ranging from a maximum of 25 per cent in Warminsko-Mazurskie to a minimum of 12 per cent in the metropolitan Warsaw area of Mazowieckie. This range is smaller than the one among Spanish Autonomias or Italian Regioni.

Finally, and to put our discussion in proper perspective, it is worth mentioning that eight of the ten richest NUTS-2 regions of the EU are large metropolitan areas, such as London, Paris or Hamburg, while eight of the ten poorest are small islands, some of which even outside Europe (e.g. Martinique or Guadeloupe).

2.2 Regional policies

Since its inception and through its many mutations, enlargements and growing ambitions, the European Union has consistently placed sustained economic growth and income convergence, at the very top of its list of policy objectives. With equal consistency, for about fifty years the European Union has pursued this double objective by means of two sets of policies: the progressive creation of a larger, deeper, and more competitive common market for goods, services and factors of production, and an activist policy aimed at subsidizing production and investment in an ever increasing number of sectors and regions. This second set of policies is explicitly aimed at assuring convergence in the per-capita incomes of member states, and of their regions. As we argue below, this choice stems from the deeply seated conviction that free trade of goods and factors through competitive markets would, by itself, never be able to bring about economic convergence across Europe. In fact, as the EU and the European Commission have repeatedly stated in dozens of official documents, free trade in competitive markets would most likely yield the opposite result; that is income divergence and increasing inequality across states and regions. Hence, the double-headed EU policy of advocating free trade, factor mobility and market competition to achieve continental growth, while at the same time subsidizing and regulating an increasing number of firms and markets, with the aim of making growth more equal across the continent. These conflicting views run deep inside the EU culture, and its policies.

The rightly infamous Common Agricultural Policy (CAP) is, in spite of its name, just the largest among such policies. It aims at increasing the activity of the European agricultural sector over and above the level that free world trade would support; and it does so through a variety of transfers and subsidies tied to the production of this or that agricultural commodity. Nevertheless, I leave the CAP aside in what follows, and concentrate only on the subset of structural policies that have an explicit regional character. There is no great loss in doing so, partly because so much has already been written about the European CAP that contributing any original thought has become almost impossible, and partly because there is nothing in the CAP which is substantially different from the rest of the EU structural policies. It consists of a set of public transfers, generally linked to production levels and quotas for specific products. It aims at keeping the price of agricultural products artificially high in order to increase the income of agricultural firms and workers. It does so because, according to the EU, without government support the European agricultural sector would suffer due to unspecified market failures, and this is socially bad. We face these same arguments when considering regional policies, so that one can safely assume that the ensuing analysis applies to the CAP as well.

I now move to a very short summary of what EU regional policies are about, the amounts of funds currently involved in them, and their allocation. The EU budget was, in 2000, equal to about 1.05 per cent of aggregate GDP, of which 46 per cent was taken by the Common Agricultural Policy and 36.5 per cent by the Structural and Cohesion Funds. Greece, Ireland, Portugal and Spain are the big net receivers, while all the others are net contributors. Relative to national GDP, the Netherlands is the largest contributor. The Irish position as a large net receiver of funds (about 4 per cent of GDP) still reflects the recent past when Irish per-capita GDP was below 90 per cent of the EU average, it is currently being phased out, and will be ended beginning with the next budget cycle (2006). From the point of view of gross flows, Germany and Italy (with 1999 €30 billion each, over the 2000–06 cycle) and France and the United Kingdom (with €15 and €16 billion respectively) should also be added to the list of great beneficiaries of regional funds. For the sake of comparison, over the same budget cycle Spain is set to receive €56 billion, Greece €25 billion, Portugal €23 billion and Ireland €4 billion (all figures in 1999 euro).

The Structural Funds (ERDF, ESF, EAGGF and FIFG) are supposed to finance projects pursuing at least one among six (three as of 2001) policy objectives. Each of them corresponds to a different subset of regions of the EU, even if the Commission makes a distinction between regional objectives which concentrate about 80 per cent of the budget, and non-regional objectives. As mentioned, objective regions are designated at NUTS-2 level. Notice that non-regional objectives are not restricted by the 75 per cent rule, and target areas are often smaller than NUTS-2 regions; for this reason it is not impossible to see structural funds flowing to special projects in regions of the EU with income per-capita above average. The Structural Funds co-finance multi-annual programmes in the member states. In contrast with the expenditure of the CAP, where payments from the fund are largely determined by formula, there is a substantial discretionary element in the spending of the Structural Funds. Taking full advantage of the Structural Funds is a labour-intensive exercise for member states, both for the technocratic standards projects are expected to meet and because of the extensive co-ordination required to satisfy the partnership principle.

The Cohesion Fund, introduced by the December 1992 European Council (Edinburgh) is the second pillar of the current EU Regional policy. The Fund aims specifically at improving the European transport networks and overall environmental conditions. Interventions do not have a regional but a national basis and eligibility requires a national GDP per capita below 90 per cent of the EU average. This has *de facto* limited the Fund to the four poorer countries (Greece, Ireland, Portugal and Spain). Ireland, which has been effectively well above the threshold since the late 1990s, is still receiving funds during the 2000–06 budget cycle.

Various suggestions contained in a European Commission communication of March 1998, *Reform of the Structural Funds*, aim at reducing the number of regions covered by the Funds. The proposals, which were not incorporated in the deliberation of the European Council of Berlin and which, as far as I know, have not yet been implemented, envision a reduction in the number of objectives from six to three and a stricter enforcement of the 75 per cent threshold for the NUTS-2 regions which are covered under Objective 1.

Should the current criteria for eligibility for Structural Funds be maintained after accession of the ten new countries, current recipients would see their transfers evaporate almost completely. For example, in the financing cycle which is intended to start in 2006, only two Spanish regions (Andalucía and Extremadura) are likely to qualify for Objective 1 funds. In Italy, only one (Calabria) may remain. At the same time, Spanish and Portuguese income per capita would most likely move above the threshold (90 per cent) for admission to Cohesion Fund transfers and the latter would also disappear. Other likely losers of funds are the Eastern Länder of Germany. At the same time, pretty much every administrative division of the new countries (exception made for the cities of Prague, Bratislava, Ljubljana and possibly Budapest) would qualify for Structural Funds support.

Pre-accession aid to the new members, a form of Structural Funds aid, has been operating since the 1994–99 budget cycle. The Commission-suggested policy for the post-accession system implies, as of now, an effective cap at

4 per cent of GDP for the receipts of any country and an overall target of spending on structural funds equal to 0.46 per cent of total EU GDP. Such limits are effective until the end of the current budget cycle (2006), after which they are open to modification. A crucial policy issue which is actively debated concerns the new levels (if any) at which such spending limits should be set. As far as the Cohesion Fund is concerned, the issue is more blurred. The latter having been created in order to facilitate complying with the requirements of the Maastricht Stability and Growth Pact (SGP) by the poorest countries of the EU-15 in the wake of the euro adoption, it is not obvious it should be maintained now that (i) the euro has been adopted, (ii) only Greece is still below the 75 per cent threshold and it is not clear it will remain there after ten new countries enter in 2004, and (iii) the largest and richest countries (e.g. France, Germany and Italy) are happily running budget deficits in violation of the SGP. Still, European policies being too sophisticated for mortal minds, we should not be surprised to find that money will be spent even after 2005 to enable member countries to comply with the Maastricht criteria.

Finally, to evaluate if the amount of resources mobilized by the Community's regional policies is large or small by historical standards, we may compare it to the celebrated (and, on all accounts, highly effective) Marshall Plan. This lasted from 1948 to 1951 and it contributed about 2 per cent of European GDP at the time in each of those four years. Over the decade 1989–99 the European Community allocated about 7 per cent of its GDP to the structural and cohesion policies. A grand total covering the whole 1975–99 period is not available, but a conservative estimate puts it at around 10 per cent of total Community GDP. The Marshall Plan funds had to be spread uniformly all over Europe, which is not the case for the European Structural and Cohesion Funds. The percentage of the population covered by the most important objectives and by the Cohesion Funds corresponds to about one third of the total European population. The ratio between resources transferred and GDP of the receiving population is, therefore, four to five times bigger than that for the Marshall Plan.

3 Regional convergence: political and academic views

Among territorial units with common fiscal and monetary policies, and under free factor mobility, one would expect uniform rates of return on investment to realize when competitive markets do what they are expected to do. To the extent that the accumulation of capital (physical or human) is the main determinant of economic growth, equality in growth rates should eventually emerge, in accordance with the predictions of endogenous growth models that assume constant returns to scale (e.g. Jones and Manuelli, 1990; Boldrin and Levine, 1997). The same conclusion holds true when one believes, as in my case, that the major driving force behind economic growth is technological innovation, either via the adoption of more productive methods/machines, or via the introduction of new goods, and that competitive markets dissipating innovator's rents are the driving force behind the adoption/imitation process. Together with free factor mobility, then, convergence of monetary, fiscal and regulatory policies, as advocated by the Maastricht treaty, should prove a sufficient condition for growth convergence across European countries and regions.

If, instead, increasing returns and local externalities are dominant, the adoption of a common currency and of common economic policies may end up fuelling further divergence. This is because, when increasing returns and locational externalities carry the day, factors of production will tend to concentrate in the most advanced areas, leaving the poorest ones behind. While, due to the aggregate increasing returns, this may yield higher aggregate growth, it will do so at the cost of increasing territorial inequality. In this case, common monetary, fiscal, and regulatory policies need to be tempered by compensating interventions. The latter seems to be the dominant view among EU's technocrats. The idea that policy convergence, and the increase in capital and labour mobility it is supposed to bring about, may cause divergence in income growth rates, is very explicitly stated in a number of policy oriented studies and it provides the logical backbone for most official reports of the European Commission. The European Commission seems to doubt the logical and factual link between deeper market integration and higher income for all participants. According to this view, it is not obvious that deeper economic integration and more free trade will generate, through market forces, higher income growth for all participants. On the contrary, the basic presumption is that deeper economic integration would favour some participants at the expense of others.

Parallel to this, another major concern of the Commission is labour mobility and inter-regional migration flows. On the one hand, the economic and social advantages of factor mobility are often stressed. On the other, one can find a number of explicit statements according to which labour market flexibility and, in particular, the inter-regional mobility of workers would not help the less prosperous regions, as all qualified workers would concentrate in the advanced ones, leaving the underdeveloped areas even worse off than without labour mobility. This concern for depopulation of certain areas and the negative aspects of migration outflows is expressed in a particularly strong form in the Cohesion Reports, which always use low population density as an index of underdevelopment; officials in Brussels do not, evidently, appreciate national parks. In order to put such concerns for migration flows in the proper perspective, one may want to take into consideration the information provided earlier about the territorial size of many of the NUTS-2 units that are the object of such concern.

3.1 Theories of economic growth and convergence

This section is not meant to be a survey of the literature, but a personal and rather impressionistic sketch of its main policy implications in relation to economic convergence across regions in the presence of free trade of goods and factors. I therefore economize on references as much as possible.

Broadly speaking, one can identify two conflicting sets of predictions about economic convergence in the theoretical literature on economic growth. The conflicting predictions stem from different, almost orthogonal, hypotheses about the sources of long-run growth and development. One class of models assumes that production technologies display constant or decreasing returns to scale, as in classical general equilibrium theory or, to go back to the dawn of modern growth theory, as in the model put forth in the 1930s by John von Neumann. For researchers working in this tradition, technological progress is the source of long-run economic growth, while capital accumulation is at most the vehicle through which technological innovations take place. Technological progress is either of the exogenous (neutral or labour-augmenting) kind, or embodied in new (human and physical) capital goods, which are adopted/accumulated via a constant return to scale mechanism. While models in this class differ in the evaluation of the most effective way to capture the economic impact of new technological advances, they share similar or almost identical predictions about long-run convergence. They all claim that, in the presence of free trade and relatively unrestrained market competition, economic convergence will eventually take place. We call this the *convergence* hypothesis.

The alternative view claims that the nature of modern technologies is such that market forces, when left to themselves, lead almost unavoidably to inequality and divergence. Again, this prediction follows from a hypothesis about the engine(s) of growth. For models in this class, there are two possible engines of growth: either increasing returns (due to some form of externality) in the aggregate production function, or increasing returns (due to fixed costs) in the technology for innovation at the micro level. In either case, these theories predict that industries and markets will organize themselves along some monopolistic equilibrium (possibly with the help of the state's visible hand) and that such a monopolistic state of affairs is necessary for growth and innovation to take place. As in the traditional microeconomic theory of innovation, models of the so-called new growth theory predict, on the one hand, that monopoly power and concentration of economic resources are necessary for innovation and growth to exist, and, on the other, that the process of economic growth must necessarily lead to increasing inequality among regions starting from slightly different initial conditions. In particular, rates of return need not be equalized across regions, and factors will flow, in a cumulative process, toward those areas or sectors where increasing returns make their payoff higher. Hence, when markets are left free to operate and no state intervention is contemplated, widespread increasing returns lead to concentration of economic activity, persistent differences in productivity and growth rates and, as a final outcome, dramatic divergence in the rates of economic growth and in overall economic conditions. I call this the *divergence* hypothesis.

Before moving on to a discussion of the two hypotheses, I should mention an apparently minor but, in my view, decisive issue that is seldom if ever addressed explicitly, that of territorial size. Neither of the two debating camps has paid particular attention to the size and structure of the territorial units over which economic convergence should be observed or should instead fail to realize. A notion of reasonably large in population size and reasonably heterogeneous in factor endowments must be implicit in the choice of a geographical unit of analysis, but is never spelled out in practical applications. Recent theoretical studies in the area of economic geography stress the tension between centripetal and centrifugal forces, congestion effects and increasing returns from agglomeration, transportation costs and gains from specialization, as the factors determining the size, distribution and heterogeneity of economic units. This does not add much to the old and traditional ideas on this matter, and I have not been able to find a single paper taking an explicit stance on the size of the territorial areas across which externalities spread. More importantly, I am not aware of any quantitative evaluation of the territorial size over which economic theories would predict agglomeration or polarization, convergence or heterogeneity. This is regrettable, as the output of such a study would certainly be crucial for the purpose of policy evaluation.

I mentioned earlier that the European Commission has elected specific regional units as the targets of the convergence process and has defined exactly the geographical level at which the persistence or disappearance of unacceptable inequalities should be measured. To the extent that scientific research can be used as a guide to policy, something must be said about the appropriateness of these units. Until now this has not been done. We are therefore left only with the common sense notions of 'reasonably large' and 'reasonably heterogeneous' to decide whether, given a territorial unit of measurement, the existence of income disparities between regions should be taken as evidence that the market mechanism does not work and advocate interventions or, instead, as the unavoidable outcome of natural heterogeneity. It is our belief that the territorial level chosen by the Commission to evaluate the process of economic convergence, i.e. NUTS-2 and NUTS-3 regions, is not appropriate for this purpose. The reason is quite simple: the regions classified at either level are too heterogeneous, in every important dimension, to allow comparability and, often, either too large to make external effects credible, or too small to make concentration of economic activity an issue of practical relevance. Further, most NUTS-2 regions and certainly all NUTS-3 regions are too small in size to expect convergence, under any reasonable set of circumstances. Indeed, one should add, most NUTS-2 and all NUTS-3 regions are so small that one should not even desire to achieve long-run income convergence across them.

A further consideration, which is of particular importance in the European context, is that the predictions of either class of growth model are conditional upon the non-existence of a large and interventionist government. This is particularly important when the convergence hypothesis is being tested against the data. We are not aware of any theoretical model predicting a convergence, no matter what. Indeed, even the frequently used (and abused) Solow (1956) model, bases its predictions on the joint hypotheses that markets are competitive and factors mobile, and that the rate of technological progress is determined independently from the saving rate, the level of work effort and the structure and extent of taxation. It is easy to see that, in most models in which long-run economic convergence is the predicted outcome under competitive conditions, the presence of government interventions and regulations would imply that convergence does not occur, even when possible.

3.1.1 *Convergence theories*

Only in the highly stylized setting of the one-sector, neoclassical growth model with exogenous technological change and identical rates of time preference, can one predict that capital/labour ratios will become asymptotically identical across countries and that a uniform growth rate of total factor productivity (TFP) will drive the growth process everywhere. Most other models of sustained economic growth under constant returns to scale predict, at most, convergence in growth rates, and only under very special circumstances convergence in levels. In fact, there is a sense in which it is *only* models in which technological progress is, at the same time, the engine of growth and exogenous, that predict convergence in level independently from initial conditions and parametric configuration. This strong version of the convergence hypothesis states that, in the long run, a common level of economic well-being will be achieved independently of initial conditions and independently of the details of national monetary and fiscal policies as long as the diffusion and adoption of technological innovations is not seriously restrained. The theoretical work-horse of this approach is an optimizing version of the classical Solow (1956) and Swan (1956) growth models. In applied investigations, the basic capital, labour, and TFP approach is augmented to take into account the effects that human capital levels, availability of land, natural resources and public goods, together with the presence of political instability, may have on the otherwise spontaneous process of economic growth. The issue, therefore, is that of the speed at which convergence occurs, as well as whether other variables, besides those just listed, have conditioning power upon the convergence mechanism. Two of the most widely quoted empirical applications of this point of view, claiming that historical and statistical evidence is in general supportive of the claim that convergence in per-capita income levels is occurring at an average rate of about 2 per cent per year, are Barro and Sala-i-Martin (1991) and Mankiw, Romer and Weil (1992).

European nations and regions are no exception to this general finding. While the data set adopted by Barro and Sala-i-Martin excludes most of the latecomers in the European Community and all the current recipients of the Cohesion Fund resources (i.e. Greece, Ireland, Portugal and Spain) they interpret their regression results as supportive of the fact that both within- and between-country convergence is taking place. The two authors argue that, over the period 1950–85, there is strong evidence that the poorer regions of the South of Italy grew faster than the richer ones in the North and that the initial gap in per-capita income levels is being progressively eroded. Similar findings are reported for the United Kingdom. As pointed out later, this conclusion is flawed both because of the methodological weaknesses of the Barro and Sala-i-Martin approach, and because of the scarce attention they pay to the time-period covered in their data set. When post-1985 evidence is taken into due consideration, economic convergence between the North and the South of Italy disappears in the middle 1970s, and never resurfaces again.

The weakest version of the convergence hypothesis insists upon the fact that, while the adoption of technological innovations is the key determinant of economic growth, the adoption process is neither obvious nor automatic, and it can easily be disrupted or seriously retarded by a number of factors. Among those that have been explicitly considered in analytical exercises, I should mention the election of bad systems of property rights inducing the establishment of positions of monopolistic power, misconceived macro- and micro-policies leading to excessive taxation, and various obstacles to free trade and the free movement of factors. The microstructure of markets and detailed aspects of the incentive system, as well as traditional macroeconomic policies, are then crucial factors establishing the pre-conditions for convergence. In this view, achieving similar capital/labour ratios or reaching common levels of human capital accumulation are neither necessary nor sufficient conditions for convergence in factor productivity and income levels. What is instead crucial is that the forces of market competition are let free to generate strong enough incentives for the mechanisms of comparative advantages and competition-driven imitation to play their role. This leads to the adoption of the most efficient production techniques by competing firms and, therefore, to convergence in TFP within similar industries and across countries. Conditional upon the different endowments of immobile factors, free trade and the competitive mechanism will lead to convergence in labour productivities and per-capita incomes (e.g. Boldrin and Levine, 1997).

From this point of view, differences in the aggregate stocks of physical and human capital, the lack of which is often taken as a distinctive signal of underdevelopment that adequate policies ought to remove, can only partially explain the observed differences in income and labour productivity. This is not to deny, obviously, that an adequate stock of capital (both public and private, both physical and human), and the adoption of stable and reasonable macroeconomic policies, are necessary conditions for economic development. The point is that they are not at all sufficient, and the crucial engine driving the growth dynamics is to be found elsewhere: in the forces of competition which spur innovation. Even if all the factors just mentioned were present in equal quantities, they could be efficiently allocated in one region and very inefficiently in another, thereby generating huge differences in realized TFP. The aim of economic policy should not be to promote saving and investment *per se*, but to allow and facilitate the efficient allocation of resources; growth should come as a consequence of the competitive race. Efficient allocation of productive factors can be achieved only when the market mechanism and price competition are left free to set incentives. An empirical advocacy of this point of view can be found in Prescott (1998) and Parente and Prescott (2000), who argue that income disparities across nations and over time are to be attributed to large variations in TFP and cannot be accounted for by reasonable measures of differences in physical or human capital. Differences in TFP, in turn, cannot be explained by 'lack of knowledge' in the poorer areas of Europe. The amount of scientific knowledge available to the average citizen of Provence is not so different from that available to the average citizen of Hamburg or West Netherlands. Nevertheless, their measured total factor productivities are almost three times apart. This is a remarkably large difference. While somewhat lower, it is the same order of magnitude as the gap between the TFP of India and that of the USA. Traditional explanations of such differences, which are coherent with most of the policies adopted until now by the European Commission, appeal to differences in the stocks of public capital and infrastructures more generally or, alternatively, to some form of intangible social or human capital available in one region and not in the other (as, e.g., in Putnam et al. (1993) or, more to the point, European Commission, 1999). The theory of endogenous innovation proposed in Boldrin and Levine (1997, 2002a, 2002b) claims that competitive rent, generated by limited capacity and costly imitation, is the fundamental reward of innovators. These are led – better: forced – to innovate by the competitive pressure of their peers who are also continuously striving to stay one step ahead of the pack.

Innovations are always embodied in either physical or human capital and, as such, costly to adopt and imitate. This leads to the creation of temporary rents, as marginal utility of the new good exceeds its marginal cost for a while. Temporary competitive rents provide entrepreneurs with an adequate reward for the opportunity cost of their innovative effort under all but the most exceptional circumstances. Beside providing a first step toward an endogenous theory of Total Factor Productivity, this class of models also implies that it is the lack of competitive conditions, the existence of monopoly power, and the distorting impact of taxes and regulations that lead to lack of economic growth in some countries or regions.

3.1.2 Divergence theories

On the opposite side of the spectrum we find a number of models predicting that, under conditions of market competition, convergence should not be expected to take place. Innovations requiring substantial fixed costs, widespread increasing returns and external effects are, within this theoretical framework, the engines of economic progress, while comparative advantages and competitive imitation play a minor or at least secondary role. The theoretical background of this literature goes back to the early work in the theory of economic growth which, after the Second World War, inspired the development policies of the fifties and sixties (big-push theories, dual labour market, demand-driven poverty traps). Its recent revival hinges on the research of Paul Krugman in the theory of international trade (see Krugman (1991), and Krugman and Venables (1995), for recent restatements) and of Paul Romer in the theory of endogenous growth (Romer, 1986, 1990). It is often referred at as 'new trade and growth theory'. A recent survey of empirical work carried out along these lines can be found in Durlauf and Quah (1998).

Independently of the actual source of increasing returns, if they materialize at the regional level any increase in the degree of trade openness will be likely to send the most productive factors flowing toward the advanced regions, where their return is higher, leaving the disadvantaged areas further behind. In its extreme version, this approach predicts that, for example, strategic complementarities and increasing returns are so pervasive that the construction of infrastructures for transportation and communication may be harmful for the poorest areas, as it facilitates emigration of the most productive factors. Two fundamental assumptions about the nature of modern technologies sustains such predictions: that all factors are reproducible and mobile, so that fixed factors and congestion play only a secondary role, and that the process of innovation and technological progress relies on fixed costs, which gives rise to widespread increasing returns. Hence the need for policies that prevent depopulation and that, more generally, create incentives for keeping the strategic factors of production in the least advanced regions. This is the strong version of the divergence hypothesis.

Several strands of the new growth theory literature have argued for different sources of increasing returns and agglomeration effects. The idea that fixed costs at the firm level matter and that, with decreasing long-run cost curves, the rich grow richer and the poor poorer, has been, and probably still is, the leading intuition behind this approach. Particular cases of this line of research identify the fixed costs with the generation of innovations (R&D activities, external effects from human capital investment) or with the accumulation of minimum stocks of physical capital and/or public infrastructures without which private investment and labour effort cannot yield the appropriate rate of return. An alternative, but substantially similar view, argues for the simultaneous presence of strong complementarities in production and widespread coordination failures in the market for productive factors. Under such circumstances, industrialization and sustained economic growth cannot take place because individual agents are unable to coordinate their investment decisions. Due either to the presence of strong and positive external effects of one investment project upon another, or to some form of minimum market size condition, or to both, individual projects are not profitable when started in isolation. Only if numerous projects are implemented simultaneously, will the realized return be high enough to justify the allocation of productive capital to the enterprise. Hence the theoretical justification for an active policy of subsidies and financial support to firms located in the poorer regions; see e.g. Ciccone and Matsuyama (1996), Matsuyama (1995), Murphy, Shleifer and Vishny (1989).

The traditional theory of regional economics also contains a long list of reasons why advanced economic activity will tend to concentrate in a few regions, leaving others behind, when free trade and market competition are setting the incentives. Among the facts making for concentration are, once again, economies of scale, economies of agglomeration, increase in labour market efficiency due to search-and-match effects, monopoly power generated by innovation leadership and, more generally, externalities associated with the generation of productive knowledge.

What we call the weak version of the divergence hypothesis argues that some minimum absolute level of the externalities-inducing factors must be achieved in order to make the process of economic growth self-sustained. While the theoretical models adopted are pretty much the same as in the previous case, poverty traps and low-growth equilibria originate here not because the ratio between the poor and the rich regions is below some critical value but, instead, because the poor regions have not managed to cross a threshold level in their endowment of the strategic inputs: human capital, public infrastructures, R&D activity and financial deepening. In the absence of political intervention or when it is too weak, some form of club convergence will be observed. Regions will cluster within different clubs, which are determined by upper and lower bounds on the endowments of the strategic factors. Convergence within each one of these classes may therefore be observed, with countries belonging to the same club growing (or stagnating) together in the long run without much reduction of between-club inequalities. This point of view has been translated into a statistical methodology and applied to both worldwide data sets and to the case of European regions. Some authors, e.g. Canova (1998) and Quah (1996), have found supporting evidence for the idea that European regions, for example, are dividing themselves up into four clusters, each one with its own asymptotically stable per-capita income level. The evidence reported in my work with Canova does not support this view; this is due in part to the use of an improved analytical methodology, but mostly to the availability of an extended and more complete data set.

All these models advocate direct government intervention in the economic arena to induce convergence. Indeed, the strong version of the divergence hypothesis might argue that, unless almost complete convergence has been attained, free trade will always generate a tendency for increasing disparities. One common feature of these models, which is particularly important for policy purposes, is the lack of a clear definition of the territorial area over which external effects are supposed to be acting in a distorting and socially inefficient way. As I already pointed out, NUTS-2 regions are extremely heterogeneous in size and population. If external effects are relevant for a region as large as Andalucia, what prevents them from propagating from Lisbon all over Portugal, or from Rome to Reggio Calabria?

4 Regional economic convergence: EU evidence

Probably the most important lesson, during the last twenty years, that empirical studies of economic growth in trade-integrated areas have taught us is that the predictions of new growth or new trade theory models are comfortably rejected by the data. This kind of models almost unanimously predict that trade openness combined with increasing returns and a variety of external effects will produce agglomeration phenomena, poverty traps, economic divergence and increased inequality. When differently endowed countries start trading with each other, the richer or more advanced win while the others lose. The rewards take the form either of a higher growth rate of income (because of faster capital accumulation or faster rate of innovation) or of a concentration of productive factors in the rich countries, or both. Agglomeration theories, which seem to be particularly popular among policy makers and technocrats involved with regional and structural policies, predict that capital and labour move toward where their complementary factor of production is more abundant, thereby leading to a concentration of economic activity in a few privileged areas and leaving the rest far behind. Hence the need for active public intervention to prevent factors (especially labour) from moving around too much and for subsidizing economic activity in poorer areas where it would not, otherwise, take place.

We are not aware of any historical experience of trade integration showing support for this kind of predictions. In fact, all recorded episodes of increased trade openness, at the national or international level, have generated the opposite outcome: poorer areas have either strictly gained terrain on the leader (in both absolute and relative terms) or have kept distances roughly constant. What we have in mind here are, for example, the increasing trade and factor mobility among the fifty states of the United States since the end of the Civil War; the increasing trade and economic integration among the initial six members of the EEC since the 1950s and then, since the end of the 1980s, among the current fifteen; the recent successful integration of Canada, US and Mexico in the NAFTA; the almost fifty years of progressive and still increasing trade integration of Japan and South East Asian countries among themselves and with Europe and the US. One is hard pressed to find a single loser in any of these episodes. It is quite important to stress that, in all but one case (the post-1980s EU), trade integration and increased factor mobility took place without much regional, structural or transfer policy compensating the poor countries for the losses due to trade integration. While the extent to which trade openness and integration have generated convergence varies greatly from one situation to the other, divergence has *never* been observed at any reasonable level of spatial disaggregation. The latter is not a minor point. The EC integrated trade first among six and then among a higher number of countries for about twenty-five years, practising very few compensatory or structural policies (exception made for the Common Agricultural Policy, the consequences of which are well known) and income differences sharply decreased both across and within the EC countries. During the last twenty years, the EU has increased the amount of funds invested in structural and regional policies dramatically, without any visible impact on the rate of economic convergence either across or within EU countries. Empirical estimates suggest, in fact, that regional convergence has come close to a halt just at the time structural and cohesion policies have been introduced (see Boldrin and Canova, 2001). East Asian countries have practised near zero compensation or structural policies. Still, their convergence to the average income of their trading partners (i.e. Europe, US, Canada and Japan) seems beyond question. The list may be continued *ad libitum*, but it would become redundant. The message is clear: opening up trade among regions that are economically heterogeneous does not lead to divergence, not spontaneously at least.

The second lesson we have learned from the practical experience of the last thirty years is that trade integration facilitates economic growth but is far from guaranteeing it, especially if appropriate internal economic policies are not adopted. Large regional aids may temporarily increase the income of recipient regions, and in this sense postpone the need for tackling serious restructuring or structural reforms, but there is no evidence that they generate higher growth rates in the long-run. Empirical evidence has consistently shown that when reasonably large territorial units are chosen for the analysis, opening up trade and allowing internal markets to work lead to a certain degree of convergence. How fast this spontaneous convergence takes place is still an open topic of debate. In fact, on average and across very many political systems and fiscal and monetary policies, the most likely result seems to be that convergence takes place in growth rates but not in levels: countries that start ahead tend to stay ahead, even if distances are somewhat reduced. Somehow, a combination of initial conditions, factor endowments and, most important, national policies seems to determine country-specific steady states (or balanced growth paths) to which individual countries converge. Such steady states are different across countries and are affected by trade policies, but trade integration alone improves the relative performances of the poorer countries only by a handful of percentage points, relative to the richer ones, not much more. In certain circumstances, convergence in levels does seem to take place but such circumstances are rare. For example, Western European countries and Japan came very close to the per-capita income levels of the USA in a period of roughly thirty years between the end of the Second World War and the oil crisis of the 1970s. However, convergence was not, and is still not, complete; in fact, since about the middle 1970s, the three groups (US, EU and Japan) have kept their relative positions approximately unchanged. For the miracles of South East Asia a large amount of convergence toward the US level has taken place, but one has the impression that this group of countries converged to some relative steady-state position that is strongly determined by national characteristics. Spain, Portugal and, to a much lesser extent, Greece have somewhat reduced their distances from the EU average income level since 1986, while Ireland has managed to overtake the EU average income level in a period of less than twenty years.

4.1 Testing for convergence and divergence

I discuss in this section some aspects of the methodologies adopted and the relation between what is being tested in the data, its theoretical interpretation and the policy implications. The sophistication of the underlying theoretical models has been matched by the sophistication of the econometric techniques, but not necessarily by the care with which theory has been mapped to the data and the empirical results interpreted. This may be due to the fact that, since its inception, the empirical literature on economic growth defined its task as that of testing a simple-minded dichotomy: convergence versus divergence. If the data show that countries with higher per-capita income in the initial period display a lower growth rate in the subsequent periods, then convergence is taking place along the lines of some, properly augmented, version of the neo-classical, exogenous growth model. On the other hand, when the data show that long-run growth rates either do not depend upon initial conditions or display a monotone increasing relation with initial conditions one can conclude that convergence is not taking place. This, in turn, is meant to imply that models such as those underlying either version of the convergence hypothesis are incorrect descriptions of reality and that we are living in a world that is better described by models where growth is due to increasing returns and agglomeration externalities, and where free trade hampers instead of facilitating economic convergence. The problem is that neither of these two conclusions is quite correct.

First, the prediction that long-run growth rates are a decreasing function of initial income or capital stock is common to both the exogenous growth, Solow-like models and to the basic class of endogenous growth, external effects models suggested, for example, by Romer (Boldrin and Rustichini, 1994, contains a proof). This does not contradict our discussion in the previous section. If an isolated Romer economy has an equilibrium at all, it is one in which it grows fast at the beginning and then it slows down converging to a balanced growth rate. Hence, *per se*, findings of conditional convergence, in which (conditional on their stocks of human and public capital) countries' growth rates are a decreasing function of their initial per-capita income, cannot support either view and should not be used to claim that perfectly competitive, exogenous growth models provide an adequate description of actual economies. To obtain a prediction of divergence, one needs to put two increasing returns economies next to each other, open up trade among them, and allow at least one of the factors to be mobile. It is free trade that, with increasing returns, generates divergence; any convergence regression that does not control for the extent of trade and factor mobility across countries contributes nothing to the issue which concerns us here. Secondly, the prediction that initial differences are maintained in the long run is common to models where external effects and market inefficiencies are present, and also to perfectly competitive models of technology adoption and growth. Consequently, should the data show that initial differences are somehow maintained and that appropriately scaled distributions of per-capita income and productivity do not tend to shrink in the long-run, there would be no reason to conclude that external effects are ruling the growth process. It is a relatively straightforward exercise to show that even club-convergence results of the type reported in Canova (1998) are consistent with fairly simple models of endogenous growth under perfect competition and constant returns to scale. Hence, in order to gather evidence on which one of the two conflicting hypotheses is more appropriate to describe economic growth in the regions of Europe, one would need to do, at least, two things. Taking trade openness and factor mobility into proper account; check if growth rates react to trade integration and if factor mobility leads to more or less concentration of economic activity across countries and regions. Examine directly if the scarcity/abundance of the factors that divergence theories deem to be the sources of increasing returns has an impact on growth rates and the interregional distribution of income per-capita. This is what Fabio Canova and I have tried to do in our empirical research on the sources of economic growth in the European Regions.

These caveats notwithstanding, I summarize next the main findings of the convergence literature. A certain amount of convergence in income levels is taking place across Europe, this process is substantial and unquestionable at the national level and much weaker and somewhat uncertain at the regional level. In particular, the evidence that, after their integration into the free trade area, the four poorest countries of the EU (Greece, Ireland, Portugal and Spain) have, to different extents, converged to, and in the case of Ireland surpassed, the EU average is striking. Further, most of the regional convergence seems to be due to the presence of a national factor. Said differently, the reduction in regional inequality across Europe is explained by the convergence of national per-capita income levels. An important periodization in the convergence patterns is clearly visible. Most observers agree that in the period since 1950 and until 1973–74 there is a strong tendency for poorer countries (and, in the limited data available, also for the poorer regions) to catch up to the European average. During the following two decades things change dramatically and the regression coefficients do not signal a continuation of the convergence process at the regional level, while it continues, and in some cases it accelerates, at the national level. National patterns become dominant and convergence coefficients become non-significant when estimations are restricted to the subset of poorer regions (basically, the Mediterranean ones, but things would not change and would even get worse if the East German Länder were added, net of intra-national transfers). These findings are also confirmed by my own investigation of the data in joint work with Fabio Canova, which I will now summarize.

Per-capita income is the product of three variables: labour productivity, the employment rate and the labour force participation rate. Traditionally, growth theory has had little or nothing to say about the last two variables: most growth models, independently of the kind of convergence hypothesis they support, take labour supply as exogenously given and assume away any kind of concern with labour market conditions. This is a regrettable fact, which should be remedied, as all the evidence available suggest that underdevelopment comes together with low labour force participation rates and high unemployment. Patterns of simple correlation between labour market indicators and per-capita GDP tend to suggest that, across European regions, high unemployment levels come together with low labour productivity. What about the evolution of regional labour productivity over time? In my work with Canova, the uniform finding is that neither convergence nor divergence seems to be taking place. Roughly, the distributions of both labour productivity and per-capita income across the regions of the EU appear to be remarkably stable over the last thirty years. Formal test statistics suggest a very weak tendency to converge, but the latter is barely significant. These patterns are very robust to regrouping of the data and different kinds of statistical techniques. Obviously, this is not meant to imply that every region remains exactly where it started thirty or more years ago. There is reshuffling of positions within the EU, with some initially poorer regions (e.g. Ireland, Limburg and the Italian North-East) becoming substantially richer than the average while some initially richer ones fall below average (e.g. part of Belgium, Liguria and the central areas of the UK). What is more important, being the recipient of structural or agricultural funds does not seem to have provided the push needed by the poorer regions to catch up, nor has it helped in significantly reducing the dispersion of per-capita income within Europe. Some recipients have done extremely well, Ireland being the preferred example, while others have done miserably, such as most of the Italian Mezzogiorno. But a number of non-recipients have also achieved high income levels – again: think of the North-East of Italy – while, as mentioned, many formerly rich non-recipients have dropped substantially in the rankings. We have also studied whether the variables considered as the sources of local increasing returns by models of non-convergence, do affect the long-run distribution of per-capita income. In particular, we have concentrated on the following: public capital stock, education level, R&D expenditure, central versus peripheral location, recipients versus non-recipients of structural and agricultural funds. In all cases, we have found no evidence of any statistically relevant difference. The distributions of growth rates remain the same, there is neither more convergence nor more divergence as the controlling variable is increased, and any evidence of a partition of the set of European regions into two (or more) separate groups determined by different levels of the five conditioning variables is absent. Our conclusion, subsequently corroborated by a number of other studies, was that there is no statistical evidence of divergence across European regions and that, in particular, the predictions of non-divergence models are drastically rejected by the data. We also concluded that, while convergence of growth rates has probably taken place, convergence of regional per-capita income does not appear in the data. Further, we also observed that when one looks at the behaviour of structural funds recipients, there is no evidence that the substantial transfers initiated in the early 1980s had any statistically significant effect on their overall growth process. Some among the receiving regions have done well during the 1985–2002 period, some modestly, and some poorly. In order to improve our understanding of the possible reasons for these differential performances, when data were available we have also looked at some individual country cases.

4.2 Mediterranean growth

With the exception of Ireland and the German Eastern Länder, the bulk of poorer European regions are concentrated in the four Southern European Countries: Greece, (Southern) Italy, Portugal and (most of) Spain. Also, these are the regions for which underdevelopment is a structural feature in the strong sense. In contrast to Ireland, they have not witnessed any growth miracle since the middle 1980s and, in contrast to the East German Länder, the relative poverty of these regions (both with respect to national and continental averages) dates back to long ago and cannot be easily attributed to a particularly bad political regime. For three of these countries we have gathered time series data on regional per-capita income, capital stock (both public and private), labour and capital income, employment levels and, for

Greece and Spain, amounts of European structural funds received. We have examined each country in turn with the purpose of answering the following questions. Are regional growth rates of labour and TFP different within each country? Can we claim that the initially richer regions grow faster, or slower, than the initially poor ones? Are capital–labour ratios systematically different across regions and are these differences helpful in explaining the differences in measured productivities? Does public capital play any special role? Do we observe a statistically significant relationship between regional indices of ERDF spending and subsequent increases in labour productivity?

4.2.1 Greece

It should be observed that, for the Greek regions as well as for those of all other countries we have considered, growth is, once again, mostly attributable to changes in TFP. This is no surprise to students of growth; since Robert Solow's original finding we have learned, over and over, that growth in per-capita income is due to growth in the overall productivity of factors and that, *per se*, pure increases in the capital/labour ratios, no matter which measure of aggregate capital is used, play only a minor role. In some cases, e.g. Greece, Spain and Southern Italy, we have found that capital/labour ratios are higher in the least developed regions, in particular when public capital is at the numerator; labour and total factor productivities are nevertheless much lower.

Greece is the poorest of the four Mediterranean areas that are objects of Brussels' attentions. Currently, its per-capita income is at about 65 per cent of the EU average. This is exactly where it was twenty-one years ago, when it first joined the EU and began receiving transfers: all the catch-up that Greece managed to do since 1960 took place before it started to receive structural funds. It is also a fact that, since accession, Greece has been the one country in Europe indulging least in market friendly internal policies, reduction of public expenditure and taxes, privatization and liberalization of markets. When looking at intra-national differences in income per capita, Greece behaves like most of Europe: differences persist but do not get worse. In particular, labour productivity in the poorest regions does not seem to catch up with that of the richest. That capital–labour ratios *per se* cannot be the explanation for the persistent differences in productivity is confirmed once again by Greek data: when public capital is added, the capital–labour ratio is higher in the poorer Greek regions than in the richer ones.

We have also tried to check whether a relation exists between movements in TFP and flow of Structural Funds. In the available data, growth rates of per-capita income, labour productivity and TFP are completely unrelated to the flow of structural funds. With Fabio Canova, we estimated very simple linear regressions of growth rates on the flows of funds. The point estimate of the relevant coefficients was more often negative than positive (in fact, only contemporaneous GDP growth was positively affected by Structural Funds) and not statistically significant in the case of labour productivity and TFP.

4.2.2 *Italy*

The long-run evolution of regional inequality in Italy displays an interesting historical pattern, which has been documented by a number of observers. All measures of productivity and income appear to converge until the first half of the 1970s. After that the process stops and relative distances between incomes remain unaltered or expand slightly. Interestingly enough, public intervention in the South, both at the Italian and European levels, either stepped up considerably or was started in the first half of the 1970s. Italian data are particularly volatile; still they do not display any long-run pattern of the type predicted by divergence theories. Labour productivity and TFP seem to converge until the middle 1970s, after which convergence comes to a halt and the still existing regional differences become persistent or tend to increase. During the same period the ratios of private to public capital stock have converged across Italian regions since the second half of the 1980s. In fact, since 1979 the ratio of public investment per-capita between the South and the North of Italy is of almost two to one. In spite of this fact, regional differences in labour productivity and TFP remain large, and simple regressions of regional TFP growth rates on measures of regional investment in public capital yield either negative or non-significant correlation coefficients.

4.2.3 *Spain*

The case of Spain is as striking as the previous two (for a complete and analytically rigorous account, see Arevalo, 2003). Regional inequalities in labour productivities have been quite persistent since the middle 1970s until the late 1990s, when they have shown signs of beginning to shrink again, somewhat resuming the convergence process of the 1960s. Both periods are characterized by Spanish growth rates substantially above the EU average. The exceptional expansion of the 1960s was brought about by the *abertura*, i.e. Spain's unilateral drop of trade tariffs and re-insertion in the international trade mechanism, after three decades of almost complete autarky. The post-1996 expansion has not been characterized by growth rates as high as in the previous period; yearly values have been around 3 or 4 percentage points, versus an average of about 8 per cent during the sixties. Still, since 1996 Spain has grown at about one percentage point a year, or more, above the EU average. While it is not obvious that the slightly more pro-market policies of the post-1996 Spanish government should be credited for this performance, a few other things are certain. The EU structural policies were not in place during the 1960s, in fact Spain was not even a member of the EU at that time. Spain entered the EU in 1986, and regional policies have not been modified since then.

Across Spanish regions and since the late 1970s, the relative endowments of public and private capital stocks converged more or less monotonically. Capital–labour ratios have also dramatically increased; they are now identical between poor and rich regions. While measures of regional endowment of capital converged, the variance of regional labour productivities remained roughly constant during the same period. The differences are very persistent, and the long-run dynamics seem to be completely dominated by a national factor and not by specific regional components. Increasing returns and agglomeration models would have predicted a behaviour of regional TFPs parallel to that of the regional capital–labour ratios. This did not occur. The amount of structural funds flowing to Spain after 1986 and, in particular, after 1990, has been particularly large. The funds were mostly allocated to the poorer regions of Spain. Nevertheless, as was the case for Greece, simple-minded regressions of productivity or per-capita income indices on previous injections of structural funds give very bad results. Most coefficients are not statistically different from zero, and the only significant ones (of FEDER funds on average growth rates three years after) are negative.

4.2.4 Aggregate performances and national policies

During the 1960s and until 1974 Spain liberalized trade unilaterally and adopted internal policies that, relatively to the previous situation, were market oriented. By 1974 its income per-capita stood at almost 80 per cent of the European average, which is where it still stands now, after almost thirty years of oscillations, in both growth rates and internal policies.[1] Irish relative per-capita income stagnated for more than twenty years, without any apparent impact from either the 1973 EU accession or the EU structural funds: by the middle 1980s its income per capita was around 65 per cent of the EU average. Since then the government fully embraced free trade, more open competition, low taxes, low public spending: Ireland public expenditure and taxes are slightly below 30 per cent of GDP, while the EU average is at about 42 per cent. Its income per capita now exceeds 115 per cent of the EU average. Look next at Greece, Portugal and the Mezzogiorno. The first one stands now at about 65 per cent of the EU average. This is exactly where it was twenty-one years ago, when it first joined the EU and began receiving transfers: all the catch-up that Greece managed to do since 1960 took place before it started to receive structural funds. It is also a fact that, since accession, Greece has been the one country in Europe that has indulged least in market-friendly internal policies, reduction of public expenditure and taxes, privatization and liberalization of its markets. Portugal seems to have done almost the opposite: it followed its neighbour Spain in unilaterally liberalizing trade in 1960, shifted to a regime of high public spending and taxation coupled with heavy state intervention in labour and product markets right after the 1974 revolution, and resumed liberalization, privatization and labour market reform in the late 1980s. Its per-capita GDP, relative to EU-15, followed a parallel sequence: from 45 to 60 per cent between 1960 and 1974, unchanged between 1974 and 1988, and from 60 to 78 per cent between 1988 and 2000. The Mezzogiorno's itinerary is slightly more complex, as it has been the object of both Italian and EU transfers at the same time. In any case, during the 1960s the flow of external funds to the Mezzogiorno was relatively low: this and the earlier one were the decades of massive labour migration to Northern Italy and Europe. By the time of the oil crisis, 1974, the Mezzogiorno per-capita GDP was about 63 per cent of the EU average. Since then, the Mezzogiorno has become one of the privileged targets of EU structural funds and the Italian Government has stepped up its subsidy and transfer policies. Migration flows came to an end and official unemployment started rising. Currently, Mezzogiorno's per-capita income is around 68 per cent of the EU average.

In this context it becomes particularly instructive to compare the fate of Ireland with that of the eight Objective 1 regions of Southern Italy. The latter group had a mean per-capita GDP equal to 69 per cent of the EU-15 average in 1988, while Ireland was still at 64 (the difference was larger, 70 versus 62 per cent in 1980). In 1996 the Italian regions were at 67 per cent of the EU-15 and Ireland was at 97. Distances have increased further since then: Ireland stands at more than 115 per cent, while the average of the eight Mezzogiorno regions stands at 68 per cent. This is quite puzzling, at least from the perspective adopted by the Commission in designing its regional policies: in the first half of the 1980s, Ireland was substantially poorer, more deprived of capital stock and infrastructure, certainly more peripheral to the EU core than Southern Italy. Hence it should have been stuck in relative poverty even more than Southern Italy was. But it was not. One possibility is that Ireland received substantially more resources than Southern Italy. But the opposite is true. We have not been able to recompile reliable data for the whole 1986–96 period. Still, over the 1994–99 budget period Ireland received Ecu 5.62 billion under Objective 1 while Southern Italy received Ecu 14.86 billion for the same Objective 1, a share of the Ecu 3.1 billion Italy receives under Objectives 2, 5a and 5b (Campania being in all those Objectives) and a share of the Ecu 1.7 billion Italy receives under the non-regional Objectives 3 and 4. Ireland only receives funding under Objective 1 and under the Cohesion Funds. The latter transferred a total of about Ecu 1.1 billion to Ireland over the 1994–99 period. The population of Ireland is 3.6 million, while that of the eight regions of Southern Italy is about 20 million. In per-capita terms, then, Ireland is slightly ahead: each Irish citizen probably received about 40 per cent more EU transfers than each Southern Italian citizen. The comparison does not end here: while Ireland cannot receive any transfer from the rest of Ireland, Southern Italy has been receiving substantial transfers from the rest of Italy since the early 1950s. The size of these transfers dwarfs that of the EU Structural Funds (see, e.g. Boldrin and Rustichini (1995) for details), thereby making the regions of Southern Italy much larger recipients of structural funding than Ireland, even in per-capita terms. Why, then, did they not grow, while Ireland did?

4.3 Central and Northern European growth

4.3.1 The CEEC-10

In joint work with Fabio Canova, Boldrin and Canova (2003), we looked at the determinants of economic growth in the ten Eastern European candidates to enter the EU between 2004 and 2008 (i.e. the eight admitted to join in 2004 plus Bulgaria and Romania) in the ten years since they abandoned socialist economic regulation, 1990–2000. Average growth rates of GDP vary substantially, from a value of −4.0 per cent per year in Bulgaria to a 7.7 per cent rise per year in Latvia. Apart from Latvia, the success stories appear to be Slovenia, with an average growth rate of 5.0 per cent, and Lithuania with 4.9 per cent. After Bulgaria, the worst performers are Romania (−0.4) Estonia (2.0) and the Czech Republic (2.0).

The relative contributions of labour and capital follow analogous patterns across countries: the capital stock has a small influence while the contribution of labour to growth is negative. To be precise, the contribution of capital to aggregate growth is fairly constant and centred at around 1.4 per cent on average. Exceptions are Bulgaria (0.6) and Latvia (0.8) on the negative side, and the Slovak (2.2) and the Czech (2.0) Republics on the positive side. In these two countries growth of the stock of capital accounts almost entirely for growth in aggregate output, with variations in the labour inputs or TFP playing a secondary role. Labour dismissals were intense during the decade of the 1990s. This is reflected in the uniformly negative contribution of the labour input, which averages at about −1.1 per cent. The fall is extremely large for Bulgaria (−4.0 per cent) and quite small for Romania (−0.001 per cent) with all the other countries in between. Qualitatively speaking, these patterns are not dissimilar from those observed in Spain and Portugal post-1975. Quantitatively, the difference is one of speed and magnitude, both of which appear to be higher in the CEECs, making their transition process even more remarkable when compared to the one that took place in the Iberian Peninsula. On average, the seriously downward phase of the transition process lasted about seven years in the CEECs: this is about half the time it took for either Spain or Portugal to start growing faster than the EU average after their transition began. The relative size of the sectors affected by the transition is also much larger in CEECs. The Spanish and Portuguese economies were heavily protected from foreign competition, had a strong presence of the state in all sectors, but, nevertheless, they were market economies. State controlled firms never accounted for more than 20 or 25 per cent of gross value added in the tradable sector. In contrast, and excluding perhaps Hungary, private enterprises never came to control more than 20 per cent of tradable economic activity in the CEECs before the socialist system collapsed.

Here, as everywhere else, TFP is the key to economic growth. Averaging over the whole CEEC-10, TFP changes have contributed growth of about 2.2 per cent per year out of a total of 2.5 per cent per year (roughly 88 per cent). However, this average masks substantial cross-country differences. For example, in Lithuania, Latvia, Slovenia and Poland, TFP growth would have implied GDP growth in excess of 4.0 per cent, had the two production inputs remained constant, while in Bulgaria, Romania and the Czech Republic the contribution of TFP changes to growth has been either negative or negligible. For Hungary and Poland, two of the largest recipients of FDI in the group, the TFP contributions are positive but not large.

4.3.2 East Germany

In contrast to the CEECs, East Germany has enjoyed the protection of its big Western brother during the transition. From an economic point of view this has meant that (i) a number of domestic income support policies, financed with taxation from the West, have shielded East German residents from the most unpleasant costs of the transition, (ii) that firms operating or installing themselves in the East received abundant public subsidies, and (iii) that the Länder of the East have been classified as Objective 1 regions, receiving structural funds from the EU. The total amount of transfers involved is enormous. For example, during the period 1991–97 the German government alone transferred to the East Länder a total of €571 billion, corresponding to about 50 per cent of their GDP over the same period. To get an idea of the magnitude involved, total lending and transfers from the World Bank to CEEC and Central Asia transition countries has equalled approximately 3 per cent of their GDP. Beside these nice windfalls, firms of the East Länder had immediate access to the EU-15 markets, and did not face the restrictions, tariffs and other administrative obstacles that apply to products and services coming from outside the EU. Given that the initial conditions in East Germany were substantially better than those of other CEECs when transition started and the plenitude of public support, how did the East Länder economy perform relative to the less fortunate CEEC-10?

It is well known that the growth performance of East Germany has been quite mediocre. After a spurt of rapid growth, right after unification, the Länder of the East have slowed down, and during the last eight years they have grown slower than the rest of the EU. Between 1995 and 2002, growth in GDP per capita has averaged close to 1.0 per cent, much lower than in any CEEC save Bulgaria and Romania. Labour productivity, which started at about one-third of the West in 1991 grew to reach 65 per cent in 1995 only to stagnate around that level ever since. During the same period, TFP has done even worse. In fact, the Länder of East Germany have the worst performance of all Europe when it comes to growth in labour productivity.

The observed slowdown is long enough to rule out any cyclical interpretation: in spite of the enormous transfers, the economy of East Germany is not converging to either the EU or the German averages. While it may be a bit too early to classify the East Länder as the Mezzogiorno of Germany, we are certainly facing another example of persistent backwardness, lower productivity, low labour force participation rates, higher unemployment and high subsidies. The analogies with the regions of the Italian Mezzogiorno go further. The backwardness or poverty of the East German Länder is, like the one of Southern Italy, quite relative. After all, GDP per capita in East Germany has reached 76 per cent of the EU average, approximately the level of Portugal and several points above the level of Greece. However, to the extent that half of this amount is financed by West Germany, it is clear that in comparing East Germany with CEECs, a much lower level, say 45 or 50 per cent of the EU average, should be taken as a true value. This places the East German Länder just below the Czech Republic, Hungary and Slovenia, both in terms of labour productivity and per-capita GDP; that is a few percentage points below where they started twelve years ago. Since the best CEECs appear to have done better and are projected to do significantly better in the near future, one should seriously ask why the extraordinary amount of resources poured into the East German economy have provided income support but failed to deliver sustained growth.

There may be several reasons why this has happened. In my opinion, the most coherent explanation has to do with the perverse effects that income support policies generate on the incentives to work, produce and invest of East German citizens. Since 1990 total employment in East Germany has fallen by 30 per cent from nine to six million, roughly the fall observed in Bulgaria, and the largest among all CEECs. As in most transition countries, the manufacturing sector has experienced the largest decline in employment, and job creation has occurred only in the construction sector. The expansion of the latter has been particularly abnormal in East Germany because West German funds for reconstruction have led to an oversized construction sector with poor or negative efficiency gains in the sector itself, which had low TFP and a low technological content to start with. Obsolete and unproductive firms have been scrapped, and despite an initial boom (1990–91) in the creation of new firms, the entrepreneurial process has stopped right after the first enthusiasm for reunification waned. The registration of new enterprises in the East, which was almost twice as large as that in the West in 1991, fell to only one-tenth of that in the West in 2000. Interestingly, over the period 1995–2002 German FDI flow to CEECs was larger than into East Germany. This is not surprising. In 1990 gross nominal wages in East Germany where 46.7 per cent of the West German level, while in 1999 they had reached 73.9 per cent of the West German level. In comparison, average labour productivity was only 31 per cent of the West German level in 1990 (implying unit labour costs 50 per cent higher in East Germany) and was 59.4 per cent in 1999 (implying unit labour costs which are still 24 per cent higher in East Germany than in the West). Unit labour costs in the CEEC-10 as a whole are substantially lower than in the average of the EU, where in turn they are lower than the unit labour costs of West Germany.

Together with the significant fall in employment, labour force participation has also dramatically declined as a consequence of generous early retirement programmes and of the large number of females exiting the labour market. Overall, labour force participation shrunk by about 7–8 per cent in the last 12 years, 50 per cent more than in the average CEEC. Income support to unemployed has become substantial: to give but just an example, one-fifth of the East German population received income support in the form of benefits or state assistance in 1999. The level of support is high both in absolute (about €1000 per capita in the first case and about €750 in the second case) and relative terms. So-called active labour market retraining programmes provide extremely generous support for participants, in some cases higher than the monthly wage earned by a low-skilled worker. Not surprisingly, they have a remarkably poor record at increasing employment. Overall, more than 60 per cent of total transfers to East Germany are for purposes of social protection. In this situation, we should expect to see stagnating growth performance, little downward pressure on wages, rent-seeking activities by non-participants and unemployed, and strong incentives to maintain the status quo – a picture which duplicates to a large extent the experience of the southern part of Italy and of a number of other provinces of Southern Spain. Subsidized income support has become a *modus vivendi* and has created incentives for its perpetuation. It has also been suggested that the abundance of assistance programmes has produced a very inefficient allocation of new capital. Funds have been used to maintain alive an inefficient and unproductive manufacturing sector and new enterprises have been established mostly in sectors with low level of competition, low level of R&D intensity and low technological content.

4.4 More on regional funds

It should be self-evident that this does not mean that the transfers involved with the structural policies made no difference for the countries and regions on the receiving end. They certainly did and still do: receiving a nice yearly cheque of an amount in between 2 and 5 per cent of national income is valuable. Net of transfers, health, and social insurance payments, public expenditure in the EU is never above 25 per cent of GDP. European transfers increase the funds available for public expenditure by ten or twenty percentage points and by much more when we look only at public investments.

Angel de la Fuente has been one of the strongest and most scientifically dedicated supporters of the idea that structural funds may be useful to economic growth. His contributions should be interpreted in the light of the previous observations. In a number of articles he has shown that the structural funds flowing to Spain were mostly used for productive investments which were, indeed, productive. That is: they contribute to GNP, proportionally to their estimated share in the aggregate production function. This is certainly correct: transfer of funds from the EU to Spain has helped the accumulation of productive infrastructure in that country. It would be really shocking if it were otherwise. But the crucial claim is not that Structural Funds are wasted. The crucial claim is that they do not alter the long-run growth rate of the recipient regions in any significant way. In my statistical work with Fabio Canova we looked in many ways to discover such an effect, but could not find it. Pedro Arevalo (2003) has carried out a painstaking and meticulous investigation of Spanish regional development since the late 1950s, using a high quality data set of both provincial and regional human, public and private capital stocks, and sectoral value-added. He shows that TFP growth accounts for the lion's share of economic growth and convergence across Spanish regions, with little left for public and private capital and a somewhat larger share for human capital. More importantly, he shows once again that, even at this very detailed and disaggregated level, one cannot find any sign of a positive impact of Structural Funds on provincial and regional TFP growth rates. While speaking against current EU regional policy is a political taboo, other people have also started looking at the question. A recent paper by Ederveen, de Groot and Nahuis (2002) is a prime example. It is relevant here also because, erroneously, a number of authors have quoted it as contradicting the earlier analyses of Boldrin and Canova. This is not the case; in fact it reinforces our findings. They use a statistical methodology which is quite different from ours, but reach the same conclusions: Structural Funds by themselves are ineffective. To be precise: their estimates show a statistically significant negative effect of Structural Funds on regional growth rates and convergence. They find a small positive effect of Structural Funds only for countries with the right policies, where the latter have to be selected carefully though. Conditioning on the most obvious right policies does not work in Ederveen *et al.* either: low inflation, low budget deficit, and a cohesive social policy are not able to make Structural Funds effective. Only high institutional quality and low corruption do. More interesting is their country-by-country breakdown of this conditional effect: in all Cohesion countries but Ireland the impact of Structural Funds is strongly negative even when one conditions on the variables measuring corruption and institutional quality. In fact, the impact is also negative in Italy and, in two cases out of three, France! As Ederveen *et al.* (2002) conclude, the current allocation of the ERDF is largely focused on the countries with negative elasticities to Structural Funds. The authors apply their methodology to the EU accession countries and show that, also in these countries and even after conditioning for institutional variables, the likely impact of Structural Funds on convergence is negative. Only openness, not surprising in the light of our discussion above, may help make the impact somewhat positive for some of the accession countries. In summary, we are not aware of any serious study showing that the growth rate of TFP, at either national or regional level, is significantly affected by EU structural policies. Overwhelming evidence shows that long-run growth is the product of increasing TFP, not just of capital accumulation. TFP growth is, indeed, a fairly mysterious object. Nevertheless, it is there in the data and, again, no piece of data shows that regional TFP growth has been affected by structural funds.

5 Concluding thoughts about policy

I stressed in the Introduction the more theoretical and strictly academic implications of my research on economic growth in the European regions: the predictions of new growth theory are soundly rejected by the data. I dedicate this concluding section to discuss the policy implications of my analysis.

The theoretical principles underlying the EU regional and structural policies are, prima facie, commendable and hard to dispute. The Commission calls for (i) concentration of funding where it is most needed, on the basis of (ii) explicit and certified planning of such intervention in (iii) cooperation with local and national authorities whose funding the EU transfers are supposed (iv) to complement (with co-funding ranging from 50 to 80 per cent of the value of the project). As is often the case, reality is quite different. We have already insisted on the lack of both common and economic sense behind the choice of NUTS-2 and NUTS-3 regions as the territorial levels at which economic convergence should be measured. We will not harp further on this point, but list it as the first natural step in a long due reform of European regional policies: select territorial units that are both homogenous and large enough to make convergence in per-capita GDP a reasonable target and coordination at the European level justifiable. Common sense suggests choosing areas with a population of at least ten million people, and economic theory in this case does not disagree with common sense. The choice of an appropriate territorial unit brings to the forefront the issue of the level at which resources should be funnelled.

Currently various sub-national administrative levels are involved, sometimes particularly small ones. Theoretically the choice of sub-national units is meant to stimulate decentralization. However, the restrictions imposed make the approach resemble a degenerate form of fiscal federalism. First, the administrative entities involved are very unequal and since the Commission imposes homogenous technical requirements on planning, financing and implementing the projects, this places a huge burden on small regions or administrative units. All but a handful of local administrations, those of the few very large regions, use the services of consulting companies located in Brussels to handle Structural Funds projects. Alternatively, they let their central governments elaborate, present, bargain and manage those projects in their behalf – not much decentralization and/or federalism. Italy, where Structural Funds for the Mezzogiorno are *de facto* handled, coordinated and almost dished out by a dedicated *Direzione Generale* at the Italian Treasury is, once again, a perfect example.

While EU funding is not supposed to replace local spending, it obviously does so because of an aggregate budget constraint at the level at which resources are being funnelled. Furthermore, as central governments are active partners in the funding process and are allocating national resources to the same regional entities to which European funds go, it is at the level of central government budgeting that substitution takes place. With the sole exception of Germany, the administrative units involved have little or no autonomous fiscal power: their resources flow from central governments which, obviously, count European Structural Funds provisions as part of total financing. Finally, the desired territorial concentration of funding is, to say the least, long gone: not a single country of the EU-15 goes without receiving some regional subsidy. Counting on a map of Europe, the NUTS-2 regions receiving some transfer under some structural objective make up about 90 per cent of the total. In fact, as I learned recently at an EU and World Bank sponsored conference on regional policies, at most 70 per cent of the total amount of funding goes to areas with a per-capita income lower than the EU average. One way or another, almost all regions of Europe need to converge to the average European income.

Despite recent, belated but somewhat positive, signals coming from Brussels' academic consultants, I am convinced that the recognition that structural and cohesion funds are just transfer payments across countries used to facilitate political bargaining and coalition building is not forthcoming. Hence, the figment of the convergence goal and of growth and efficiency enhancing objectives is likely to be kept, scientific evidence to the contrary notwithstanding. In this case, two reforms should still be advocated. One is a drastic lowering of the maximum income for admission to funding. A level equal to 50 per cent of the EU average would, in our view, be a good choice, allowing funds to really be concentrated where they are most needed. Secondly, a drastic reduction of the number of objectives to be pursued is to be recommended (as proposed by the Commission in 1998 and being implemented currently). In our view objective 1, properly rephrased to focus on structural deficiencies (especially large public goods, transportation and communication infrastructures and environmental protection), is the only one that should be retained on a permanent basis. Criteria for the allocation of funding should also be radically modified. First, I would, contrary to much common wisdom, de-emphasize the support for small and medium enterprises. Policies of support to small and medium size firms should be the task of national governments via properly designed fiscal and labour market legislation and by granting to small firms easier access to financial markets. It is my view that such national policies are by far more effective (when properly implemented) and relevant than some general subsidies coming from Brussels, linked to complicated business plans the elaboration of which is often too demanding for truly small companies. Anecdotal evidence and common sense both coincide in suggesting that supporting small and medium enterprises via structural funds reduces to supporting those firms that look small, have good political connections, and a comparative advantage in rent-seeking (rather than value-added) activities. Secondly, I would also recommend insisting quite strictly on the public good nature of the projects to be financed. This I advocate for three simple reasons. First, both theory and empirical evidence suggest that if there is anything like a poverty trap, this is caused by the shortage of the basic productive public goods. Secondly, together with favourable fiscal and labour market environments, this is the kind of public good that generates the absolute advantage (in the sense of Jones, 2000) crucial to attract mobile factors of production, FDI in particular. Thirdly, no matter how corrupt the allocational system for the production of such large public goods may be, it allows more control from the EU and engenders less collusion between the private sector and the political system than the subsidization of a large number of small private enterprises.

Note

1. See Chapter 5 of this volume for graphs of relative per-capita GDP of the EU countries over time that show patterns similar to those described here.

References

Arevalo, P. (2003) 'Crecimiento y convergencia en España y sus regiones: 1960–2000', Doctoral Dissertation, Universidad Carlos III de Madrid, Madrid, Spain.

Barro, R.J. and X. Sala-i-Martin (1991) 'Convergence across States and Regions', *Brookings Papers on Economic Activity*, no. 1, pp. 107–82.

Boldrin, M. and F. Canova (2001) 'Inequality and Convergence in Europe's Regions: Reconsidering European Regional Policies', *Economic Policy*, no. 32, pp. 205–45.

Boldrin, M. and F. Canova (2003) 'Regional Policies and EU Enlargement', in B. Funck and L. Pizzati (eds), *European Integration, Regional Policy, and Growth* (Washington DC: The World Bank), pp. 33–93.

Boldrin, M. and D.K. Levine (1997) 'Growth under Perfect Competition', mimeo, Universidad Carlos III and UCLA, October.

Boldrin, M. and D.K. Levine (2002a) 'Perfectly Competitive Innovation', Federal Reserve Bank of Minnesota Staff Report no. 303, March.

Boldrin, M. and D.K. Levine (2002b) 'Factor Saving Innovation', *Journal of Economic Theory*, vol. 105, pp. 18–41.

Boldrin, M. and A. Rustichini (1994) 'Growth and Indeterminacy in Dynamic Models with Externalities', *Econometrica*, vol. 62, pp. 323–43.

Boldrin, M. and A. Rustichini (1995) 'La crisi italiana. Note sul Federalismo possibile', in F. Giavazzi *et al.* (eds), *La Costituzione Fiscale* (Bologna: Mulino), pp. 79–180.

Canova, F. (1998) 'Testing for Convergence Clubs: A Predictive Density Approach', mimeo, Universitat Pompeu Fabra, March.

Ciccone, A. and K. Matsuyama (1996) 'Start-up Costs and Pecuniary Externalities as Barriers to Economic Development', *Journal of Development Economics*, vol. 49, pp. 33–60.

Durlauf, S. and D. Quah (1998) 'The New Empirics of Economic Growth', NBER Working Paper no. 6422, February.

Ederveen, S., H.L.F. de Groot and R. Nahuis (2002) 'Fertile Soil for Structural Funds? A panel data analysis of the conditional effectiveness of European Cohesion Policy', mimeo, Netherlands Bureau for Economic Policy Analysis.

European Commission (1999) *Sixth Periodic Report on the Social and Economic Situation and Development of the Regions of the Community* (Brussels: Commission of the European Communities), February.

Jones, R.W. (2000) *Globalization and the Theory of Input Trade* (Cambridge MA: MIT Press).

Jones, L.J. and R. Manuelli (1990) 'A Convex Model of Equilibrium Growth: Theory and Policy Implications', *Journal of Political Economy*, vol. 98, pp. 1008–38.

Krugman, P. (1991) 'Increasing Returns and Economic Geography', *Journal of Political Economy*, vol. 99, pp. 483–99.

Krugman, P. and A. Venables (1995) 'Globalization and the Inequality of Nations', *Quarterly Journal of Economics*, vol. 110, pp. 857–80.

Mankiw, G., D. Romer and D. Weil (1992) 'A Contribution to the Empirics of Economic Growth', *Quarterly Journal of Economics*, vol. 107, pp. 407–37.

Matsuyama, K. (1995) 'Complementarities and Cumulative Processes in Models of Monopolistic Competition', *Journal of Economic Literature*, vol. 33, pp. 701–29.

Murphy, K., A. Shleifer and R. Vishny (1989) 'Industrialization and the Big Push', *Journal of Political Economy*, vol. 97, pp. 1003–26.

Parente, S. and E. Prescott (2000) *Barriers to Riches* (Cambridge, MA: MIT Press).

Prescott, E. (1998) 'Needed: A Theory of Total Factor Productivity', *International Economic Review*, vol. 39(3), pp. 525–51.

Putnam, R.D. *et al.* (1993) *Making Democracy Work* (Princeton, NJ: Princeton University Press).

Quah, D. (1996) 'Twin Peaks: Growth and Convergence in Models of Distribution Dynamics', *Economic Journal*, vol. 106, pp. 1045–55.

Romer, P. (1986) 'Increasing Returns and Endogenous Growth', *Journal of Political Economy*, vol. 94, pp. 1002–37.

Romer, P. (1990) 'Endogenous Technical Change', *Journal of Political Economy*, vol. 98, pp. S71–S102.

Solow, R. (1956) 'A Contribution to the Theory of Economic Growth', *Quarterly Journal of Economics*, vol. 70, pp. 65–94.

Swan, T. (1956) 'Economic Growth and Capital Accumulation', *Economic Record*, vol. 2, pp. 334–61.

7

EU Accession and the Catching Up of the Central and East European Countries*

Arjan M. Lejour
CPB Netherlands Bureau for Economic Policy Analysis, The Hague, Netherlands

and

Richard Nahuis
CPB Netherlands Bureau for Economic Policy Analysis, The Hague, and Utrecht University, Netherlands

1 Introduction

This chapter explores the consequences of the enlargement of the European Union (EU) with the Central and Eastern European Countries (CEECs). We examine the consequences of the CEECs' entitlement for Structural Funds support and the impact of economic integration as such. We are interested in the question whether EU accession helps these countries to catch up to EU income levels. On average, income per capita in purchasing power terms is hardly a third of that in the EU. In the 1990s this gap has not been reduced. The question is whether the accession to the EU could be a help in closing this gap.

The integration process on which we focus involves the accession to the internal market, the equalization of external tariffs and free movement of labour. Although these are not all the potential effects of the eastern enlargement, they capture some of its main economic dimensions. Other effects of enlargement, e.g. those associated with the subsequent accession to EMU and changes in the Common Agricultural Policy, are not explored here, in part because these effects are still subject to considerable policy uncertainty.

The CEECs are relatively poor, so they are likely to be entitled to substantial support in the Structural Funds programme. We assess the impact thereof by estimating the size of the transfers the CEECs are likely to receive from the EU. We do so by developing three scenarios: one where the current rules are applied to the CEECs in the future without taking the cap on the maximum support into account; a second one where we do apply the maximum cap;

* The authors acknowledge Sjef Ederveen, Enrico van Exel, Joeri Gorter, Henri de Groot and Ruud de Mooij for contributions and discussion.

and a third where the rules are seriously reformed. For the most plausible scenario we assess the impact on economic growth and the potential caveats. According to our estimates the large transfer sums under the heading of this programme lift economic growth in the CEECs by 0.1 per cent to 0.2 per cent per year.

The other economic effects are assessed by combining econometric estimates with model simulations. While the implications of a common external tariff and the free movement of labour can be analysed in a straightforward manner, the analysis of accession to the internal market requires a more subtle approach. Previous studies have analysed this shock by means of an exogenous across-the-board reduction in trade costs (see e.g. Baldwin, Francois and Portes, 1997; Keuschnigg and Kohler, 2000; Breuss, 2001). Our analysis deviates from this approach in two ways. First, we take account of the sectoral variation in trade costs since enlargement of the internal market is likely to have disproportional effects on some industries.[1] Secondly, rather than simulating a 'best-guess' reduction in trade costs, we estimate gravity equations to derive the size of the shock. More specifically, for 16 different industries, we derive the potential trade between the EU and the CEECs from gravity equations. The estimates provide an indication of trade flows when CEECs are full members of the EU. Comparing this potential trade with actual trade, we can derive an estimate of the tariff equivalent of the barriers to trade. These barriers are then assumed to be removed when the CEECs accede to the EU.

We adopt a CGE model for the world economy, called WorldScan, to explore the implications of EU enlargement in its three dimensions. The model, calibrated on the most recent version of the GTAP database, has a number of features which make it appropriate for analysing the impact of enlargement. In particular, the model makes an explicit distinction between, on the one hand, six regions in the EU and, on the other hand, Poland, Hungary and the other accession countries. Moreover, the model distinguishes between 16 industries so that we are able to explore which industries will be most affected by EU-enlargement. Thus, combined with the gravity approach, the model does justice to the sectoral variation in the reduction in trade costs.

Our simulations suggest that EU enlargement yields large gains for the CEECs and a modest welfare improvement for the EU. This conclusion is consistent with previous model simulations of EU enlargement. For instance, Brown *et al.* (1997) estimate welfare gains for the CEECs between 3.8 and 7.3 per cent, and around 0.1 per cent for the EU. Baldwin, Francois and Portes (1997) find a real income gain of 1.5 per cent for the CEECs and more modest effects for the EU. Breuss (2001) reports effects on real GDP between 4 and 9 per cent for the CEECs and about one tenth of that for the EU. Our findings tend to be somewhat larger than the effects reported in those previous studies. This is because of the relatively large shock associated with the accession to the internal market which, in contrast to the previous studies, is based on empirical research.

Combining the effects of the customs union, internal market, migration, and that of the Structural Funds programme, consumption could increase by about 15 per cent in the CEECs (nearly 13 per cent due to the first three elements and a higher growth rate for about 20 years due to the transfers). In terms of consumption per capita compared to the EU-15, the increase is about five percentage points. This is a substantial increase, but a long way from equal consumption levels.

The rest of the chapter is organized as follows. Section 2 discusses the current state of the accession countries in terms of catching up. Section 3 describes the Structural Funds programme. The economic effects of this programme are presented in Section 4. Section 5 demonstrates the shock of EU-enlargement in three dimensions: the shift towards a customs union, accession to the internal EU market and free movement of labour. Section 6 analyses the implication of these shocks for both the EU and accession countries. Finally, Section 7 concludes.

2 The challenge

EU enlargement brings new challenges for the EU to reduce the income disparities between the current Member States and the CEECs. The last decade is not characterized by a convergence process. Indeed, Table 7.1 reveals that, during 1989–99, EU GDP per capita grew by 22 per cent while that of the CEECs in 1999 is no higher than in 1989. Hence, the first decade of transition is characterized by a divergence in income levels between the EU and the CEECs. The exception is Poland, where the average growth rate during the last decade is more or less equal to that of the EU.

Table 7.1 Convergence and divergence between the CEECs and the EU 1989–99, per capita

	Real GDP in 1999 (1989 = 100)	*Average growth rate 1994–99*
Poland	122.0	5.8
Romania	73.7	−1.4
Czech Republic	95.1	1.6
Hungary	99.6	3.4
Bulgaria	70.7	−1.8
Slovak Republic	103.3	5.6
Lithuania	63.5	3.2
Latvia	59.4	2.9
Slovenia	105.3	4.2
Estonia	78.5	4.3
Mean CEECs	100	3.6
EU-15	122	2.4

Source: Boeri *et al.* (2000), Eurostat and authors' calculations.

Comparing the first and second columns of Table 7.1, we see that there is an enormous difference between the first five years of transition and the last five years. In particular, after a sharp fall in GDP in the early years of transition, the CEECs have in the second half of the 1990s, on average, returned to their pre-transition level of welfare. During the last five years, the average growth rate in the accession countries was 3.6 per cent per year. Poland and Slovakia even grew by an annual rate of almost 6 per cent. Compared to the annual growth rate of 2.4 per cent in the EU, these figures suggest that accession countries have reached a phase of convergence towards the EU-15. This, however, does not hold for all countries. For instance, Bulgaria and Romania also experienced a decline in GDP during the last five years. Also the Czech Republic features a poor track record.

To converge to the average EU level in the coming years, the CEECs need to grow substantially faster than the EU. In particular, if the difference in growth rates were to remain 1.2 per cent annually, i.e. the average over the past five years, it would take 83 years before the accession countries have moved to the average EU-15 level. This is long by any standard. If CEECs would aim to converge at a faster rate, for instance within a period of 20 years, this would require an annual growth rate of at least 7 per cent per year. Hence, catching up of the CEECs requires a formidable effort.

Several factors might contribute to the convergence of accession countries to the EU average, including market integration, domestic reform and EU policies. Regarding the first component, one may think of trade integration, inflows of FDI and the associated technology transfers, free mobility of labour, and increasing competitive forces from the EU. This chapter provides a quantitative assessment of these effects in Section 6. Secondly, ongoing transition may stimulate growth. For instance, a further development of government and legal institutions in the CEECs, including administrative capacity, may enhance trust and certainty with respect to property rights (Knack and Keefer, 1997). Moreover, the creation of a civil society with appropriate coordination mechanisms, structural reform in many sectors and investments in human capital will contribute to economic growth. The final factor that may enhance growth in the CEECs is transfers. An assessment of the EU transfer policy is an issue to which we now turn.

3 A brief description of the current cohesion policy

The European cohesion policy has two pillars: the Cohesion Fund and the Structural Funds. The Cohesion Fund was introduced in the Maastricht Treaty as support for the least developed member states to meet the criteria to enter the EMU. More specifically, member states with a GDP per capita in purchasing power parities of less than 90 per cent of the EU average are eligible for support from the Cohesion Fund. The €18 billion which is available for the period 2000–06 is allocated by objective criteria over the four countries eligible: Spain (62 per cent), Greece (17 per cent), Ireland (4 per cent) and Portugal (17 per cent). Expenditures (co-)financed by the Cohesion Fund are restricted to areas related to transport and environment. The distribution between those two areas was roughly half and half in the previous planning period (1993–99).

The second pillar of the European cohesion policy, the Structural Funds, is much larger in terms of budget and more complicated in terms of institutions. Its general aim is to enhance cohesion and to reduce welfare differences among the regions of EU. More precisely, since the Berlin meeting of the European Council, the Agenda 2000 agreement spells out that the Funds are to meet three objectives: support for (1) Regions whose development is lagging behind, (2) Economic and social conversion of areas facing structural difficulties, and (3) Adaptation and modernization of policies and systems of education, training and employment. Table 7.2 shows the allocation of Funds to these objectives. In addition to Objectives 1, 2 and 3, there are four types of community initiatives and two (minor) types of support which are listed merely for completeness. As is clear from Table 7.2, Objective 1 is by far the largest objective in terms of budget. Eligible Objective 1 regions

Table 7.2 Allocation of Structural Funds over receiving countries 2000–06

	Objective 1	*Objective 2*	*Objective 3*	*Total*	*Per capita*[c]
	€ million				€
Belgium	625	433	737	1 795	180
Denmark	0	183	365	548	141
Germany	19 958	3 510	4 581	28 049	343
Greece	20 961	0	0	20 961	1 973
Spain	38 096	2 651	2 140	42 887	1 087
France	3 805	6 050	4 540	14 395	248
Ireland[a]	3 088	0	0	3 088	833
Italy	22 122	2 522	3 744	28 388	497
Luxembourg	0	40	38	78	183
Netherlands	123	795	1 686	2 604	167
Austria	261	680	528	1 469	180
Portugal	19 029	0	0	19 029	1 927
Finland	913	489	403	1 805	355
Sweden[b]	722	406	720	1 848	215
United Kingdom[a]	6 251	4 695	4 568	15 514	266
EU-15	135 954	22 454	24 050	182 458	490

[a] Includes the PEACE (2000–04) programme.
[b] Including special programme for Swedish coastal areas.
[c] Includes support under Financial Instruments for Fisheries Guidance.

source: http://europa.eu.int/comm/regional_policy/ag2000/finan_nl.htm

are: (i) NUTS 2 regions whose per capita GDP is less than 75 per cent of the Community average; (ii) Finnish and Swedish regions with an extremely low population density; and (iii) the most remote regions such as French overseas departments, the Canary islands, the Azores and Madeira.

Annual expenditure in 2000–06 on European cohesion policy – the Cohesion Fund and Structural Funds together – amounts to €40 billion. This is 40–41 per cent of the total EU budget or, alternatively, 0.35 per cent of GDP in the EU. Annual expenditure in the early 1990s was only €14 billion. This implies a tripling of the budget during the last decade, an expansion that cannot be explained by inflation and enlargement alone.

The allocation of the funds over regions eligible is fairly complicated and a detailed discussion is beyond the scope of this chapter. Suffice it to note that the EU takes into account the relative wealth of a region, the relative wealth of the country that a region belongs to, population and to some extent unemployment. Table 7.2 also indicates the allocation of funds over the current 15 EU member states. It shows that there is something in every member state that makes it eligible to receive support from the Funds. Poor countries typically receive more support than rich regions. Indeed, Figure 7.1 shows the relation between GDP per capita in a country and the amount of support from Structural Funds policy. It reveals that, on average, a 1 per cent higher income per capita yields a 3 per cent smaller amount of funds. However, even the richest countries receive some support. Regions eligible for Objective 1 support are by definition not eligible for support for other Objectives. Greece, Ireland and Portugal are (almost) fully covered by Objective 1. Hence, they do not receive funds for other Objectives.

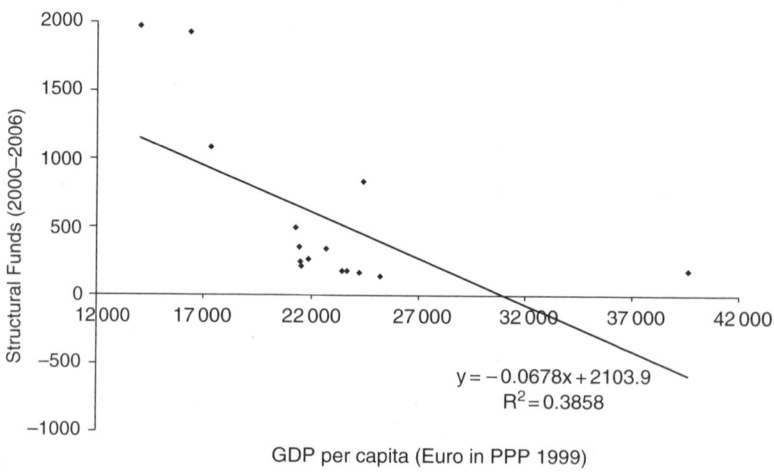

Figure 7.1 Relation between income and Structural Funds support, per capita

Pre-accession support for candidate member states completes the picture on cohesion policy. An €11 billion programme (PHARE, 2000–06), to strengthen institutions and implement the *acquis communautaire*, prepares accession countries for EU membership. There is a somewhat smaller programme (ISPA) that resembles the Cohesion Fund.

4 The impact of Structural Funds on the accession countries

In order to assess the impact of Structural Funds on the accession countries we need to take two steps. The first is to estimate what the future allocation of structural funds will look like. The second step is to estimate the impact of the funds on output.

4.1 The allocation of funds under three scenarios

A substantial amount of structural funds is only going to be allocated to the accession counties in the next financial period that runs from 2007–13. Until that period, the allocation of EU funds is already determined. To calculate the expected allocation of funds we need to make several assumptions:

- Accession: 10 in 2004 and 2 (Romania and Bulgaria) in 2007 (to calculate EU averages we use the EU-27 (−1, as we lack data for Malta)).
- Economic growth: we assume 2.5 per cent real growth for the current members and 4 per cent for the accession countries.
- We assume that the within-country distribution of regional income does not change.
- We do not adjust for changing PPPs in the future.
- For population development we use the middle projection of the UN.
- All data are provided by Eurostat.

The first scenario is that the current rules will be applied to the accession countries too. I refer to the Objective 1 rules only. As most accession countries' regions do qualify for this Objective and the Objectives are mutually exclusive, this is a realistic approach. Table 7.3 indicates the allocation of funds that would occur (the current EU members that would not receive any funds are left out in the table).[2]

The first two columns provide information about income and relative income, both in PPPs. The third column shows the amount of funds allocated to the regions per country. As can be seen, the current members receive €27 billion in the next 7-year period (compared to €136 billion in the previous period under Objective 1, see Table 7.2). The last line in the third column shows that the total budget for Objective 1 would roughly double (compare again to Table 7.2). The third column, however, ignores one important rule: the amount of support that a country receives from the EU should not exceed 4 per cent of its own GDP. The second scenario is the one where this rule is

Table 7.3 Scenario 1 and 2 Structural Funds support: the current rules apply also in the future (2007–13)

	GDP per capita 2002 PPP €	*Relative GDP EU=1*	*Effective Objective 1 policy (mln.)*	*Obj. 1 Total with 4% cap (mln.)*	*Per capita*	*% of GDP 2007–13*
			Scenario 1	*Scenario 2*		
Germany	25 285	1.22	4 373	4 373	53	0.0
Greece	16 333	0.79	7 476	7 476	701	0.7
Spain	19 818	0.95	5 162	5 162	131	0.1
France	23 819	1.15	1 871	1 871	31	0.0
Italy	23 806	1.15	7 086	7 086	124	0.1
Portugal	18 242	0.88	1 123	1 123	114	0.1
Total EU15			27 091	27 091		
			Scenario 1	*Scenario 2*		
Czech Republic	14 750	0.71	22 483	21 525	2 113	4.0
Estonia	9 584	0.46	3 633	2 082	1 554	4.0
Hungary	12 722	0.61	18 684	18 684	1 892	3.8
Lithuania	7 351	0.35	9 037	4 320	1 192	4.0
Latvia	7 239	0.35	5 579	2 478	1 100	4.0
Poland	9 087	0.44	99 333	63 110	1 622	4.0
Slovenia	17 574	0.85	0	0	0	0.0
Slovak Republic	11 996	0.58	13 039	7 990	1 474	4.0
Cyprus	16 505	0.79	0	0	0	0.0
Malta	..	..	..	..	..	..
Bulgaria	5 652	0.27	16 522	5 035	627	4.0
Romania	6 761	0.33	53 043	13 801	627	4.0
Total Accession countries			241 352	139 026		
Total EU+ Accession countries			268 443	166 118		

applied. For most accession countries this rule is binding as is revealed by the last three columns.

If this rule is going to apply to the accession countries the budget rise for Objective 1 is limited. But *if* the 4 per cent cap is going to apply to the accession countries the distribution of the funds is at odds with common sense: the poorest accession countries (Bulgaria or Romania) receive lower per capita support than the relatively rich accession countries such as Poland, Hungary and the Czech Republic. Moreover, wealthy countries such as Italy still receive funds whereas Cyprus does not.

Table 7.4 Scenario 3 Structural Funds under a national criterion (2007–13): Objective 1 with a 5% cap

	GDP per capita 2002 PPP €	*GDP index EU = 1*	*Total €mn*	*Per capita €*	*As % of GDP 2007–13*
				Scenario 3	
Greece	16 333	0.79	8 328	781	0.73
Spain	19 818	0.95	6 753	171	0.13
Portugal	18 242	0.88	4 403	447	0.45
Total EU15			19 485		
Czech Republic	14 750	0.71	10 371	1 018	1.93
Estonia	9 584	0.46	2 572	1 920	4.94
Hungary	12 722	0.61	13 551	1 372	2.76
Lithuania	7 351	0.35	5 400	1 490	5.00
Latvia	7 239	0.35	3 097	1 375	5.00
Poland	9 087	0.44	78 796	2 025	4.99
Slovenia	17 574	0.85	1 026	519	0.51
Slovak Republic	11 996	0.58	8 197	1 512	4.10
Cyprus	16 505	0.79	78	96	0.08
Malta	..	..	..	..	..
Bulgaria	5 652	0.27	6 294	784	5.00
Romania	6 761	0.33	17 252	784	5.00
Total Accession countries			146 633		
TotalEU + Accession countries			166 118		

A third scenario is more sensible as it bases redistribution on a national criterion. One way to improve redistributive efficiency is to concentrate support to Member States with a GDP per capita below the EU average. This would however imply a serious reform of the rules.[3] We assume that the amount of support to a country falls linearly with its income per capita. We also assume now that the discussion about the cap is going to lead to an increase in the cap to 5 per cent of GDP. The results of this scenario are presented in Table 7.4. For reasons of comparability we allocate the same amount of funds as results from scenario 2. We see that in the EU-15, only Greece, Portugal and Spain would receive support. About six-sevenths of the budget now flows to the new member states. Some new member states would still receive the maximum support of 5 per cent of GDP. This cap implies still that accession countries with lower levels of GDP per capita receive less support than countries that are richer. This reduces redistributive efficiency. Alternative formulae regarding the support per Member State, or eliminating the cap on the maximum support per country altogether, could alleviate this perverse distributional effect of cohesion support. This would however imply that a country such as Romania would receive about 20 per cent of GDP as a transfer; something many people would assess to be unwise.

To wrap up: the first scenario is not plausible as, for example, Romania would receive about 20 per cent of GDP as a transfer. The third scenario is less plausible than the second as the rules need to be reformed fundamentally. This is unlikely as unanimity voting applies to the Structural Funds programme. The second scenario requires no strong reform and the budgetary consequences are, for the EU as a whole, not severe (we ignore, however, transitional measures, which might turn out costly). Thus we take scenario 2 as starting-point for further analysis.

4.2 What do the transfers imply for economic development?

Cohesion support has the potential to encourage convergence across regions. This is clearly illustrated by various model simulations, either carried out within the EC or by outside researchers. However, Structural Funds and the Cohesion Fund are not necessarily effective in this respect. Indeed, there are several possible caveats that may reduce the growth effect of cohesion support, such as crowding out, inappropriate spending and rent-seeking. Although the EC tries to minimize these adverse unfavourable by-products of cohesion support, ex-post evaluations should say how effective it really is in stimulating economic convergence across regions. On the basis of various case studies of the impact of Structural Funds on growth, it is hard to make an objective quantitative assessment. The evidence from econometric studies is mixed: some studies report a positive, some an insignificant, and some even a negative impact of Structural Funds.

Meta-analysis suggests that the potential growth elasticity of cohesion support is 0.18. Model simulations on average suggest that an amount of cohesion support equal to one percent of GDP yields 0.18 additional percentage points in annual growth of GDP per capita. Meta-analysis also reveals, however, that the actual growth elasticity from econometric studies is a mere 0.04, almost five times smaller. The challenge is thus to reform cohesion policy such that this gap is bridged.

The current rules imply that a country can receive a maximum amount of cohesion support equal to 4 per cent of its GDP. Applying an average growth elasticity of cohesion support of 0.18, we find that cohesion policy can potentially boost the growth rate in the CEECs by an additional 0.7 per cent per year. When taking the econometric studies as the starting-point, the number would be somewhat more than 0.1 per cent higher growth. The question is which is more plausible?

4.3 How effective are the funds?

There are numerous reasons why the funds are probably not so effective in reducing income disparities in the EU. The first reason – we already discussed – is that a substantial part of the Structural Funds still goes to relatively wealthy countries. A second reason is that the EU funds for economic development might crowd out funds generated by domestic taxation.

A third reason for the weak (expected) performance for which there is ample anecdotal evidence is: government failures leading to inappropriate spending and rent seeking. The anecdotal evidence is complemented by Ederveen, de Groot and Nahuis (2002) who estimate the conditional effectiveness of the Structural Funds. Hence they estimate the growth-effect of Structural Funds given the quality of the government. The latter is proxied by a corruption-perception index and other measures of institutional quality. They find that structural funds contribute positively to growth only in countries with a high institutional quality. None of the accession countries for which data are available meet the minimum criterion.

For these three reasons we argue that an informed guess should be at the lower end of the results discussed in the previous section – between 0.1 per cent additional growth and 0.7 per cent – hence roughly 0.1 or 0.2 percentage points additional growth. This implies that for all countries except Slovenia and Cyprus we guesstimate an additional growth effect of 0.1–0.2 per cent. Over a period of about 20 years this would imply an increase in income of about 2 per cent to 4 per cent. The next section assesses the impact of economic integration as such.

5 Shock of enlargement

This section discusses three shocks of EU-enlargement: (i) a gradual removal of the remaining formal trade barriers in agriculture and food processing and the adoption of the common external tariff (CET), (ii) accession to the internal market, and (iii) free movement of labour. Section 6 analyses the economic implications of these shocks with the WorldScan model. This model is presented briefly in the last part of this section. We do not analyse some other potential implications of enlargement such as accession to EMU, changes in the Common Agricultural Policies of the EU, or changes in EU policies with respect to the Structural Funds.

5.1 Towards a customs union

Accession of the CEECs to the EU implies a move from an almost free-trade area towards a customs union. This means that all remaining bilateral formal trade barriers between the CEECs and the EU will be abolished. In 1997, these barriers were present in both agriculture and several manufacturing sectors. In accordance with the Europe agreements, the bilateral tariffs for manufacturing products had been removed by 2002. The abolition of these tariffs can thus not be directly ascribed to accession to the EU. Therefore, we do not include the Europe agreements in our analysis. Instead, we focus on the bilateral tariffs that are not covered by the Europe agreements, namely those in agriculture and food processing.

Table 7.5 Bilateral and external tariffs in agriculture and food processing in the CEECs and the EU

	Export tariffs		*Import tariffs*		*External import tariff*	
	Agriculture	*Food*	*Agriculture*	*Food*	*Agriculture*	*Food*
Levied by CEECs						
Hungary	−2.1	−1.7	22.7	35.6	15.9	32.0
Poland	0.0	−0.3	38.4	63.3	26.7	63.3
CEEC-5	0.0	−3.5	24.6	41.0	17.6	48.9
Levied by EU-15					7.3	36.1
Hungary	−2.1	−5.2	17.3	33.2		
Poland	−3.0	−4.4	22.0	41.7		
CEEC-5	−3.0	−5.4	9.4	30.4		

Source: Dimaranan and McDougall (2002).

Apart from abolishing bilateral trade barriers, the move towards a customs union means that the external tariffs in the CEECs with respect to third countries will be set equal to the common external tariff (CET) of the EU. This holds for both agriculture and food processing and all manufacturing sectors.

As shown in Table 7.5, most regions in the EU and the CEECs provide export subsidies for agricultural products and food processing. Hungary provides an export subsidy of 2.1 per cent of the export value in agriculture and 1.7 per cent in food processing. Compared to the CEECs, export subsidies of the EU are larger. Hence, the EU stimulates its exports of agricultural and food products more than the CEECs do. The bilateral import tariffs in agriculture and food processing in these countries are substantial, both in the CEECs and the EU. Compared to the EU, the import tariffs imposed by the CEECs are somewhat larger. Import tariffs in Poland are especially high, while Hungarian tariffs are among the lowest.

For agricultural products, we see that the external tariff of the EU is lower than that of the accession countries. In food processing, the EU tariff is higher than in Hungary but lower than in Poland and CEEC-5. Among the accession countries, Hungary imposes the lowest external tariffs. The external tariffs for manufacturing products are also relatively low for Hungary, but still higher than the CET. The Polish external tariffs are the highest in most sectors.

5.2 Accession to the internal market

The second component of EU enlargement involves the accession of the CEECs to the internal market. This will affect the economies of the CEECs and current EU members in several ways, for instance via trade, FDI, domestic investment and so on. Our focus is on the trade effect.

Accession to the internal market may increase trade for at least three reasons. First, a number of administrative barriers to trade will be eliminated or at least reduced to levels comparable to those between current EU members.

Here, one can think of reduced costs of passing customs at the frontier, such as shorter delays and fewer formalities. Secondly, and probably more important, is the reduction in technical barriers to trade. The Single Market reduces these technical barriers by means of mutual recognition of different technical regulations, minimum requirements and harmonization of rules and regulations.[4] Finally, risk and uncertainty will be mitigated by the CEECs' accession to the EU. One type of risk is the possibility that somewhere in the link from producer to consumer some agent defaults. This is especially important for goods moving from East to West as export credit guarantees are less well developed in the CEECs. Another is political risk, a risk more relevant for goods moving from West to East (as insurance does not cover these risks and as democracies are thought to be less stable in the CEECs). These risks and uncertainties may form substantial impediments to trade.[5]

In discussions about the EU internal market programme of 1992, researchers had great difficulty in measuring the economic gains. The same holds true in assessing the enlargement of the internal market with new members. Today, however, we can observe how the internal market functions by comparing the trade intensity inside the EU with the trade intensity between two otherwise equivalent countries that are not part of the EU. We follow such a procedure to measure the economic consequences of accession to the internal market by estimating gravity equations at the industry level.

Gravity equations explain bilateral trade flows as a function of GDP (per capita) of the exporting and importing countries, the distance between the capitals of countries, a set of dummies, and the bilateral import and export tariffs between countries. Besides these variables we include an EU dummy that equals unity if both countries are currently members of the EU and otherwise is zero. Our main interest is in the estimated coefficient for the EU dummy. It reveals that in ten out of sixteen industries, the dummy has a positive and significant coefficient. Hence, in these sectors, bilateral trade is systematically higher if two countries are both members of the EU. The insignificant dummies may either refer to industries where the internal market has not progressed much or where technical barriers to trade are unimportant.[6]

How to interpret these numbers? For industries with an insignificant dummy, we assume that accession to the internal market has no impact on trade. For other sectors, the dummy is used to calculate the potential trade increase. In particular, we assume that EU membership implies that the dummy would change from zero to one for bilateral trade patterns between the EU and the CEECs. After having determined the potential trade increase per sector, the next step is to compute a trade barrier that corresponds to this potential trade increase if it would be removed. We do this by computing Samuelsonian iceberg trade-cost equivalents, which we refer to as non-tariff barriers (NTBs). Iceberg costs are modelled as part of the goods that melts away during the process of trade. We use the demand (or Armington) elasticities from WorldScan to infer the NTB between the EU and the accession

Table 7.6 Percentage increase in total exports per country on basis of EU dummy

	Total exports	*Exports to EU-15*
Hungary	44	65
Poland	30	50
CEEC-5	32	52
EU-15	2	51[a]

[a] This figure refers to export from the EU-15 towards the CEEC-7.

Source: Authors' calculations.

countries that would create the potential trade increase according to our estimates. This methodology implies that, once we abolish the NTBs in the WorldScan model, we arrive at the (ex-ante) trade levels that correspond to the predictions from the gravity model. If the potential trade increase is high, then the current barrier must be high.

The weighted average NTB where sectoral output shares are used as weights is 6.7 per cent for CEEC exports to the EU, and 7.0 per cent for EU exports to the CEEC. This is within the range of a 5 to 10 per cent reduction in real trade cost, which was used in previous studies to simulate the impact of accession to the internal market (see e.g. Baldwin, Francois and Portes, 1997; Keuschnigg and Kohler, 2001; Breuss, 2001).

The potential trade increase per sector can be used also to calculate the aggregate trade increase per country. To that end, we multiply the existing trade shares of the corresponding sectors with the potential trade increases. The results are reported in Table 7.6. We see that exports increase most substantially for Hungary, namely by almost 44 per cent. Exports towards the EU even rise by 65 per cent. For Poland and CEEC-5, these figures are somewhat smaller. Total exports rise by approximately 30 and 32 per cent, respectively, and exports to the EU by 50 and 52 per cent of their original values. This difference is mainly because Hungarian exports are more specialized in industries with a large trade increase such as agriculture, textiles, machinery, electronic and transport equipment and other services. The aggregate increase in exports for EU countries is only 2 per cent, which is much smaller than for the CEECs. This is because only a small fraction of total exports of EU countries is geared to the CEECs.[7]

The aggregate trade increases of Table 7.6 are more or less consistent with other findings in the literature. For instance, the more recent aggregate gravity equations report an increase in bilateral trade on account of the EU dummy of the order of 30 to 60 per cent (Brenton and Gros, 1997; Fidrmuc and Fidrmuc, 2000). Similarly, the results by Baldwin, Francois and Portes (1997) suggest an aggregate increase in bilateral trade of around 30 per cent. Studies that do not explicitly refer to the EU report even higher estimates. For instance, McCallum (1995) and Helliwell (1996) suggest that a typical Canadian province trades 22 times more with another Canadian province than with a comparable neighbouring US state. This implies that borders matter substantially. As another illustration outside the context of EU enlargement, Frankel and Rose (2000) find that joining a free trade area triples trade and that joining a currency union triples trade once more! This would imply that our estimates provide a lower bound on the trade effects of enlargement, especially if one believes that EMU will be the next step for the CEECs after accession to the EU.

5.3 Free movement of labour

Regarding the impact of EU-enlargement on migration, we rely on a study conducted by Boeri et al. (2000). They use historical immigration figures for Germany to estimate migration as a function of wage differentials, employment differentials and a set of dummy variables. By substituting current wages and employment levels, and assuming free movement of labour from the first day of accession, the authors compute the likely implications of EU-enlargement on German immigration from the CEECs. These figures are then extrapolated to the other EU-countries on the basis of historical migration patterns between the CEECs and respective EU countries.

Then assuming accession in 2002 for the ten candidate member states, Boeri *et al.* predicted an inflow of 335 000 immigrants in the first year after accession to the EU. This flow gradually declines in subsequent years. In 2020, the stock of migrants in the current EU countries would have grown to 2.4 million, which is approximately 2.6 per cent of the total population in the CEECs (see Table 7.7).

The study by Boeri *et al.* also indicates the origin and destination of migrants. For instance, it suggests that 30 per cent of all migrants originate

Table 7.7 Migration by source and destination in 2020

	Thousands of persons	*Percentage of population*
CEEC-7	−2 400	−2.6
Hungary	−150	−2.1
Poland	−750	−1.9
CEEC-5	−1 500	−3.4
EU-15	2 400	0.6
Germany	1 575	2.0
France	60	0.1
United Kingdom	100	0.2
Netherlands	25	0.2
South Europe	180	0.2
Rest of EU	460	1.2

Source: Boeri *et al.* (2000) and own calculations.

from Poland, 7.5 per cent from Hungary and the rest from the other accession countries. These shares depend not only on the size of countries, but also on the incentives for migration, such as wage levels and employment rates. As the income gaps of Poland and Hungary with the EU are smaller than for the CEEC-5, migration shares are somewhat lower for Hungary and Poland than their population sizes might suggest at first glance. From the migrants of the CEECs, 65 per cent will move to Germany, 2.5 per cent to France, 4 per cent to the UK, 1 per cent to the Netherlands, 7.5 per cent to Southern Europe and 20 per cent to the rest of Europe. Of this latter group, approximately 12 per cent of the immigrants will go to Austria.

5.4 WorldScan

WorldScan is a computable general equilibrium model for the world economy.[8] The model is calibrated on the basis of the GTAP database, version 5 (Dimanaran and McDougall, 2002) with 1997 as the base year. The database allows us to distinguish between a large number of regions and sectors. In particular, the EU is divided into six regions: Germany, France, UK, Netherlands, South EU (comprising Italy, Spain, Portugal and Greece) and Rest of EU. The accession countries are divided into three regions: Poland, Hungary and CEEC-5 (comprising Czech Republic, Slovak Republic, Slovenia, Bulgaria and Romania). For each region, we distinguish sixteen sectors. These consist of agriculture, raw materials, ten manufacturing sectors and four service sectors.

The heart of the model relies on neoclassical theories of growth and international trade. Sectoral production technologies are modelled as nested CES functions with value-added and intermediate inputs. Value added is produced in a Cobb-Douglas function by combining labour, capital and in some sectors a fixed factor. The intermediate inputs are combined in a CES function. With respect to trade, WorldScan adopts an Armington specification. In particular, commodities from different origins are imperfect substitutes, which explains two-way trade between regions and which allows market power of each region. In the long run, trade patterns are determined by Heckscher-Ohlin mechanisms, that is, based on factor endowments.

Enlargement of the EU with 7 countries (referred to as the CEEC-7) implies an increase in the EU population by around 26 per cent, while GDP will rise only by a mere 4 per cent. Trade patterns of the CEECs are primarily geared to the EU (see Table 7.8).

6 Economic impact of enlargement

This section explores the economic implications of using WorldScan to simulate the three shocks discussed in the previous section. We present the total effects on consumption and GDP per capita and on the terms of trade.

Table 7.8 Direction of exports as percentage of GDP in 1997

	EU	*ROW*	*CEEC-7*	*Total*
Hungary	34	16	4	54
Poland	14	9	1	25
CEEC-5	26	15	2	44

Source: Dimanaran and McDougall (2002).

With respect to consumption we discuss the importance of the three separate shocks. For the sectoral effects, we refer to Lejour, de Mooij and Nahuis (2001).

In the experiments below, we assume that Poland and Hungary enter the EU in 2004 and the CEEC-5 in 2007. All shocks are implemented gradually. The effects are evaluated in the year 2020, in which a new stable equilibrium is achieved.

The elimination of import and export tariffs and adoption of the common external tariff affects relative prices. This causes two effects. First, it affects relative prices of intermediate inputs, investment and final goods. This changes the demand for the different goods from different origins, leading to trade creation and trade diversion. Trade creation will cause a reallocation in production in all countries, resulting in efficiency improvements and an associated expansion in output. The second implication is that it affects the terms of trade, that is, the price of exports relative to imports. Although an improvement in the terms of trade may have adverse effects on production, it can improve welfare since it raises the value of its produced goods, relative to imported goods. This welfare gain is reflected in higher consumption.

These mechanisms are also present for the accession to the internal market. The channels through which NTBs affect the economies in WorldScan are also similar to those of tariffs. Hence, the abolishment of NTBs changes relative prices, causes trade creation and trade diversion, changes the terms of trade and affects the incentives to invest. There are, however, two major differences. First, in contrast to tariffs, NTBs involve income effects since they reflect real trade costs,such as waiting time at borders or the time devoted to customs formalities. In particular, NTBs are modelled as iceberg costs, the idea being that a share of the commodities melts away during the process of trade. Removing these costs will typically cause a terms-of-trade gain in both countries. To understand this, note that we measure the terms of trade as the price of exports relative to imports that holds just outside the domestic border. For imports, the price includes cost of freight (the iceberg costs and the c.i.f. – inclusive of cost, insurance and freight - that are present in the database) but not import taxes. For exports the price is f.o.b. (free on board) and includes export taxes but excludes the iceberg costs. Lower NTBs can thus raise the price of exports relative to imports in both countries.

Table 7.9 Macro effects of EU accession by CEECs, percentage change from 2002 baseline

	Consumption per capita				*GDP per capita*	*Terms of trade*	*Population*
	CU	*IM*	*Migration*	*Total*			
CEEC-7	2.3	9.3	1.3	12.9	10.6	6.7	−2.6
Hungary	2.6	13.8	1.1	17.7	12.0	8.5	−2.1
Poland	3.6	9.0	0.8	13.6	11.1	6.2	−1.9
CEEC-5	0.9	8.2	1.6	10.6	5.6	6.9	−3.4
EU	0.0	0.2	−0.2	0.0	0.0	0.6	0.7
Germany	0.0	0.4	−0.7	−0.2	−0.4	1.0	2.0
France	−0.2	0.1	0.0	−0.1	−0.1	0.4	0.1
UK	0.1	0.1	−0.1	0.1	0.0	0.4	0.2
Netherlands	0.1	0.4	−0.1	0.5	0.2	0.6	0.2
Southern Europe	0.0	0.2	−0.1	0.2	0.0	0.7	0.2
Rest of EU	0.0	0.3	−0.4	0.0	−0.1	0.5	1.2

Notes: The baseline is the simulation without the three shocks. For the internal market (IM) the values are changes compared to the CU simulation; for migration they are changes compared to the IM simulation. The values on consumption per capita do not necessarily add up, due to rounding.

Source: WorldScan results.

The second difference between import tariffs and the NTBs is that the latter are symmetric between the EU and the CEECs. Hence, abolishing the iceberg costs implies that each sector experiences two shocks: fiercer competition on the home market as the relative price of foreign varieties falls, and a better competitive position on the foreign market.

The macroeconomic effects of accession are presented in Table 7.9. It reveals that the CEECs gain a lot. On average consumption per capita increases by 12.9 per cent and GDP per capita by 10.6 per cent. The difference is due to the positive terms of trade effect of 6.7 per cent. The effects in the EU are very limited. For the analysis we split the change in consumption per capita in changes caused by the customs union (CU), the internal market (IM) and migration. It may be seen that the admission to the internal market has the largest effects. This is not only the case for consumption but also for GDP and terms of trade. These effects are discussed in more detail below.

The macroeconomic implications of accession to the internal market (IM) are substantial for the CEECs. On average, GDP and consumption increase by 5.3 and 9.3 per cent, respectively. The increase in GDP for Hungary is 9 per cent, while GDP in Poland and CEEC-5 increases by 5.8 and 3.4 per cent (not shown here). For all countries, consumption growth is higher than the growth in GDP because of the substantial terms-of-trade gain. For Hungary, the extra consumption growth due to accession to the internal market is almost 1 per cent annually (between 2004 and 2020). For CEEC-5, the increase is 0.5 per cent per year (calculated, for comparability, between 2004 and 2020).

The terms-of-trade gain of 6.7 per cent is also for the largest part due to the internal market. The EU experiences a much smaller gain. This different magnitude in the terms-of-trade effect is due to the large trade share of the CEECs with the EU as compared to the EU's trade share with the CEECs as shown in Table 7.8.

The effects on consumption and GDP for Hungary are larger than for Poland and CEEC-5. The reasons are threefold. First, the trade shock for Hungary is relatively large, as Hungary has a comparative advantage in sectors that experience the largest decline in NTBs. Second, Hungary is relatively open, so that a larger share of its GDP is affected by the removal of NTBs. Third, Hungary expands in sectors that are relatively capital-intensive. Accordingly, the capital stock expands substantially.

Table 7.9 shows that consumption per capita increases by 2.3 per cent as a result of the customs union. Behind this aggregate figure, there are differences among countries. Poland and CEEC-5 experience a small terms-of-trade loss. This is due to the abolishment of export subsidies by the EU, and the relatively large reduction in external tariffs by Poland and CEEC-5. The terms-of-trade losses imply that the change in GDP exceeds that in consumption. However, the abolition of the large initial price distortions in Poland renders the Polish efficiency gains from trade creation also relatively large. Furthermore, the lower investment prices induce extra capital accumulation. Accordingly, the consumption and GDP effects of the customs union are relatively large in Poland.

In contrast to Poland and CEEC-5, Hungary experiences a terms-of-trade gain. The reason is that both current import tariffs of Hungary vis à vis the EU and its external tariffs are lower than for Poland and CEEC-5. The Hungarian external tariffs are sometimes even lower than the CET of the EU (in agriculture, and food processing) so that accession to the EU involves an actual increase in the Hungarian external tariff. The terms-of-trade improvement for Hungary, together with the positive effects of trade creation, is responsible for an increase in consumption by 2.6 per cent. This effect is smaller than for Poland. This is partly because the initial bilateral tariffs between the EU and Hungary are lower (so that less efficiency improvements can be reaped) and because the price of investment goods in Hungary falls less than in Poland.

Our results for the economic implications of the customs union and the internal market are larger than previous studies have reported (see e.g. Baldwin, Francois and Portes, 1997; Brown et al., 1997; Breuss, 2001). These studies simulated a uniform 5 or 10 per cent reduction in trade costs to explore the impact of accession to the internal market. Such a shock is no more than an eye-ball view on accession to the internal market, however. In contrast, our approach is based on the empirical findings of 16 gravity estimations. As discussed in section 2, the weighted average of our NTBs suggest a reduction in real trade costs of around 7 per cent. The reason why we find large effects of accession to the internal market is mainly due to the dynamic effects of increased capital accumulation. Indeed, a major part of the GDP increases is due to additional investment associated with a higher return to capital and the lower producer cost of investment goods. These dynamic efficiency gains are not always fully captured in previous studies.

We now explore the economic implications of the migration shock presented in Table 7.7. Table 7.9 reveals that consumption per capita rises in the CEECs due to the reduced supply of labour. The reason is that capital is not perfectly mobile across countries. Hence, the lower supply of labour increases the capital/labour ratio in these countries. This raises the marginal product of labour and thereby raises wages. For similar reasons, consumption per capita in Germany and the Rest of the EU decrease. Indeed, the lower capital/labour ratio causes a decline in the productivity of labour in these countries and thus a fall in wages.[9] The effect remains small because of the modest increase in the population size. It seems however to dominate the effects of the customs union and the internal market in Germany and the Rest of EU. In other EU countries, immigration has a negligible impact on per capita consumption because of the small number of immigrants.

7 Conclusions

Does EU membership really help the CEECs in catching up to the EU income levels? Based on the analysis in this chapter the answer is undoubtedly positive. On average, GDP increases by about 13 per cent and consumption by 15 per cent in these countries. These gains will mainly materialise from an efficient working of the internal market. The effects of the customs union, migration and the structural funds are more modest.

Although these effects are significant, the CEECs are far away from comparable welfare levels to the EU. In that respect, EU accession is not sufficient, but it is a major step in the catching-up process. Moreover, we have neglected the effects of FDI flows in this analysis. As a result of accession, FDI inflows to these countries will increase, as the period leading up to accession has already shown us. The prospect of the internal market reduces the risk and uncertainty of foreign investment. These new investments will have a positive effect on production and growth. These effects can be substantial. There are not only direct effects but also indirect effects due to technology spillovers from foreign subsidiaries to the home firms.

The effects of trade and FDI seem to be more important than financial transfers from the EU to the new members. The recent past has shown that cohesion funds have a minor effect on productivity in the receiving countries. In spite of the large sums involved – often 3 to 4 per cent of GDP for the receiving countries for at least a decade – they only raise productivity and economic growth by about 0.1 to 0.2 per cent per year. Based on findings set out in this chapter, we therefore conclude that it seems more effective that countries put their human and financial efforts into facilitating the smooth functioning of the internal markets for goods, services and capital than into trying to increase transfers from Brussels towards Central and Eastern Europe.

Notes

1. Keuschnigg, Keuschnigg and Kohler (2001) also differentiate the reduction in trade costs between industries on the basis of non-tariff barriers reported by the OECD.
2. The regional details behind this table are available upon request from the authors. For the accession countries most regions indeed qualify for support under Objective 1 (exceptions are the areas including Prague and Budapest, Slovenia and Cyprus). For the current members only Greece still has a lot of regions that qualify for substantial support.
3. IBO (2001) analyses the distribution of funds under several similar systems.
4. For a detailed discussion of these approaches and their effect on trade, see Brenton, Sheehy and Vancauteren (2001).
5. Conforming to the internal market *acquis* may also involve costs for CEEC producers, especially environmental norms and labour market regulations (safety and health). These costs are not included in the analysis. Part of these costs, however, may be compensated by the EU through the Structural Funds. Transfers and costs may thus cancel out.
6. We refer to Lejour, de Mooij and Nahuis (2001) for estimation results. Given space here, we concentrate on the macroeconomic effects.
7. The 2 per cent refers to the increase inclusive of intra-EU trade. If we would use the trade data exclusive of intra-EU trade, we would arrive at a trade increase of approximately 5 per cent.
8. See CPB (1999) for more details.
9. Migration also increases the rate of return on capital, which creates a migration surplus. The higher rate of return to capital, however, does not raise the capital stock sufficiently to prevent a decrease in GDP per capita since capital is not perfectly mobile. For this reason, our results on the GDP effect of immigration differ from studies where capital is mobile.

References

Baldwin, R.E., J.F. Francois and R. Portes (1997) 'Costs and Benefits of Eastern Enlargement: The Impact on the EU and Central Europe', *Economic Policy*, no. 24, pp. 127–76.

Boeri, T. *et al.* (European Integration Consortium) (2000) The impact of Eastern enlargement on employment and labour markets in the EU Member States, Report for the European Commission, Berlin.

Brenton, P. and D. Gros (1997) 'Trade Reorientation and Recovery in Transition Economies', *Oxford Review of Economic Policy*, vol. 13, pp. 65–76.

Brenton, P., J. Sheehy and M. Vancauteren (2001) 'Technical Barriers to Trade in the European Union', *Journal of Common Market Studies*, vol. 39, pp. 265–84.

Breuss, F. (2001) Macroeconomic Effects of EU Enlargement for Old and New Members, WIFO Working Paper no. 143/2001 (Vienna: WIFO).

Brown, D., A.V. Deardorff, S. Djankov and R.M. Stern (1997) 'An Economic Assessment of the Integration of Czechoslovakia, Hungary and Poland into the European Union', in: S.W. Black (ed.), *Europe's Economy Looks East: Implications for Germany and the European Union* (Cambridge: Cambridge University Press), pp. 23–60.

CPB Netherlands Bureau for Economic Policy Analysis (1999) *WorldScan: The Core Version* (The Hague: Central Planning Bureau).

Dimaranan, Betina V. and Robert A. McDougall (2002) *Global Trade, Assistance, and Production: The GTAP 5 Data Base*, Center for Global Trade Analysis, Purdue University.

Ederveen, S., H.L.F. de Groot and R. Nahuis (2002) Fertile soil for structural funds? A panel data analysis of the conditional effectiveness of European cohesion policy, CPB Discussion Paper no. 10, The Hague.

Fidrmuc, J. and J. Fidrmuc (2000) Integration, disintegration and trade in Europe: evolution of trade relations during the 1990s, Working Paper no. 2000-12, CentER for Economic Research, Tilburg.

Frankel, F.A. and A.K. Rose (2000) Estimating the effect of currency unions on trade and output, NBER Working Paper no. 7857.

Helliwell, J. (1996) 'Do National Borders Matter for Quebec's Trade?' *Canadian Journal of Economics*, vol. 29, pp. 507–22.

IBO (2001) Financing structural policy in the perspective of EU enlargement (in Dutch), Ministry of Economic Affairs, The Hague.

Keuschnigg, C. and W. Kohler (2000) 'Eastern Enlargement of the EU: A Dynamic General Equilibrium Perspective', in Glenn W. Harrison, Svend E. Hougaard Jensen, Lars Haagen Pedersen and Thomas F. Rutherford (eds), *Using Dynamic General Equilibrium Models for Policy Analysis* (Contributions to Economic Analysis no. 248) (Amsterdam: North-Holland), pp. 119–70.

Keuschnigg, C., M. Keuschnigg and W. Kohler (2001) 'The German Perspective on Eastern EU Enlargement', *The World Economy*, vol. 24, pp. 513–42.

Knack, S. and P. Keefer (1997) 'Does Social Capital Have an Economic Payoff? A Cross-Country Investigation', *Quarterly Journal of Economics*, vol. 112(4), pp. 1252–88.

Lejour, A.M., R.A. de Mooij and R. Nahuis (2001) EU enlargement: Economic implications for countries and industries, CPB document no. 11, The Hague.

McCallum, J. (1995) 'National Borders Matter: Canada–US Regional Trade Patterns', *American Economic Review*, vol. 85, pp. 615–23.

8

Measuring the Economic Impact of the Eastern European Enlargement on an EU Member State: The Case of Italy*

Rossella Bardazzi and Maurizio Grassini
University of Florence, Italy

> 'One of the greatest tasks for the EU is to heal the division of Europe and to extend the same peace and prosperity to the central and eastern European countries that the present EU countries have'
>
> Source: (Agenda 2000).

1 Introduction

This chapter focusses on the economic implications of European Union enlargement, with particular reference to the Italian economy. Enlargement may be viewed as the merging of two groups of countries; the present EU Member States: Austria, Belgium, Denmark, France, Finland, Germany, Greece, Holland, Ireland, Italy, Luxembourg, Portugal, Spain, Sweden and United Kingdom (EU-15); and the Central and Eastern European Countries (CEECs): Cyprus, the Czech Republic, Estonia, Hungary, Latvia, Lithuania, Malta, Poland, Slovakia, and Slovenia. The main factor to be considered here is the creation of a Customs Union and Single Market which enlargement would involve.

From a methodological perspective, the economic impact of enlargement may be evaluated for the new economic area as a whole or for each Member State individually.[1] The accession, provided it takes place in the proper

* The empirical results reported in this chapter are part of a project funded by the European Commission under Study BUDG/B1/001. We benefited from comments by the participants at the presentation of the report at the European Commission (January 2002), at ISAE (March 2002) and at the presentation of the paper at the XIII World Congress of IEA (Lisbon, September 2002). We also thank Wilhelm Kohler (Coordinator of the European project) and Mario Nava (Policy Advisor of the European Commission President) for their helpful suggestions and discussions. The usual disclaimers apply.

institutional framework, will foster economic growth and prosperity in both the Candidate Country and the existing Member States. Clearly, the positive impact will be much more significant for the Candidate Countries than for the existing EU countries.

As for any research, the results need to be viewed in the context of the instruments applied, the level of aggregation adopted, and the data employed if we are to obtain a correct understanding of the analysis. The present study has been done using a system of multi-sectoral models linked by means of an international trade model. The group of models, as well as the international trade model, constitute the INFORUM (INterindustry FORecasting at University of Maryland)[2] system. The Italian model in the system is named INTerindustry Italian MOdel or INTIMO. This interlinked system has allowed us to obtain unprecedented results relating to the effects of EU enlargement on a specific Member State, Italy.

The present study, which spans a period of ten years (2001–10), refers to a baseline scenario where the CEEC growth path is not strengthened by the benefits of economic integration. In the alternative scenarios, a widespread assumption that makes our simulations easily comparable with those of previous (and forthcoming) studies has been presumed: the Candidate Countries' GDP rate of growth exceeds that of the EU-15 by about 2 per cent annually.[3] Under the Europe Agreements applicant countries have made considerable progress towards full participation in the single market. Nevertheless, trade is still restricted by a bundle of tariffs mainly concentrated on agricultural and food products and by a range of border and non-border measures. The impact of the complete removal of these residual barriers to free trade is examined in this study.

Focussing on the Italian economy, the first conclusion reached concerns the evaluation of the direct and indirect impact of the assumed increase of the applicant countries' GDP growth rates. Since the econometric model of the Italian economy is based on the sectoral detail of the country's input-output tables, we have used a sectoral representation of the economy to measure the impact of the applicants' demand for goods and services; namely, their import structure. Since historical data on trade between the CEECs and the EU indicate the concentration of the import–export flows in a clearly defined bundle of commodities, we have investigated the effect of this trade specialization on the performance of the Italian economy.

The simulation design allows us to compare the impact of the trade between Italy and a CEEC with the more significant effect of the EU-15 trade with the CEEC. In the first case, we have two countries, Italy and the CEEC, and in the second case, we have two country-sets, EU-15 and the CEEC, with Italy constituting a single region of the EU. This second case allows us to measure the indirect effect of the Eastern European enlargement on Italy. Furthermore, there is a third scenario where the composition of the CEEC's imports is considered. This experiment provides evidence that in the case of Italy – which is close to the Eastern EU border – the indirect impact on the GDP rate of growth is even more important than the direct one. The transmission of the increase generated by enlargement is as important as the direct trade with the new entrants. While the effect of the increase on exports induced by a growing demand for goods by the CEEC is preserved throughout the simulation period, that increase is doubled by the indirect effect. Moreover specialization in the CEECs' imports generates a further increase in the GDP rate of growth, so that the total increase amounts to a factor of circa 2.6 with respect to that found in the case of Italy/CEEC.

This result clearly demonstrates that Eastern enlargement is not simply a question of boundaries. In particular, it is clear that – for countries such as Spain – the indirect effect of Eastern enlargement may be much more significant than the direct effect. Furthermore, the sectoral analysis of foreign trade – together with the sectoral evaluation of its impact – is crucial for understanding the effects of enlargement. The importance of a sectoral representation of the economy becomes clearer when the removal of tariffs and non-tariff barriers (NTBs), which mainly concern agriculture and food industry products, have been evaluated. NTBs still apply and constitute the bulk of measures hampering international trade between the CEECs and the EU. Moreover, these measures are concentrated on particular products. For example, the international trade model used in this study examines information on 120 commodities; here, the NTBs – specifically singled out for simulating their removal – account for about 15 per cent of the range of commodities considered by the model.

As regards the simulation results for the removal of tariffs and NTBs, two alternative scenarios have been formulated: in the case of NTBs it is impossible to measure the precise size of their mark-up effect on price formation; the two scenarios refer to a generous effect in terms of Baldwin's hypothesis which assumes an overall reduction of 10 per cent (Baldwin, Francois and Portes, 1997), and to a conservative hypothesis similar to that proposed by Keuschnigg and Kohler (1999).

The chapter is organized as follows. Section 2 presents the key data on Candidate Countries (CCs) and the structure of Italian foreign trade. The modelling approach used for dealing with the main economic issues involved with enlargement is briefly described in Section 3. In Section 4, the baseline and the simulation scenarios are described, while in Section 5 the structural changes in the Italian economy produced by Eastern enlargement are presented. Finally, results and conclusions are underlined in Section 6.

2 Key data on the Candidate Countries

2.1 Macro data

The CCs rank very differently in terms of their 'applicability' for full membership. In the year 2000, for example, they accounted for 45 per cent of EU population but only 7 per cent of EU GDP, with GDP per capita varying from

Table 8.1 Key data on the 13 candidate countries in 2000

	Population (millions)	*Area (km²)*	*GDP (€bn)*	*GDP in PPS(€bn)*	*Population*	*Area*	*GDP*	*Index of GDP in PPS*
					(as % of EU-15)			
Bulgaria	8 191	11 971	13.0	5 400	2.2	0.4	0.2	24.0
Cyprus	755	9 251	9.5	18 500	0.2	0.3	0.1	82.1
Czech Republic	10 278	78 866	550.0	13 500	2.7	2.5	0.6	59.9
Estonia	1 439	45 227	5.5	8 500	0.4	1.4	0.1	37.7
Hungary	10 043	93 030	495.0	11 700	2.7	2.9	0.6	51.9
Latvia	2 424	64 589	7.7	6 600	0.6	2.0	0.1	29.3
Lithuania	3 699	65 300	12.2	6 600	1.0	2.0	0.1	29.3
Malta	388	316	3.9	11 900	0.1	0.0	0.0	52.8
Poland	38 654	312 685	171.0	8 700	10.3	9.8	2.0	38.6
Romania	22 456	238 391	40.0	6 000	6.0	7.5	0.5	26.6
Slovakia	5 399	49 035	20.9	10 800	1.4	1.5	0.2	47.9
Slovenia	1 988	20 273	19.5	16 100	0.5	0.6	0.2	71.5
Turkey	64 818	769 604	217.4	6 400	17.2	24.1	2.5	28.4
EU-15	376 455	3 191 000	8 526.0	22 530	100.0	100.0	100.0	100.0

Source: Eurostat (2001).

between 24 per cent of the EU average in Bulgaria to 82 per cent in Cyprus (see Table 8.1).

Given this variation in the 'applicability' ranking, the Candidate Countries have over time been classified as either 'front-runners' or 'latecomers'. At the Luxembourg Council in December 1997, a group of five CEECs (the Czech Republic, Estonia, Hungary, Poland and Slovenia) were selected for EU membership in 2002. In 2001, all the candidates were posed on the same starting line. In December 2001, on the basis of the *Strategy Paper* and the *Regular Report on Enlargement*, the Laeken Council concluded that ten CCs would be ready for membership in the year 2004, making a modest 'enlargement' of the former group. These candidates were the front-runners in the so-called Luxembourg Group together with the two Baltic republics of Latvia and Lithuania, the islands of Cyprus and Malta, and Slovakia. For the time being, the other candidates, Bulgaria, Romania and Turkey were not scheduled to become EU members before the year 2007 (i.e. they were not covered by the *Agenda 2000* horizon). These three countries constituted a relatively large proportion of the population of the original group of candidates; therefore, the 'size' of the enlargement has been significantly re-scaled.

On the basis of the data contained in Table 8.1, Table 8.2 summarizes the data on the Luxembourg Group, the 'New 5', and the Laeken Group (namely, the Luxembourg Group plus the 'New 5'). It also outlines statistics on the Southern enlargement of Greece, Portugal and Spain which joined the EU-9 in the 1980s.

The population of Greece, Portugal and Spain amounted to 21.6 per cent of the EC-9 in 1985, while the Laeken Group is slightly below 20 per cent of the EU-15. As regards GDP, the Eastern candidates for enlargement have a GDP of slightly over 4 per cent, rising to 9 per cent in terms of PPS. The Southern enlargement generated an increase of GDP of 10.4 and 14.3 per cent

Table 8.2 The Eastern and Southern enlargements: population and GDP

(Percentages)

	Population	*GDP*	*GDP in PPS*	*Per capita GDP in PPS*
Eastern (as of 2000)				
Luxembourg Group	16.6	3.5	7.5	45.3
New 5	3.4	0.6	1.4	41.1
Laeken Group	19.9	4.2	8.9	44.6
EU-15	100.0	100.0	100.0	100.0
Southern (as of 1985)				
Greece, Spain, Portugal	21.6	10.4	14.3	65.9
EC-9	100.0	100.0	100.0	100.0

Source: Eurostat (2001) and DG ECFIN (April 2001).

respectively for the EC countries. These differences are reflected in the relative level of GDP per capita in PPS. While the average GDP per capita for Greece, Portugal and Spain amounted to two-thirds of that of the EC-9, per capita GDP for the Candidate Countries does not amount to 50 per cent of that for the EU-15.

The comparative data on population and GDP in Table 8.2 suggest that from a macroeconomic perspective, the impact of the CCs on the EU economy is likely to be small. Indeed, the weight of the 'Laeken Group' is relatively smaller than that of the 'Southern enlargement group' which was relatively smoothly absorbed by the EC-9. However, the low level of income of the future members will cause a significant EU transfer in the name of economic cohesion. Nevertheless while the impact of the Eastern enlargement on the economy of the EU as a whole or on that of single Member States is generally considered modest, the budgetary implications are likely to be highly significant.

Generally speaking, the Member States lacked a clear overall strategy to tackle the effects of the collapse of Communism. The first reaction was to set up the PHARE programme of assistance in December 1999. Subsequently, the European Council agreed on the plan to negotiate Association Agreements with individual countries (April 1990). This plan, which in several respects marked a turning point, was called 'Europe Agreements' and has characterized the relationships between the European Community (and subsequently the European Union) and the CEECs throughout the 1990s. One objective of the Agreements was to promote trade liberalization by removing trade barriers and encouraging the CEECs to direct economic activity towards the western European markets. In this way the trade flows of the Candidate Countries were diverted from East to West, and their shares of EU imports and exports indicate the progress made in terms of integration with the EU economy (see Table 8.3). The EU shares of CCs' imports range from 44 to 68 per cent, whilst their share of exports go from a minimum of 47 per cent for Cyprus to over 76 per cent for Estonia. For the EU as a whole, each CC represents a negligible share in terms of both end market and supplier.

The preparations for enlargement that were initiated by the Europe Agreements immediately after the collapse of the Soviet Union have yielded positive results. The PHARE programme which involved EU assistance in steering the CEECs' economy towards a market economy, the positive effect of a remarkable flow of foreign direct investment (FDI), and the generous removal of many European trade barriers, have all helped stimulate the growth of the CCs. The average GDP rates of growth in the years 1995–99 shown in Table 8.4 reveal a very successful process of 'catching up' which has highlighted the performance of the Laeken Group of countries. One task of the enlargement process is to respond to the existing division within Europe by extending the benefits of peace and prosperity to the present EU's neighbours; the speed with which the CCs are currently moving is certainly encouraging, at least for the near future (see the last three columns of Table 8.4).

Table 8.3 Relative EU shares of the Candidate Countries' imports and exports in 2000 (*percentages*)

Candidate Countries	*EU's share in CCs' imports*	*EU's share in CCs' exports*	*CCs' share in EU imports*	*CCs' share in EU exports*
Bulgaria	44.0	51.1	0.3	0.3
Cyprus	55.9	47.7	0.1	0.3
Czech Republic	62.0	68.6	2.1	2.5
Estonia	62.6	76.5	0.3	0.3
Hungary	58.4	75.1	2.1	2.5
Latvia	52.4	64.6	0.2	0.2
Lithuania	43.3	47.9	0.2	0.3
Malta	59.9	33.5	0.1	0.3
Poland	61.2	69.9	2.3	3.6
Romania	56.6	63.8	0.7	0.9
Slovakia	48.9	59.1	0.7	0.7
Slovenia	67.8	63.8	0.6	0.9
Turkey	48.8	52.3	1.7	3.2

Source: Eurostat (2001).

Table 8.4 GDP rates of growth of Candidate Countries

Candidate Countries	*Average GDP growth rate at constant prices 1995–99 (%)*	*GDP growth rate at constant prices in 2000 (%)*	*Spring 2003 forecasts*			
			2001	*2002*	*2003*	*2004*
Bulgaria	−1.8	5.8	4.0	4.3	4.5	5.0
Cyprus	4.0	4.8	4.0	2.0	2.0	3.8
Czech Republic	1.5	2.9	3.2	2.0	2.8	3.9
Estonia	4.6	6.9	5.0	5.6	4.9	5.1
Hungary	3.3	5.2	3.7	3.3	3.7	4.1
Latvia	3.2	6.6	7.9	6.1	5.5	6.0
Lithuania	3.2	3.3	5.9	5.9	4.5	5.0
Malta	4.5	5.0	−0.8	3.0	3.1	3.7
Poland	5.7	4.0	1.0	1.3	2.5	3.7
Romania	−0.6	1.6	5.7	4.9	4.9	5.0
Slovakia	5.0	2.2	3.3	4.4	3.7	4.5
Slovenia	4.2	4.6	3.0	3.0	3.4	3.7
Turkey	3.9	7.2	−7.4	7.8	3.7	4.5
EU	2.4	3.3	1.6	1.1	1.3	2.4

Source: Eurostat (2001) and European Commission, ECFIN (2003a,b).

2.2 Sectoral data

The accession of the CCs, provided it takes place within the proper institutional framework, should foster economic growth in both the CEEC and the EU Member States. Obviously, the impact will continue to be skewed as the positive impact on the applicants will be much more significant than the equivalent impact on the EU-15 which is generally expected to be modest. But this result is strictly related to the level of aggregation; from a macroeconomic perspective, the enlargement may have a negligible effect, while a sectoral impact may be substantial in some cases.

Table 8.5, which provides sectoral import-export data according to the Chapters of Combined Nomenclature (CCN) of the Harmonized System, contains those with a share over the total EU-15 exports to and imports from the CEEC-10 – the Leaken Group of ten countries – greater than 1 per cent. In part due to the CCN definition, about five Chapters cover 50 per cent of the trade flows between the EU-15 and the Laeken Group. This group of CCN largely dominates the bilateral flows between the EU-15 and single CCs. During transition, these commodities have maintained and even increased their trade significance with EU countries. Indeed, specialization of trade has been detected in a number of EU Member States. In France and Italy the trends of import–export flows are very similar and close to the EU average. In Germany these flows show the same – albeit less sharp – trend towards specialization; and in Spain import–export flows concentrate on a remarkably limited bundle of commodities. This observed structural change in EU/CEEC trade flows deserves closer investigation; meanwhile, it is to be noted that this fact appears to confirm the emerging pattern in trade specialization detected by Baldone, Lasagni and Sdogati (1997) in the early 1990s.

2.3 The international trade pattern of a Member State: the case of Italy

The statistics provided by SISTAN (*Sistema Statistico Nazionale*, National Statistical System) and ISTAT (*Istituto Nazionale di Statistica*, National Statistical Institute) contained in the Italian Trade Centre (ITC) Report (2002) cover a sizeable amount of data on Italy's trade patterns (exports and imports), including information on commodities for 19 economic sectors and for Italian trade partners. Table 8.6 shows the CEEC shares in the Italian trade flows in year 2001. The CEEC average share in each EU Member State's foreign trade is about 3 per cent (Eurostat, 2001); these shares vary across the Member States and across the sectors. At a glance, the CEEC sectoral shares in Italian foreign trade are above the EU average, caused by the relative boundary position of Italy with respect to the Eastern European countries. In particular, the intra-trade for textiles, clothing, leather goods is remarkable. These sectors are those where the outsourcing has been well

Table 8.5 Sectoral shares of EU total exports and imports in 1998

EU exports to CEEC-10		*EU imports from CEEC-10*	
Machinery and mechanical appliances	19.74	Electrical machinery and equipment	12.33
Electrical machinery and equipment	13.79	Machinery and mechanical appliances	11.13
Motor vehicles and parts thereof	12.21	Motor vehicles and parts thereof	9.94
Plastic and plastic products	5.09	Clothing accessories (not knitted)	8.80
Paper, paper product and pulp	2.72	Clothing accessories (knitted)	5.45
Articles of iron and steel	2.59	Furniture, lamps and lighting fittings	4.60
Optical and precision instruments	2.46	Wood and articles of wood	3.94
Pharmaceutical products	2.32	Iron and steel	3.89
Iron and steel	2.17	Articles of iron and steel	3.45
Mineral fuels	1.75	Mineral fuels	2.90
Other chemical products	1.59	Plastic and plastic products	2.07
Furniture, lamps and lighting fittings	1.53	Footwear	1.85
Paints and varnishes	1.44	Aluminium and articles thereof	1.78
Man-made staple fibres	1.32	Edible fruits and nuts	1.58
Organic chemicals	1.22	Rubber and articles thereof	1.51
Cotton	1.08	Other textile articles	1.39
Rubber and articles, perfumery	1.06	Glass and glassware	1.15
Aluminium and articles thereof	1.06	Organic chemicals	1.10
Essential oils, cosmetics, perfumery	1.06	Paper and paper products	1.09
Clothing accessories (not knitted)	1.02	Copper and articles thereof	1.05
Hides, skins and leather	1.00	Cotton	0.98
Total	78.23	Total	81.98

Source: Eurostat, COMEXT.

developed in the recent decades. Some sectoral import shares are much different in size with respect to the corresponding export shares; these differences may be important when evaluating the impact of the removal of trade barriers that is part of the enlargement process: price changes of products used as intermediate consumption goods and those of commodities for final use, both hit the competitiveness of domestic industries, but with opposite effects.

Table 8.6 CEEC-10 imports and exports percentage shares in sectoral Italian foreign trade by product group in 2001

	Imports	*Exports*
Agriculture, forestry and fisheries	6.5	6.2
Mining	0.0	4.4
Food & tobacco	1.4	0.6
Textile industries	20.9	9.1
Clothing	17.8	11.0
Leather goods, shoes	25.0	9.6
Wood products	10.1	2.1
Paper products	3.0	6.6
Petroleum products	5.3	7.4
Chemical products	0.6	5.3
Rubber and plastic products	4.0	7.5
Non-metal minerals and products	15.4	3.4
Metal products	6.2	9.4
Machinery	3.2	5.7
Precision instruments	1.0	11.0
Motor vehicles	5.2	5.9
Other transport equipment	0.4	1.2
Furniture	16.4	1.1
Other manufactured products	4.5	1.2

Source: ICE-ISTAT (2002).

3 Economic issues and the modelling approach

3.1 Trade effects: the Bilateral Trade Model (BTM) and the system of multisectoral models

The problem faced in this study is the evaluation of the EU's Eastern enlargement on the economy of a single Member State. The enlargement surely concerns the two groups of countries directly engaged in the process. However, each EU-15 member state and each CEEC trades with almost every other country in the world. Trade creation, trade diversion and trade specialization related to the enlargement influence world trade. Therefore, the description of the modelling approach begins with the trade model that links the multisectoral models in the system.

The trade model incorporates the argument: 'Developments in productivity are the result of many different factors, but depend largely on investment performance, which determines the structure and size of the capital stock and enables the penetration of new technologies in the economy. A higher rate of investment growth raises the capital available per worker and thereby – ceteris paribus – labour productivity. A high rate of innovation in a context of strong investment growth also increases the quality of the capital stock.' (Excerpt from the *Broad Economic Policy Guidelines* (European Commission,

2002)). In fact, the world commodity trade model used is the Bilateral Trade Model (BTM) created and originally estimated by Qiang Ma (1996), which is continuously being revised and updated. The basic idea underlying this trade model was formulated in the late 1960s (see Armington, 1969a,b, and Rhomberg, 1970, 1973); subsequently a number of studies tackled estimation problems involved in the construction of this kind of trade model (see, e.g., Nyhus, 1975 and Fair, 1984). BTM is estimated using a bilateral database, WTDB, released by Statistics Canada and made available to the Inforum Research Centre. This database provides high quality and up-to-date information on commodity trade, which covers world commodity trade and makes the bilateral model genuinely 'global'. The raw data set has been subjected to two aggregations. One concerns the commodity classification, where the large number of commodity flows have been reduced to a set of 120 trade flows. The second is geographical so that the number of trading countries has been reduced from 200 to about 60, including the countries of the system of multisectoral models[4] and other countries or groups of countries (for instance, the transitional economies of Eastern Europe, the OPEC countries, South Africa, other developing Asian countries, and major South American countries). The data allow us to construct bilateral trade flow matrices for 120 commodity groups. Each matrix has a number of rows and columns that are related to these 60 countries. The BTM database is ready to accommodate this huge number of countries and the present working version is tailored to the existing country models in the system. The structure of the data allows us to investigate the trade structure of other countries not yet included in the system of models and, hence, to tackle problems such as those considered in this research.

The BTM takes the sectoral imports from each country model and allocates them to the exporting countries within the system by means of import share matrices computed from the trade flow matrices; imports demanded from a country by all its trading partners equal its exports. Hence, exports turn out to be endogenous in the interlinked system. The key work of the model is to calculate the movement in 120 import-share matrices. Each cell (i.e., each import share) of these matrices, which records a non-null trade flow, is modelled by means of an equation. For each exporter country, each importer country and each commodity considered in the model, the non-null trade share is explained by (a) the effective price of the good in question relative to the world price of the good as seen from the importer country, (b) an index of the capital stock in the industry of the exporter country relative to an index of world average capital stock in the industry in question as seen from the importer country, and (c) a peculiar time trend suitable for dealing with bounded variables.

The BTM work begins with the collection of prices, imports and capital investments, but we see that the share equations require capital stock data which are intentionally not collected from the country models, even if they are endogenously computed. Capital stock data made available from official national statistics are largely based on different criteria, and may not always be comparable (as required in the above equation). Consequently, we chose to compute capital stocks directly from statistics taken from a 'comparable' perpetual inventory model where comparability is mainly based on the use of a common depreciation rate. The idea behind a relative capital stock as an explanatory variable is that technical progress is part of new investments. A capital stock that contains more recent investments may render the industry more competitive. In other words, an industry can buy market share by investing. In order to accentuate this assumption, the capital stock is computed from investments, and the depreciation rate is consequently chosen as a strategic variable. (At present, it is equal to 8 per cent.)

The BTM links the models of the Inforum system, which consists of multisectoral models of Western Europe (Germany, France, Spain, Austria, the UK, Belgium and Italy), the Far East (China, Japan, South Korea and Taiwan), and Central-North America (Canada, the United States and Mexico).[5] Each country model has been constructed by the country partner so that it embodies the peculiarities of the economy as observed and understood by the model builder. As described in Grassini (2001), a more descriptive name for these models might be Interindustry Macroeconomic Models (IMM) or Multisectoral Macroeconomic Models (MMM); 'interindustry' and 'multisectoral' stress the presence of an input–output structure and the detailed representation of the industries in the economy; and 'macroeconomic' emphasizes that the usual variables of macroeconomics are covered.[6] Inforum models are rooted in data: an enormous database is necessary to support a proper IM model given the underlying belief that a model incorporating as much past economic outcomes as possible will have a better chance of accurately simulating policy changes than a model that incorporates less information.

Like macroeconometric models, Inforum models use regression analysis on a time-series. Therefore, parameters in behavioural relations are econometrically estimated using observed economic outcomes and not calibrated by the model builder. A distinctive property of these models is their 'bottom-up' approach; that is, the macro totals are obtained by summing the industry details.

Inforum models are explicitly dynamic, with real dates on each year's solution, and the researcher also knows the dynamic path by which the new solution is reached, which may have enormous practical implications for those policy makers who are often just as interested in the path to equilibrium as they are in the ultimate equilibrium point. Predictions of time paths are naturally computed at the industry level: the macro dynamics are simply the result of the industry dynamics. For example, we will show that, after enlargement, sectoral growth paths are not at all steady over time, with accelerations, decelerations, recessions and recoveries occurring along the simulation horizon. Therefore, an economic analysis of the enlargement effects based only upon the comparison between two equilibria would be misleading: the model should offer guidance as to how sectors may cumulate gains and losses along the path, so that policy makers may consider potential policy actions.

The integration of the Italian Inforum[7] model into a family of interlinked models has a number of important advantages for the analysis of the questions under consideration. In contrast to any economic analysis with a 'stand alone model' of a national economy, it enables the consideration of a number of indirect effects of enlargement. The following list cites just a few of these relevant effects operating through the European economies on a specific Member State:

- changes in the demand for Italian commodities as intermediate products by other EU countries due to additional imports from CEECs to present EU members other than Italy;
- changes in the demand for Italian consumption goods by other EU countries induced by income effects caused by economic growth in present member states due to enlargement;
- changes in the demand for Italian capital goods from other EU countries due to the same economic reasons explained above;
- substitution effects in trade with CEECs between commodities of EU member states – Italy included – due to changes in competitiveness, caused by the impact of the removal of trade barriers on relative prices.

3.2 Migration and population: the Demographic Projection Model (DPM)

The accession of the CEECs to the EU is likely to have a significant impact on the conditions of migration. The free movement of workers is defined by Art. 39 (*ex* Art. 48) of the EC Treaty and is one of the fundamental liberties granted under Community law. As described by the DG for Economic and Financial Affairs in a document on enlargement, 'indeed, given that barriers to trade, FDI and other capital movements have already been largely removed, the free movement of persons and workers constitutes the probably most significant dimension in economic integration to change after accession compared to the status quo' (European Commission, ECFIN, 2001, p. 40). Not surprisingly, a debate on the consequences of potential migration has provoked the fear in many countries that the increase in EC populations due to Eastern labour flows may lead to a deterioration of the labour-market position of the local workforce and to wage reduction and job losses. In response, several proposals have been put forward in order to introduce a flexible system of transitional arrangements such as those applied at the accession of Greece, Portugal and Spain. These concerns are particularly acute in countries which are likely to be net recipients of migratory flows, such as Germany and Austria.

Numerous studies have been made on the impact of post-enlargement labour migration generally analysing the problem with reference to a set of factors including income differentials, the situation of the labour market, economic expectations and demographic trends in the CEECs. The forecasts vary according to the methodology used and the underlying assumptions made.[8] After accession, the early annual flows from the CEEC-10[9] are estimated at around 120 000 workers (or 335 000 persons) in the oft-quoted study by the European Integration Consortium (2000). This projection declines until the end of the decade to 50 000 workers (or 145 000 persons). Following the assumptions implicit in the model, around two-thirds of the annual flow will be absorbed by Germany, whilst one-tenth will be accounted for by Austria, the second highest recipient. Despite the disparities in per capita income and wages between the EU-15 and the CEECs, recent immigration from these countries to the EU has been very low. In recent years, the emigration flows from CEECs have displayed a downward trend. The nature of these flows has altered and are now characterized principally by short and frequent movements both from East to West and between the CEECs themselves.[10] Another relevant factor for migration is the dynamics of demographic trends both in the host and source countries. As shown in Table 8.7, demographic projections for the CEECs have characteristics similar to most Western countries: population decline and population ageing.

Our model includes a well-elaborated Demographic Projection Model (DPM). The role played by DPM is to produce projections of Italian population by age and gender (Bardazzi, 2001). As with any other demographic model,

Table 8.7 Demographic projections for the CEECs, Italy and the EU

	Population (thousands)		*Difference*		*Percentage aged 60 or over*	
	2000	*2050*	*Absolute*	*Percentage*	*2000*	*2050*
Poland	38 671	33 004	−5 667	−14.7	16.6	35.6
Slovenia	1 990	1 569	−421	−21.2	19.2	42.4
Czech Republic	10 269	8 553	−1 716	−16.7	18.4	40.1
Hungary	10 012	7 589	−2 423	−24.2	19.7	36.2
Estonia	1 367	657	−710	−51.9	20.2	35.9
Sub-total	64 309	53 422	−10 887	−16.9		
Romania	22 480	18 063	−4 417	−19.6	18.8	34.2
Bulgaria	8 099	5 255	−2 844	−35.1	21.7	38.6
Slovakia	5 391	4 948	−443	−8.2	15.4	36.8
Latvia	2 373	1 331	−1 042	−43.9	20.9	37.5
Lithuania	3 501	2 526	−975	−27.8	18.6	37.3
Sub-total	41 844	32 123	−9 721	−23.2		
Total CEEC	106 153	85 545	−20 608	−19.4		
Italy	57 536	44 875	−12 661	−22.0	24.1	42.3
European Union*	375 276	331 307	−43 969	−11.7	21.9	35.3

Source: United Nations (2003), except for * from United Nations (2000).

DPM is tailored to generate medium- to long-term projections. DPM relies upon scenarios concerning fertility rates by age, mortality rates from one age to the next, and net immigration by age and gender. The hypothesis regarding net immigration is the most unpredictable of the components of population projections and is the one to be modified if we believe that enlargement will change the migrant flow from CEECs to Italy. The demographic projections produced by DPM are then used in INTIMO to model private consumption (the system of demand includes the age structure of population), the labour market (demographic evolution changes the labour force), and government expenditure (health expenses and pensions clearly depend on the age structure of the population).

4 Simulation scenarios for EU enlargement

In April 2003, the European Parliament voted in favour of the accession to the EU of ten CCs – Cyprus, the Czech Republic, Estonia, Hungary, Latvia, Lithuania, Malta, Poland, the Slovak Republic and Slovenia – with which accession negotiations were concluded on December 2002.[11] Parliament also welcomed the statement made at the Copenhagen European Council that the EU should aim to admit Bulgaria and Romania by 2007 provided these countries continue with modernization and reform and comply with the Copenhagen criteria. On 16 April the Accession Treaty was signed at a special meeting in Athens. Membership was constitutionally ratified by each CC, the new Member States joining the EU on 1 May 2004.

These historic events have changed rapidly the overall framework of EU enlargement. This chapter describes a study, funded by the European Commission in 2001, which investigates the costs and benefits for Italy after enlargement. At the time, the accession negotiations were far from being concluded and neither the number of new Member States nor the accession date were known. Although the simulation scenarios may have been modified by the historic events, our methodological approach and empirical results may still be significant and may be applied in future alternative scenarios.[12]

4.1 The 'baseline' scenario

The baseline scenario refers to the future economic performance of the domestic economy without EU enlargement. The design of this reference forecast requires us to make assumptions about some exogenous variables, described below, to provide a credible path for 'business-as-usual' growth. The GDP growth in the CCs is assumed to follow the average rate of growth for other countries in the system. In other words, we assume that the CCs grow at a pace close to that of the main industrialized countries, that is, Western Europe, the United States, Canada and Japan. In fact, one can say that the EU support and assistance to the CC in the past decade has already produced higher growth rates and that this catching-up process would have lost steam if the accession process had been stopped.

Each country model, linked by the Bilateral Trade Model, produces sectoral price projections. For BTM, these are adjusted by assumed exchange rates to produce indexes of effective prices.[13] At present BTM details exchange among these individual countries (14) and two regions, 'other OECD', and 'the rest of the world'. Industry-specific trade-weighted averages of the country prices are then taken as the prices of the two remaining regions. Since all CC fall into one or the other of these two regions, the basic assumption of the baseline scenario is that these countries have 'average' prices relative to those in the countries of the model, where 'average' is the average over the 14 countries examined. As mentioned above, BTM distributes the imports of each country among supplying countries. This means that each country model endogenously computes (sectoral) import requirements; BTM converts these requirements into the exports of the other countries. Symmetrically, each country model in the system receives from BTM its (sectoral) exports as the sum of the import requirements of the other countries. The amount of (sectoral) exports of each country will vary according to the shares of imports captured from each of the other countries in the system. Hence, exports do not belong to the set of the scenario variables; indeed (sectoral) exports of each country in the model system are endogenous.

As for Italian government expenditure, we assume that the Stability and Growth Pact, which imposes budgetary discipline and improvement on the budgetary procedure, will force national governments to limit their expenditure to a growth rate approximately equal to, or slightly below, that expected for GDP. Considering the volume of the Italian public debt, a low profile growth in government expenditure is realistic.[14]

INTIMO is a dynamic multisectoral econometric model. The other models in the system, such as BTM, are also fully dynamic. Hence, the evaluation of different scenarios is carried out year-by-year over a future period. Indeed, different shocks may take place in different years in the future, and their effects need to be evaluated year-by-year over the period of simulation which is 2001–10.

4.2 The simulation scenarios

4.2.1 Preliminary analysis

Alternative scenarios have been designed and tested in order to analyse the economic implications of enlargement on the Italian economy. Complexity, plausibility and feasibility of simulations can vary and be influenced by the structure of the model at hand. In our case, we have decided to fully exploit the features of our system of models linked by international trade flows. Therefore, we have tested some preliminary simulations gradually approaching our final and comprehensive scenario. This analysis has helped us to draw some conclusions about the relative importance of international trade in evaluating the impact of enlargement on an EU Member State. Although many studies produce trade-induced effects emanating from the idea that enlargement is primarily a custom-union issue,[15] these analytical approaches fail to consider the full interdependence of the EU single market by not having a model for bilateral trade flows. The results give the impression that trade effects are trivial for the EU – and for individual Member States – while more relevant for the Candidate Countries. These findings are implicit in a modelling approach where the CEECs are linked either to the EU as a whole or to an individual Member State with an exclusive mutual connection. Therefore, 'estimates of the impact of enlargement for the present EU tend to be limited given its much larger economic size.... For the new member states, the consensus of economists is that the gains are likely to be proportionately much larger, reflecting the fact that 70 per cent of their exports go to the present EU (only 4 per cent of EU exports currently go to the new member states) and that their economies are far smaller' (Kok, 2003, p. 36). Our simulations show a significant trade effect on Italy which is mainly due to the economic interrelations with other EU Member States and to enlargement through international trade flows.

As for the migration problem, it is important to note that the number of legal foreigners residing in Italy and coming from CCs only amounts to 8.35 per cent of the total number of resident migrants. Moreover, in Poland and Romania, the most populated Candidate Countries, the expected population reduction by the year 2050 will be approximately 15 and 20 per cent, respectively (see Table 8.7). If these projections are confirmed in the future, applicants will no longer have a positive demographic surplus to export. In addition, the 'catching-up process' will narrow income disparities between the CCs and EU-15 members and will increase labour demand in the Candidate Countries, thus absorbing a higher proportion of the workforce. To summarize, in the past Italy has not been a migratory pole for Eastern migrants, given its geographical location and prevailing economic conditions, and there is little reason to believe that this situation will change dramatically in the near future. Therefore, in our study we assume that there will be no change in migration flows in the simulation scenarios, based on the hypothesis that any potential variation in the number of migrants will be so low as to leave the labour market and the economy as a whole largely intact. Then, in our demographic projection model the assumption about net migration is maintained as in the baseline scenario.

A first group of simulation scenarios (whose detailed results are shown in Bardazzi and Grassini, 2003) assumes that CCs' GDP will grow by 2 per cent more annually, compared to the baseline. The rapid growth of the applicant countries' GDP growth should be considered an appropriate assumption, as economic integration caused by enlargement will mean that the newcomers' economies will be pulled towards EU levels of prosperity, resulting in a faster

GDP rate of growth for over another decade. Since we do not have models for the CCs, nothing can be said about the shifts in the composition of their final demand. On the resource side, however, we assume that imports will grow as rapidly as GDP, so that their resource structure remains unchanged. Higher levels of imports from the CCs will mean higher exports for the countries in the model system. This preliminary exercise does not include any change of prices due to the reduction of tariffs. When we consider only the direct effect of the CC increase in imports on the Italian economy – as an increase of Italian exports to these countries – no account is taken of the enlargement effects on other EU Member States. In this case the estimated increase in Italian GDP – compared to the baseline scenario – is very modest; and falls from 0.2 to 0.13 along the simulation interval. We can assume, however, that changes in CC imports have implications for all economies and that this in turn affects each country's outputs, and therefore the imports from every other country. Hence, Italian exports are determined by the changes in the imports demanded by the countries in the system. Our results highlight the relevance of these indirect effects of the EU enlargement on Italy: the estimated increase in GDP is roughly twice the previous one at the beginning of the simulation period and develops smoothly up to a maximum of a factor of about 2.5 at the end of the horizon. This result shows that the trade-induced effects of EU enlargement cannot be analysed only in terms of geographical distance with the CEECs and bilateral trade flows *vis-à-vis* to the future Member States: for more peripheral countries – such as Portugal – indirect effects generated through trade flows with Germany may still be significant.

4.2.2 Deepening the specialization of trade

In the 1990s, the CCs overcame the deep crisis which occurred after the crash of the socialist economies. During this decade, trade between the EU and these countries increased as the 'catching-up' of the applicants took off (see Table 8.3). When the transition began, the import–export composition was concentrated on a small bundle of goods. During the transition, these commodities have maintained and even increased their importance in trade with the EU countries, accounting for about 60 per cent of the total commodity trade.

Since this specialization occurred during the period of reconstruction towards market-oriented economies, we may well assume that this specialization will persist in the near future, that is, over the time span of the present study. Indeed, this trend towards specialization may well be the result of the good use that applicants have made of their negotiations with the EU and programmes such as PHARE. Other direct advantages may be generated by their access to the Structural Funds; indirect advantages, coming from FDI flows, are expected to remain substantial if the CEECs continue to focus on integration with the countries of Western Europe. All these elements generate investments, and the concentration on trade may therefore be related to the accumulation process. In fact, many of the items listed in Table 8.5 relate to equipment or its production.

Hence, we have investigated the effects of changes in the CC import structure on the Italian economic structure, assuming a further deepening of trade specialization stimulated by foreign investment and sub-contracting. This simulation produces an increase in Italian exports and imports that shows the highest difference with respect to the baseline scenario, a divergence of over 1 per cent increase in exports. The increase in imports is much lower, at about 0.6 per cent. The trade balance produces an increase in GDP close to 0.5 per cent compared to the baseline; consequently, the accelerator pushes investments up and the increase in disposable household income – which implies an increase in household consumption – adds another stimulus to GDP growth. Therefore, Italy would gain from a deeper specialization of CC trade structure as the relevant partner in trading machinery, equipment and motor vehicles.

4.3 The scenarios removal of tariffs and NTBs

4.3.1 CCs and the Single Market[16]

So far, our analysis has ignored the removal of trade and non-trade barriers following the EU enlargement to the East. From a modelling perspective, this means linking the CC growth effects and trade specialization as assumed in the previous section with a change in relative prices due to the removal of barriers.[17]

The structure of (residual) tariffs for agricultural products imposed by the EU on imports from the CC and by these countries on imports from EU have been estimated using data on customs duties to an 8-digit level of detail. To design this scenario, these customs duties for CCs have been approximated by the import-weighted average of tariff rates set by the Czech Republic, Hungary and Poland.[18] These computed tariff rates are shown in Table 8.8.

Since the effect of the elimination of EU tariffs on CC products is equivalent to a reduction in import prices, we model such an effect as a reduction in the relative prices of Italian imports in the import equation of the Bilateral Trade Model.[19] This allows us to evaluate the effect, at the sectoral level, of the removal of the remaining tariffs. It is worth noting that we do not consider the potential effect on Italian exports of the removal of tariffs by CEECs on products originating in Italy. *Therefore, the potentially negative impact on Italian output from accession is likely to be overestimated by our simulation.*

NTBs are impediments to trade such as: (a) quantitative restrictions; (b) price control measures; (c) import licensing; (d) different standards; and (e) other technical requirements and customs procedures. It is commonly

Table 8.8 Average tariff rates on Italian trade with the Czech Republic, Hungary and Poland (*percentages*)

	On exports to the Three	*On imports from the Three*
Unmilled cereals	36	21
Fresh fruits & vegetables	12	13
Other crops	3	6
Livestock	17	12
Fishery	5	9
Meat	32	21
Dairy products and eggs	24	64
Preserved fruits, vegetables	24	14
Preserved seafood	28	16
Vegetable, animal oils, fats	8	1
Grain mill products	18	31
Bakery products	24	16
Sugar	35	18
Cocoa, chocolate, etc	25	11
Food products n.e.c.	17	7
Prepared animal feeds	6	1
Alcoholic beverage	34	6
Non-alcoholic beverage	34	6
Tobacco products	31	29
Paints, varnishes, lacquers	1	1
Scrap, used, unclassified	1	0
Average of above	20	14

Source: EU Market Access Database and TARIC Consultation.

believed that the effect of the removal of NTBs should be substantial. Unfortunately, the available information on NTBs is mostly qualitative, and it is difficult to translate it into a quantitative index useful for investigating the impact of NTBs on trade. Therefore it is not uncommon to model the effect of NTBs by relying solely on judgement. For instance, Baldwin, Francois and Portes (1997) guess that the elimination of NTBs between the EU and CCs could be equivalent to a 10 per cent reduction in trade costs, that is, a 10 per cent reduction in customs duties. Keuschnigg and Kohler (1999) follow the same approach, but opt for a more conservative 5 per cent.

Although our analysis relies on the same kind of judgement as Baldwin, Francois and Portes (1997), our study is innovative in two respects. First, we provide estimates for two different scenarios in order to evaluate the sensitivity of trade flows, and thus present two alternative hypotheses on the effect of the removal of NTBs. Secondly, we take into account that the incidence of NTBs differs across sectors and thus distinguish between three different *ad valorem* equivalents of NTBs so as to develop the full potential of our sectoral model.

To evaluate the extent to which EU imports are subject to NTBs in the various sectors, we use 'trade coverage ratios' for each EU sector. Coverage ratios are provided by Wang (2000) who uses information on NTB indicators contained in the Trade Analysis and Information System (TRAINS) database of UNCTAD. TRAINS provides information on the effect of NTBs for each Harmonized System item (6-digit level).[20] Depending on the corresponding 'trade coverage ratios' we distinguish between three types of product sector, heavily protected, mildly protected and unprotected by NTBs (see Table 8.9).

Table 8.9 NTB coverage ratios by product group

Heavily protected product sectors		*NTBs*
2	Fruits and vegetables	34
6	Cotton	53
7	Wool	27
12	Coal	52
18	Meat	19
27	Food products n.e.c.	64
29	Alcoholic beverages	20
32	Yarns and threads	81
33	Cotton fabrics	52
34	Other textile products	88
36	Wearing apparel	88
49	Synthetic resins, man-made fibres	79
57	Product of coal	52
65	Basic iron and steel	10
67	Aluminium	50
Mildly protected product sectors		*NTBs*
3	Other crops	1
10	Fishery	6
28	Prepared animal feed	3
35	Floor coverings	1
47	Basic chemicals	3
52	Soap and toiletries	2
53	Chemical products, n.e.c.	1
58	Tyres and tubes	1
59	Rubber products, n.e.c.	1
73	Metal containers	5
75	Hardware	5
93	Radio, TV, phonograph	1
94	Other telecom equipment	1
106	Motor vehicles	2
107	Motorcycles and bicycles	2
108	Motor vehicle parts	2

Source: TRAINS and Wang (2000).

4.3.2 The two scenarios

To estimate the impact of the reduction of the NTBs imposed by the EU we perform two alternative simulations:

(1) A first *conservative* scenario (see Keuschnigg and Kohler, 1999) assumes that the removal of NTBs is equivalent to the abatement of a 10 per cent tariff rate in the heavily affected sectors and a 5 per cent tariff rate in the mildly affected sectors.
(2) A second *generous* scenario (see Baldwin, Francois and Portes, 1997) assumes that all sectors are to a certain extent protected by NTBs, whose effect is on average equivalent to a 10 per cent tariff rate. This scenario assumes that the removal of NTBs is equivalent to the suspension of tariffs equivalent to 15, 10 and 5 per cent in the heavily, mildly and (apparently) unprotected sectors, respectively.

In the following Section we examine the effect of removing trade protection in the form of both tariffs and NTBs. In order to highlight the negative impact of trade liberalisation on some sectors of the Italian economy, we present such effects as deviations from simulation with the specialisation of CCs.

5 The impact of the enlargement on structural changes in the Italian economy

Over time all economies face structural changes which can be detected in changes in the composition of aggregated economic variables. The sectoral composition of any national economy a century ago is very different from its present structure. The transition from the old to the new structure may be a relatively smooth process. The mutation of an economic sectoral structure is determined by different and changing sectoral rates of growth. According to the designed scenarios, the enlargement modifies the sectoral composition of final demand as well as the composition of (sectoral) resources. Clearly, these changes are reflected in the rates of growth of sectoral output. Table 8.10 reports the most rapidly growing sectors for the years 2001–03 and 2008–10 for the Baseline. Then, the output growth rates for the scenario of 'Specialisation of CCs' are compared with the case of the 'Removal of Tariffs' preserving the NTBs for the years 2008–10 (Table 8.11). Finally, the complete removal of tariffs and NTBs is simulated with the cases of the 'conservative' and the 'generous' scenario and results for selected sectors are presented in Table 8.12 for 2008–10.[21]

In Table 8.10, the Baseline is represented at the starting point, period 2001–03, and at the end of the horizon, period 2008–10. At a glance, we can see that the rates of growth mark a general reduction for the top 25 sectors at least. 'Building and construction' is the sector with the highest growth rate for the period 2001–03, but falls to 9th position in the years 2008–10,

Table 8.10 Structural changes in the Baseline Scenario. Top 25 product sectors in descending order with respect to the rate of output growth

Baseline *average output rates of growth in years 2001–03*		*Baseline* *average output rates of growth in years 2008–10*	
27 Building and construction	6.272	26 Other manufacturing industry	6.185
11 Agricultural and industrial machinery	6.064	15 Other transport equipment	4.740
10 Metal products	5.229	22 Leather goods and footwear	2.865
15 Other transport equipment	4.908	34 Communication	2.757
7 Primary metals	4.704	39 Private health services	2.380
13 Electrical goods	4.368	37 Real estate	2.239
8 Stone, clay and glass products	4.207	30 Hotels and restaurants	2.146
12 Office, precision and optical instruments	3.925	7 Primary metals	2.128
34 Communications	3.822	27 Building and construction	2.108
25 Plastic and rubber products	3.743	31 Inland transport services	2.065
31 Inland transport services	3.719	35 Banking and insurance	1.965
26 Other manufacturing industry	3.706	11 Agricultural and industrial machinery	1.885
23 Timber, wood products & furniture	3.654	38 Private education services	1.856
39 Private health services	3.216	40 Recreation and culture	1.741
35 Banking and insurance	3.201	12 Office, precision and optical instruments	1.736
36 Other private services	3.198	33 Auxiliary transport services	1.681
33 Auxiliary transport services	2.911	23 Timber, wood products and furniture	1.608
14 Motor vehicles	2.907	8 Stone, clay and glass products	1.557
37 Real estate	2.883	19 Alcohol and non-alcoholic beverages	1.515
38 Private education services	2.738	36 Other private services	1.470
24 Paper and printing	2.659	24 Paper and printing	1.395
30 Hotels and restaurants	2.505	25 Plastic and rubber products	1.350
29 Wholesale and retail trade	2.297	10 Metal products	1.319
40 Recreation and culture	2.121	29 Wholesale and retail trade	1.087
19 Alcohol and non-alcoholic beverages	1.892	18 Other foods	1.077

Table 8.11 Structural changes in the specialization of CCs and tariff-removal scenarios. Top 25 product sectors in descending order with respect to the rate of output growth

Specialization of CCs *average output rates of growth in years 2008–10*		*Tariff removal* *average output rates of growth in years 2008-10*	
26 Other manufacturing industry	6.277	26 Other manufacturing industry	6.343
15 Other transport equipment	5.180	15 Other transport equipment	5.366
11 Agricultural and industrial machinery	4.129	11 Agricultural and industrial machinery	3.695
34 Communications	3.154	7 Primary metals	3.121
7 Primary metals	3.126	34 Communications	3.112
22 Leather goods and footwear	2.701	22 Leather goods and footwear	2.817
31 Inland transport services	2.651	31 Inland transport services	2.595
39 Private health services	2.599	39 Private health services	2.577
35 Banking and insurance	2.519	37 Real estate	2.472
37 Real estate	2.498	35 Banking and insurance	2.469
10 Metal products	2.495	12 Office, precision and optical instruments	2.456
24 Paper and printing	2.430	30 Hotels and restaurants	2.361
30 Hotels and restaurants	2.382	38 Private education services	2.276
25 Plastic and rubber products	2.365	10 Metal products	2.241
38 Private education services	2.327	24 Paper and printing	2.232
12 Office, precision and optical instruments	2.322	25 Plastic and rubber products	2.190
33 Auxiliary transport services	2.217	33 Auxiliary transport services	2.157
13 Electrical goods	2.167	23 Timber, wood products and furniture	2.036
36 Other private services	2.088	36 Other private services	2.024
40 Recreation and culture	2.055	40 Recreation and culture	2.022
27 Building and construction	1.983	27 Building and construction	2.011
23 Timber, wood products and furniture	1.811	8 Stone, clay and glass products	1.885
19 Alcohol and non-alcoholic beverages	1.771	19 Alcohol and non-alcoholic beverages	1.823
8 Stone, clay and glass products	1.753	13 Electrical goods	1.781
14 Motor vehicles	1.606	29 Wholesale and retail trade	1.531

Table 8.12 Structural changes in the tariff-removal and NTBs scenarios. Top 25 sectors in descending order with respect to the rate of output growth

Conservative scenario (0–5–10) average output rates of growth in years 2008–10		*Generous scenario (5–10–15) average output rates of growth in years 2008–10*	
26 Other manufacturing industry	6.330	26 Other manufacturing industry	6.311
15 Other transport equipment	5.332	15 Other transport equipment	5.266
11 Agricultural and industrial machinery	3.711	11 Agricultural and industrial machinery	3.995
7 Primary metals	3.126	34 Communications	3.183
34 Communications	3.125	7 Primary metals	3.180
22 Leather goods and footwear	2.826	22 Leather goods and footwear	2.785
31 Inland transport services	2.607	31 Inland transport services	2.682
39 Private health services	2.586	39 Private health services	2.629
37 Real estate	2.483	35 Banking and insurance	2.536
12 Office, precision and optical instruments	2.482	37 Real estate	2.530
35 Banking and insurance	2.477	10 Metal products	2.492
30 Hotels and restaurants	2.379	12 Office, precision and optical instruments	2.435
38 Private education services	2.288	30 Hotels and restaurants	2.431
10 Metal products	2.277	38 Private education services	2.350
24 Paper and printing	2.231	24 Paper and printing	2.347
25 Plastic and rubber products	2.218	25 Plastic and rubber products	2.333
33 Auxiliary transport services	2.168	33 Auxiliary transport services	2.236
23 Timber, wood products and furniture	2.065	27 Building and construction	2.113
36 Other private services	2.036	36 Other private services	2.111
27 Building and construction	2.035	13 Electrical goods	2.090
40 Recreation and culture	2.032	40 Recreation and culture	2.083
8 Stone, clay and glass products	1.903	23 Timber, wood products and furniture	2.000
19 Alcohol and non-alcoholic beverages	1.835	8 Stone, clay and glass products	1.900
13 Electrical goods	1.825	19 Alcohol and non-alcoholic beverages	1.852
29 Wholesale and retail trade	1.545	29 Wholesale and retail trade	1.616

while 'other manufacturing industry' rises from 12th position to the top of the list at the end of the simulation period. So 'real estate' from the period 2001–03 to the period 2008–10 rises from the 19th to the 6th position. In Table 8.11, in the 'Specialisation of CCs' scenario, 'building and construction' continues its downward trend, ranking 21st in the years 2008–10. This sector is stimulated by investments, and throughout the decade we witness a drop in the growth rate of investment so that consequently 'building and construction' drops towards the bottom of the list together with 'stone, clay and glass products' which supplies intermediate input to 'building and construction'. The growth of 'metal products' and 'electrical goods' slows down while some service sectors ('communication', 'inland transport services', 'banking & insurance', 'private health services', 'hotels and restaurants') have risen towards the top of the list. The sector of 'motor vehicles' halves its growth rate, dropping to last position. 'Other manufacturing industry' and 'other transport equipment', which occupy the first and second place respectively with growth rates of around 6 per cent annually, appear to be the winners in the anticipated structural change.

Table 8.11 reports the average rates of growth of sectoral output respectively for the 'Specialisation of CCs' scenario and the 'Removal of tariffs' scenario for the years 2008–10. The 'Removal of tariffs' scenario is based on a reduction on import prices from CC for those sectors where tariffs still apply. Although the reduction in import prices due to the removal of residual tariffs only concerns a small group – the 'agricultural' and 'food industry' sectors – directly, we can also detect changes in the ranking of a wide range of industries. These changes are modest, but noticeable; for example, 'electrical goods' report a rate of growth reduction of 0.4 per cent.

The structural changes in the 'removal of trade barriers' scenarios are shown in Table 8.12. The conservative scenario is on the left side and the generous is on the right side. We see many changes in the two lists, but there is no significant reshuffling. Incidentally, if we consider the highest and the lowest rates of growth in each list, we can say that the range of rates of growth narrows as we move from the conservative to the generous assumption. This allows us to say that the higher the reduction of import prices due to the removal of trade barriers, the lower the extent of structural change. In our simulation experiments we can also deduce that the intensity of structural change is correlated with the performance of the economy by looking at the output or at GDP.

6 Final remarks

The impact of the European enlargement on Italy has been evaluated by disentangling the scenarios so that we can see separately the effects of the new prosperity of the applicants and the removal of persisting trade barriers.

The effect of the new prosperity of the applicants has been viewed with regard to the increase of their imports from the EU and not in terms of the effect of the enlargement inside the CEECs' economies. This is characteristic of all studies of Enlargement which are viewed exclusively from one side, the member state.

In the first place, the effect of an increase in imports to the CEECs from the EU has been simulated considering the case of (a) Italy with respect to the CEECs, and (b) the EU-15 with respect to the CEECs; and then going on to focus on the specific effect of (b) on the Italian economy. From this comparison we learn that the effect of the enlargement on the Italian economy, which occurs indirectly through its impact on the other European economies, is about the same (in size) as the direct effect. Furthermore, a concentration of the CEEC imports (as well as exports) in a small group of commodities reveals a trend towards 'specialization' which indeed affects all EU countries. This evolution of the CEEC demand for imports from the EU-15 adds a further modest but clear benefit to the Italian economy.

Tariff barriers, which mainly regard agricultural and food industry commodities, have been estimated at a very detailed level and affect a total of 22 product sectors (out of 120 in the BTM), according to the commodity detail of the Bilateral Trade Model used here. As regards the simulation results for the removal of non-tariff barriers, two alternative scenarios have been formulated.

Hence, at the macroeconomic level, the cumulative impact on the Italian economy of the new prosperity of the applicants (measured as an increase in import growth rates), and the removal of tariffs and non-tariff barriers is clearly positive. Despite the generally positive impact of enlargement, some sectors are better off, whilst others do not benefit very much from the reshaping of the EU production structure, and others are directly hit by the reduction of import prices, that is, 'agriculture' and 'food industries', and suffer a clear, albeit temporary, drop in competitiveness. If we examine sectoral performance, we find that 'milk and dairy products' suffered an upsurge of (foreign) competitiveness, thus forfeiting the gains generated by the expansion of the CEECs' economies and subsequently falling during recession. The sector 'other manufacturing industry' does not appear to have been much affected by the enlargement and remains a highly dynamic sector. Other sectors tend to decelerate following the removal of trade barriers, but subsequently regain a good pace of growth. Sectoral growth paths are not steady over time, with accelerations, decelerations, recessions and recoveries which lead to different 'final' scores. Table 8.13 presents an evaluation of enlargement in two columns respectively headed 'average', which gives the percentages of the difference between the cumulated outputs of the 'generous scenario' and the cumulated outputs of the 'baseline' in the interval 2001–10, and '2010' which reports percentages relative to the difference of total outputs in the last year examined. This second column reflects our preference

Table 8.13 Percentage differences in sectoral output between 'generous' scenario and baseline

Sectors	*Average 2001–10*	*2010*
Total	**2.5**	**4.9**
Agriculture, forestry and fisheries	0.7	1.6
Coal, oil and products	2.4	3.7
Electricity, gas and water	2.2	4.2
Manufacturing	**3.9**	**7.7**
Primary metals	4.1	8.2
Stone, clay and glass products	1.4	2.5
Chemical products	1.8	3.8
Metal products	5.4	10.4
Agricultural and industrial machinery	9.1	18.5
Office, precision and optical instruments	3.9	7.1
Electrical goods	7.2	13.8
Motor vehicles	8.2	17.4
Other transport equipment	2.0	4.0
Meat and preserved meat	1.0	1.9
Milk and dairy products	−0.3	−0.2
Other foodstuffs	1.1	2.2
Alcohol and non-alcoholic beverages	1.1	2.3
Tobacco	−1.5	−3.0
Textiles and clothing	0.9	2.1
Leather goods and footwear	1.4	2.2
Timber, wood products and furniture	1.5	2.9
Paper and printing	3.4	7.1
Plastic and rubber products	4.8	9.2
Other manufacturing industry	1.1	1.9
Building and construction	0.3	0.2
Services	**2.1**	**4.0**
Recovery and repair services	2.6	5.4
Wholesale and retail trade	2.3	4.5
Hotels and restaurants	1.4	2.6
Inland transport services	2.7	5.3
Sea and air transport services	1.4	2.9
Auxiliary transport services	2.4	4.7
Communications	2.8	3.8
Banking and insurance	1.4	4.8
Other private services	2.3	5.4
Real estate	1.2	2.6
Private education services	1.6	4.4
Private health services	0.1	2.2
Recreation and culture	3.2	3.0

for analysing the simulations by 'level' rather than 'rate of growth' of output; the rate of growth is fully satisfactory for short-term analysis where a single period rate of growth contains all the information about the path for the time interval. We see that, in general, the average values are lower than those measured in '2010'. This is because the 'average' contains the structural shocks generated by the removal of trade barriers. The column '2010' gives a good picture of the effects of the enlargement according to the scenarios considered. In particular, the real effects of the enlargement are measured by cumulating the annual gains (or losses) in order to obtain a more accurate impression of the impact in a given year. Although a number of studies conclude that the impact of the enlargement (on the EU-15 countries, groups of countries or single countries) is expected to be modest, we should stress that if the impact turns out to have a given sign, what matters is its cumulative effect over time. In the case of Italy a relatively substantial expansion will affect some sectors ('agriculture and industrial machinery', 'electrical goods', 'motor vehicles, 'metal products'), whilst others (mainly 'food industries' and 'tobacco') will lose their relative importance. A cumulative output rate of growth of over 10 per cent (at the end of the 2000s) will indicate a sizeable sectoral impact.

A multisectoral model is particularly useful when investigating the impact of our scenarios on the structure of Italian industry. First, the anticipated increase in exports generated by the demand of the CEECs in their process of 'catching-up' exerts a clear Keynesian demand effect so that all industries benefit in varying degrees in terms of output growth. Clearly, the removal of tariffs and NTBs interferes with these results. In order to evaluate such interference, we must consider that the removal of trade barriers increases the competitiveness of imports from the CEECs. These imports, which constitute part of the resources, will be used to feed intermediate and final consumption. If we examine import composition, we find that some imports tend to feed intermediate consumption whilst others figure directly in final consumption, such as for example, goods produced for household consumption. Hence, the effect of more competitive imports may vary across sectors.

Figures 8.1–8.6 highlight the impact of the new prosperity of the CEECs represented in the 'Specialization of CEECs' scenario and the changes due to the removal of trade barriers in the 'conservative' and 'generous' scenarios. In each sector, the output index (2001 = 1) shows higher growth in the 'Specialization of CEECs' scenario, confirming the positive benefit of the Keynesian effect due to the increase in imports for the CEECs. For 'agriculture, forestry and fisheries' (Figure 8.1), the removal of trade barriers has a negative impact on sectoral performance in terms of output, particularly when moving from the 'conservative' to the 'generous' scenario. In 'milk and dairy products' (Figure 8.2), the removal of trade barriers is even more severe; all the benefits of expansion, stimulated by higher exports, are lost, and sectoral output falls below the 'baseline' track until the end of the period when it once again

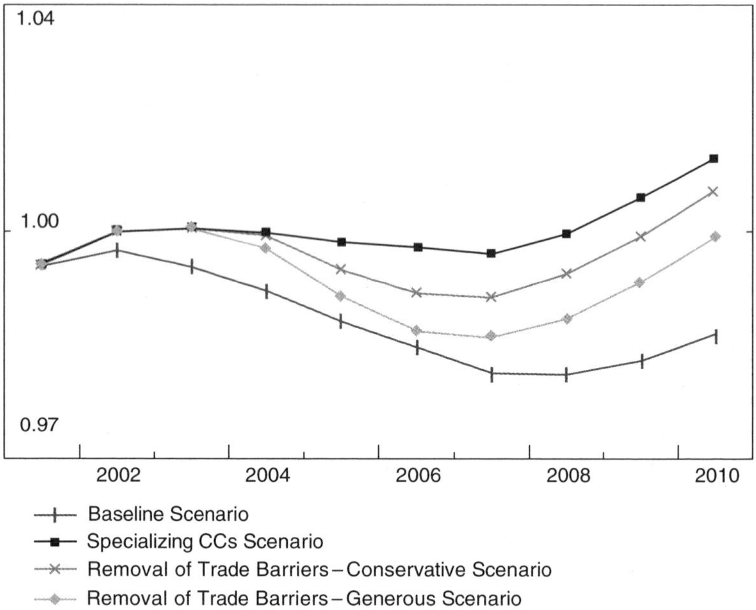

Figure 8.1 1 Agriculture, forestry, fishery: output index

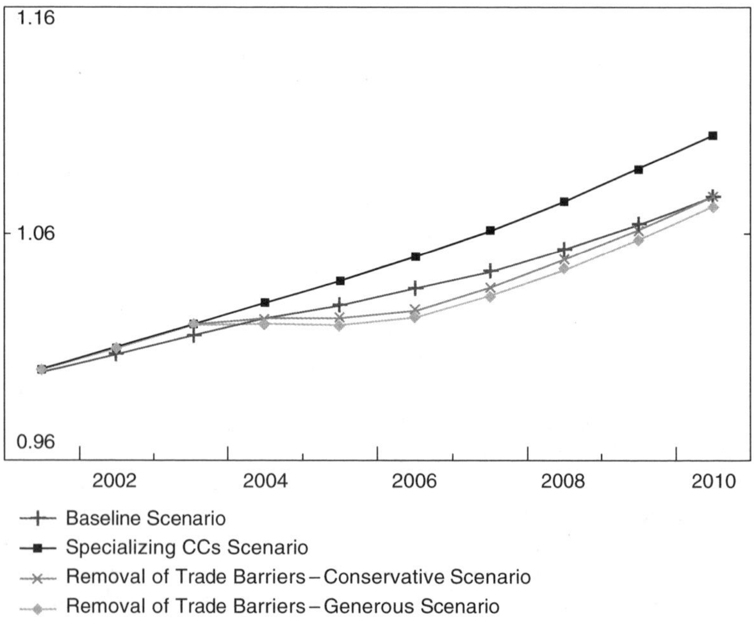

Figure 8.2 17 Milk and dairy products: output index

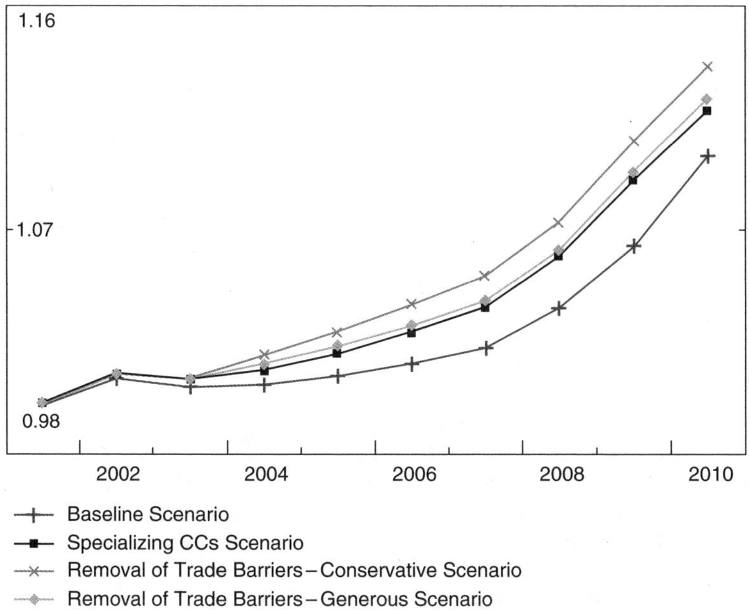

Figure 8.3 22 Leather, shoes and footwear: output index

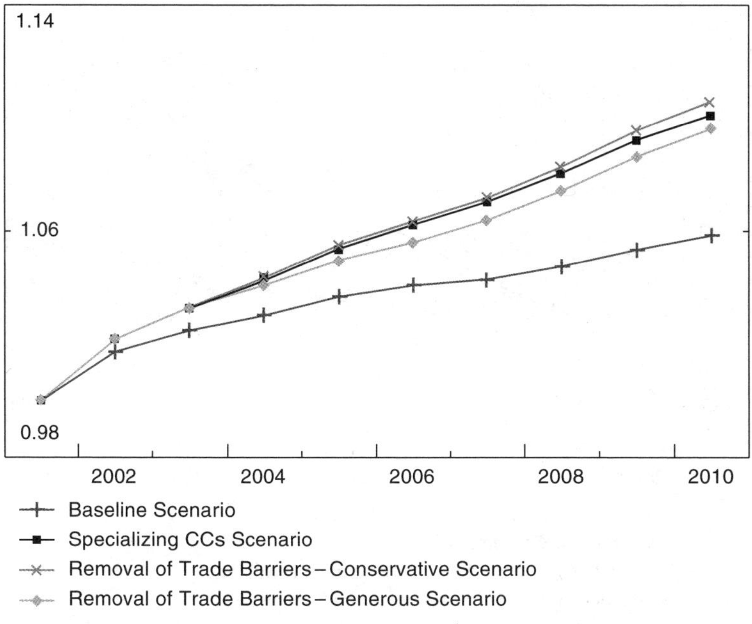

Figure 8.4 9 Chemical products: output index

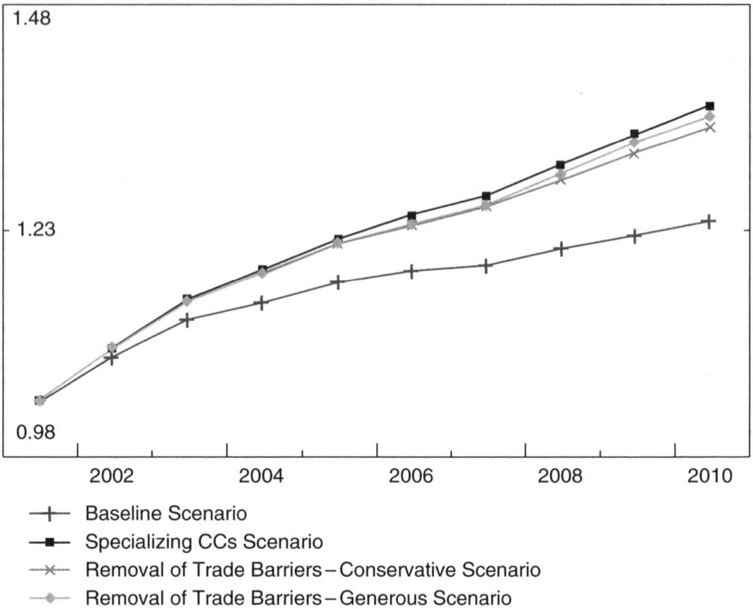

Figure 8.5 10 Metal products: output index

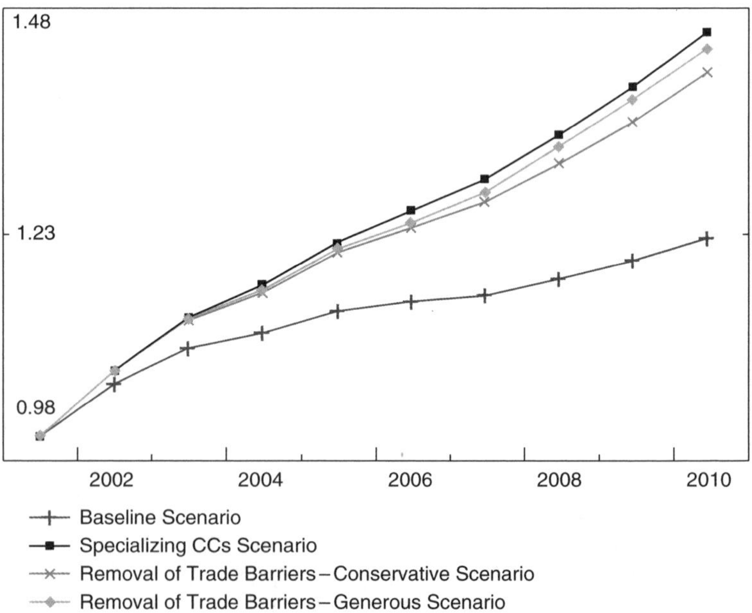

Figure 8.6 11 Agricultural and industrial machinery: output index

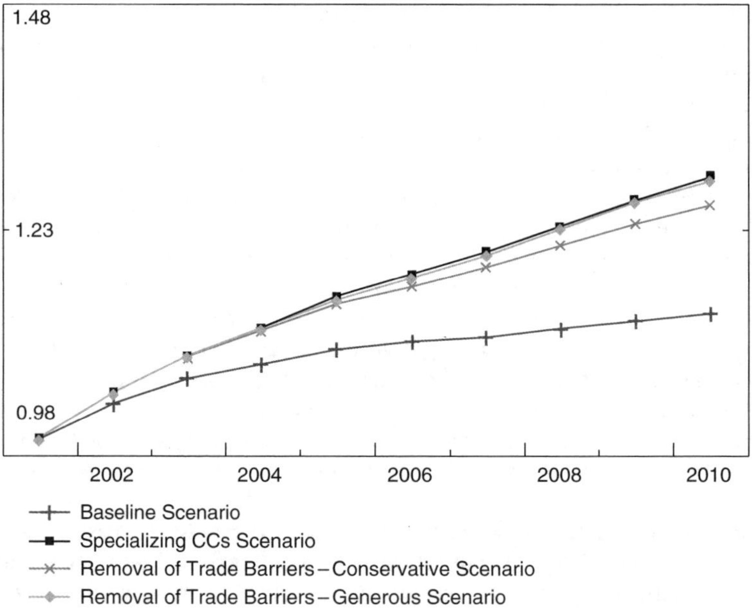

Figure 8.7 13 Electrical goods: output index

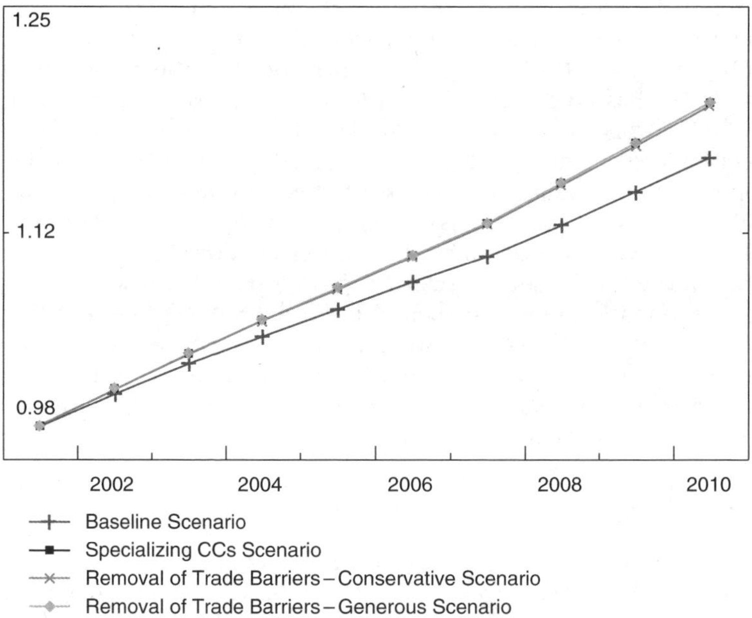

Figure 8.8 40 Recreational and cultural services: output index

approaches the 'baseline' level. In contrast, the removal of trade barriers improves the sectoral performance for 'leather, shoes and footwear' (Figure 8.3); in particular, the 'conservative scenario' stimulates further growth while the 'generous scenario' tends to undermine this stimulus. This means that according to the 'conservative scenario' commodities with reduced import prices generally constitute intermediate consumption for this sector, whilst in the 'generous scenario' the import price reduction is more likely to affect sectoral competition in final consumption products.

In Figure 8.4, the expansion of 'chemical products' is slightly improved under the 'conservative scenario', but clearly deteriorates with the 'generous scenario'. Figures 8.5 and 8.6 illustrate two cases where the removal of trade barriers generates a negative effect which is more severe for the 'conservative' than for the 'generous' scenario. On closer examination, the input structure of these two sectors ('metal products' and 'agricultural and industrial machinery') reveals that those imports absorbed as inputs mainly belong to the group of commodities not covered by the 'conservative scenario'.

The last two Figures (8.7 and 8.8) present evidence of the case where the 'generous scenario' does not modify the performance related to the 'conservative scenario' ('electrical goods') and also presents the case where there is no effect due to the removal of trade barriers ('recreational and cultural services'). The explanation in the case of 'recreational and cultural services' is simple: no imported commodities prove to be relevant for sectoral production, and no imported service competes with it on the final demand side.

In terms of GDP, studies of the impact of Eastern enlargement on a single Member State or on the EU-15 generally conclude that the impact is modest, negligible or has no discernable sign (see e.g., Baldwin, Francois and Portes, 1997; European Commission, ECFIN, 2001). We cannot confirm such conclusions given that they usually are based on analytical tools that are inappropriate for evaluating the sort of effects examined in this study. It should be noted that the process of enlargement entails the evaluation of the pulling of the CEECs' economies, their processes of trade specialization, and the removal of commodity-specific tariffs and trade barriers. This requires a 'meso-economic' approach where the sectoral representation of the economy may help to highlight the structural changes induced by these factors. Underlying macro-variables such as GDP or 'total output' result in changes in the structure of the economy, as can be seen in this study. These changes certainly merit policy makers' attention.

Notes

1. The European Commission has funded several studies on this topic. A recent report by Kok (2003) analyses the EU enlargement from a European point of view addressing the main challenges which this process poses. Other

studies viewing Enlargement from a national standpoint may be found at http://europa.eu.int/comm/budget/financing/enlargement_en.htm.

2. The Inforum work on economic modelling and forecasting is documented at the web site inforumweb.umd.edu.
3. Romano Prodi in his lecture of 10 September 2002 (chapter 2 of this volume) observed that 'depending on the degree of structural reform undertaken, enlargement-induced additional growth for the new members ranges from 1.4 to 2.7 per cent'. In fact, applied studies may differ in their assumptions about expected growth for CCs after accession. Our hypothesis of a growth rate of 2 per cent higher than the EU-15 is somewhat in the middle between a more conservative assumption of about 1.5 per cent above the no enlargement scenario as in Baldwin, Francois and Portes (1997), and a more optimistic scenario of about 2.5 per cent more than the baseline as in European Commission-ECFIN (2001).
4. The United States, Mexico, Canada, Japan, South Korea, China, Taiwan, the UK, France, Germany, Italy, Spain, Austria and Belgium and two areas comprised by the rest of the OECD countries and 'the rest of the world'.
5. There are many economic analyses carried out using Inforum country models. Here we refer to special sessions devoted to Inforum models at the International Conferences on Input-Output Techniques in 1989 (Keszthély, Hungary) and 1998 (New York). Papers presented at the first conference are collected in a special issue of *Economic Systems Research*, vol. 3, no. 1, 1991. Contributions presented at the XII International Conference in New York may be found on the web site www.iioa.at.
6. Here, we do not compare the peculiarities of these kinds of models with those of other macroeconomic or multisectoral models. However, see West (1995) for a synoptic presentation of CGE models, classic input-output models and input-output + econometric models. For a comparison of macroeconomic models see also Almon (1991); see also Monaco (1997) who gives an interesting evaluation of different kinds of macroeconomic multisectoral models from the perspective of a model builder and user.
7. Bardazzi and Grassini (2003) contains a schematic overview of the Italian Multisectoral Model (INTIMO) and of the various behavioural equations.
8. For the summarized results from some of the main studies, see European Commission (2001). One of the most detailed works is a study commissioned by the DG for Employment and Social Affairs, European Integration Consortium (2000).
9. The Czech Republic, Hungary, Poland, Slovenia, Slovakia, Estonia, Latvia, Lithuania, Malta and Cyprus.
10. For a recent report on migration in Central and Eastern Europe, see OECD (2001).
11. This achievement was reached at the Copenhagen European Council (12–13 December 2002).
12. The design of scenarios presented in this section draws heavily on Bardazzi and Grassini (2003).
13. It is assumed that the exchange rates among the key currencies in the baseline as well as in the other scenarios will not vary much over time. The US$/€ exchange rate rises steadily from the present 0.90 to 1.00 by 2010 on the assumption that the widely-held view that the euro is undervalued is not just wishful thinking in the EU. The £/€ ratio remains constant at 0.630 on the expectation that the UK will monitor this rate, rather than the £/US$, and try to maintain it. The yen/€ ratio rises from 110 to 117 and indicates a slight but progressive weakening of the Japanese currency. The scenarios were designed before the 2002/03

appreciation of the €. We still think that in the long run our hypothesis will hold. However, the stability of the exchange rates between the EU and the new associate Member States will not seriously affect the international trade flows within Europe.

14. In the present scenario as well as in the other scenarios designed in this study, the rate of growth of real government expenditure is assumed constant during the simulation period and equal to 2.2 per cent.
15. For references, see note 1.
16. This section is heavily drawn from Bardazzi and Grassini (2003).
17. We thank Elisa Quinto and Alessandro Missale for their contributions on the design of the following scenario variables.
18. First, we have calculated the unweighted average tariff rate on imports originating from the EU for each country at the 4-digit level (data have been taken from www.mkassdb.eu.int, the database of the EU). Then, for each of the three CCs the average tariff rates for the 24 agricultural sectors (2-digit sectors), have been computed as a weighted average of the 4-digit rates, using as weights the value of Italian exports to the country (data on Italian exports have been taken from the COMEXT database) in question (see Table 8.8, first column).

    The structure by sector of Italian tariffs on products originating in the Czech Republic, Hungary and Poland has been computed using data on EU customs duties reported in the TARIC Consultation database (this database can be found at the web site http://europa.eu.int/comm/taxation_customs/dds/cgi-bin/tarchap of the European Commission or at the web site www.finanze.it of the Italian Ministry of Finance). We have again used the above procedure. First, we have computed the average of tariffs at the 4-digit level from the detailed data at the level of 8-digits and, then, the weighted average rate per sector using data on Italian imports for the three countries under examination. In the case of specific duties we have computed total tariff revenues using the volume of Italian imports of the particular product from the COMEXT database and then constructed the *ad valorem*-equivalent tariff rate. The average tariff rates by sector are reported in the second column of Table 8.8.
19. More precisely, a reduction of the average tariff rate per sector from its actual level to zero is considered equivalent to a change in the relative price of imported goods for the corresponding sector.
20. 'Coverage ratios' for each (2-digit) sector are computed as the percentage of imports (per sector) that are covered by at least one of the following NTBs:
    (a) Tariff Measures (other than *ad valorem*) such as tariff quota and temporary duties;
    (b) Price Control Measures countering the damage caused by the application of unfair practice of foreign trade/unfair foreign trade practices;
    (c) Standards and Other Technical Requirements, including quality, safety, health and other regulations;
    (d) Automatic Licensing Measures;
    (e) Monopolistic Measures;
    (f) Quantity Control measures that are however absent in EU-CEECs trade, having been lifted by the Europe Agreements.
21. Further sectoral results for personal consumption expenditures, prices, imports and exports cannot be shown here. These detailed results can be found in Grassini et al. (2001) and Bardazzi and Grassini (2003).

References

Almon, C. (1991) 'The INFORUM Approach to Interindustry Modeling', *Economic Systems Research*, vol. 3, no. 1, pp. 1–7.

Armington, P.S. (1969a) 'A Theory of Demand for Products Distinguished by Place of Production', *IMF Staff Papers*, vol. 16, pp. 159–76.

Armington, P.S. (1969b) 'The Geographical Patterns of Trade and the Effects of Price Changes', *IMF Staff Papers*, vol. 16, pp. 179–97.

Baldone, S., A. Lasagni and F. Sdogati (1997) 'Emerging Patterns of Trade Specialization EU-CEECs', in S. Baldone and F. Sdogati (eds), *EU-CEECs Integration: Policies and Markets at Work* (Milan: Franco Angeli), pp. 143–90.

Baldwin, R.E., J.F. Francois and R. Portes (1997) 'The Costs and Benefits of Eastern Enlargement: The Impact on the EU and Central Europe', *Economic Policy*, vol. 12(24), pp. 125–76.

Bardazzi, R. (2001) 'Cohort, Age and Year Effects on Italian Household Consumption', in M. Grassini (ed.), *Contributions on Multisectoral Modelling* (Florence: Centro Editoriale Toscano), pp. 193–220.

Bardazzi, R. and M. Grassini (2003) 'Methodological Framework and Simulations for Evaluating the Impact of the EU Enlargement on the Italian Economy', *Rivista di Politica Economica*, March–April, pp. 31–78.

European Commission (2001) 'The Free Movement of Workers in the Context of Enlargement', *Information Note*, March.

European Commission (2002) *Broad Economic Policy Guidelines, European Economy*, main edition, no. 4 (Luxembourg: Office for Official Publications of the EC).

European Commission, ECFIN (2001) 'The Economic Impact of Enlargement', *Enlargement Papers*, no. 4, June.

European Commission, ECFIN (2003a) *European Economy*, Spring 2003, Economic Forecasts no. 2/2003.

European Commission, ECFIN (2003b) *European Economy*, Spring 2003, Economic Forecasts for the Candidate Countries: *Enlargement Papers*, no. 15, April.

European Integration Consortium (2000) *The Impact of Eastern Enlargement on Employment and Labour Markets in the EU Member States*, Study commissioned by the Employment and Social Affairs DG of the European Commission.

Eurostat (2001) 'EU Enlargement: Key Data on the Candidate Countries', Eurostat News Release, 129/2001, 13 December .

Fair, R.C. (1984) *Specification, Estimation, and Analysis of Macroeconomic Models*, (Cambridge, Mass.: Harvard University Press).

Grassini, M. (2001) 'The Core of the Multisetoral Inforum Model', in M. Grassini (ed.), *Contributions on Multisectoral Modelling* (Florence: Centro Editoriale Toscano), pp. 7–32.

Grassini *et al.* (2001) 'Eastern Enlargement of the EU, Economic Costs and Benefits for the EU Member States: the Case of Italy', Study prepared for the Commission of the European Communities DG Budget, Final Report, December.

Italian Trade Centre (ICE)-SISTAN-ISTAT (2002) *Commercio Estero e attività internazionali delle imprese Annuario 2001, L'Italia nell'economia Internazionale, Rapporto ICE 2001–2002* (Rome: ICE).

Keuschnigg, C. and W. Kohler (1999) 'Eastern Enlargement to the EU: Economic Costs and Benefits for the EU Member States: the Case of Austria', Study prepared for the Commission of the European Communities DG Budget, Final Report, September.

Kok, W. (2003) *Enlarging the European Union – Achievements and Challenges*, Report to the European Commission (Florence: Robert Schuman Centre for Advanced Studies, European University Institute).

Monaco, R.M. (1997) 'A Brief Review of Alternative Approaches to Intersectoral Policy Analysis and Forecasting', Inforum Working Paper.

Nyhus, D. (1975) *The Trade Model of a Dynamic World Input-output Forecasting System*, Inforum Research Report, no. 14, Interindustry Forecasting Project at University of Maryland, Department of Economics, University of Maryland.

OECD (2001) *Migration Policies and EU Enlargement: the Case of Central and Eastern Europe*, OECD Proceedings (Paris: OECD).

Qiang Ma (1996) *A Multisectoral Bilateral Trade Model*, PhD Dissertation, University of Maryland (available at http://inforumweb.umd.edu).

Rhomberg, R.R. (1970) 'Possible Approaches to a Model of World Trade and Payments', *International Monetary Fund Staff Papers*, vol. 17, pp. 1–26.

Rhomberg, R.R. (1973) 'Towards a General Trade Model', in R.J. Ball (ed.), *The International Linkage of National Models* (Amsterdam: North-Holland), pp. 9–20.

United Nations (2000) 'Replacement Migration: Is it a Solution to Declining and Ageing Populations', Population Division, Department of Economic and Social Affairs (New York: United Nations).

United Nations (2003) 'World Population Prospects: The 2002 Revision', Population Division, Department of Economic and Social Affairs (New York: United Nations).

Wang, Qing (2000) *Trade Flows and Trade Protection: A Multi–Country and Multi–Sectoral Investigation*, PhD Dissertation, University of Maryland.

West, R.G. (1995) 'Comparison of Input–output, Input–output + econometrics and Computable General Equilibrium Impact Models at the Regional Level, *Economic Systems Research*, vol. 7(2), pp. 209–27.

9

Dynamic Paths of the European Economy: Simulations with an Aggregate Model of the EMU as a Part of the World Economy*

Alberto Bagnai
University of Rome I, Italy

1 Introduction

The development of the European economy is a subject of remarkable interest in the current debate on the world economy. The performance of the Economic and Monetary Union (EMU) in terms of growth and unemployment is still unsatisfactory in comparison with that of the United States and of the European non-EMU countries, especially the United Kingdom. This has led some authors to investigate the existence of a deflationary bias in EMU monetary and fiscal policy rules (see for instance Altavilla and Marani, 2002). What is probably more significant, the concern that a restrictive monetary policy from the ECB might hinder the weak recovery of the EMU is shared by multilateral agencies such as the OECD (see Cotis, 2003) and the IMF (see chapter 1 and figure 1.5 in IMF, 2003).

While these analyses focus more and more on the aggregate outcomes of the euro area (EMU unemployment rate, EMU rate of growth, and so on), empirical evidence on the behaviour of the European economy as a whole is still scarce. Thus, it is of some interest to take part in the extensive debate on these topics by putting forth some simulation experiments related to the future developments of the European economy, carried out with an updated version of an aggregate model of the European Union (Bagnai and Carlucci,

* The author thanks Francesco Carlucci and the participants at the European Union session of the IEA Congress (Lisbon, September 2002) for their helpful comments. Research assistance by Valeria Perotti and Antonio Pesce is gratefully acknowledged. This work was partially funded by the University of Rome 'La Sapienza' (research project on Institutions, Growth and International Coordination) and its Faculty of Economics (research project on The Linkage of Macroeconometric Models for International Economic Policy Simulation).

2003). In this updated version an aggregate submodel for the euro area is embedded in a model of the world economy that includes four other submodels: for the United States, Japan, the United Kingdom (whose economy represents about 70 per cent of the European non-EMU countries in terms of real GDP) and the rest of the world.[1] The model version utilized in this chapter represents the Japan, UK, and rest of the world (ROW) blocks by a set of trade relations, while the euro area and US blocks are each represented by a structural economic model consisting of about 60 equations with 50 exogenous variables.[2] The economic structure and the estimation methods of the two estimated submodels (those for the euro area and the US) follow closely Bagnai and Carlucci (2003), with some extensions set forth below in Section 2.

The simulations compare the dynamic paths of the European economy in the next five years (2003–07) under a set of alternative scenarios. The first one investigates the impact of a stronger recovery of world demand on the euro area's macroeconomic performance. This experiment aims at assessing to what extent the economic recovery of the EMU, which nowadays essentially relies on US growth, could be accelerated by economic growth in the UK and emerging markets. The second scenario envisages a temporary increase in the export prices of the rest of the world, thus simulating the impact on the recovery of an 'oil-price shock'. Although the outcome of the Iraqi war of 1990 averted a supply-side shock of this kind, an evaluation of its impact is interesting nevertheless, in the light of the persistent political instability in the Middle East. The third simulation expounds the results that the EMU would achieve if it followed a more expansionary monetary policy in the next five years.

The proposed scenarios are highly stylized, but this does not reduce their likelihood, and it certainly increases the readability and transparency of the simulations' outcomes. In any case, the experiments are not intended to provide, and should not be construed as, genuine forecasts. In order to be reliable, a forecast must take into account, among other things, a fuller representation of global economic interdependence, which will be achieved in the near future by completing the estimation of the UK and Japan submodels, and a detailed characterization of economic-policy measures, which lies outside the scope of the present work. In particular, both the EMU and the US block feature an inflation-targeting monetary rule à la Taylor (1993), but fiscal policy rules were left unspecified. Therefore, the deficit/GDP ratios are examined in a situation in which the automatic stabilizers are allowed to operate fully.

As stated before, the structure of the model utilized in the simulation, as well as the main revisions embodied in the present version, are described in Section 2. Section 3 presents the simulation results and Section 4 provides a number of conclusions.

2 Model structure and properties

2.1 Theoretical framework and econometric issues

The main feature of the model utilized in the simulations is that it represents Europe as a single country, following an approach originally proposed by Dramais (1986), and utilized since then by other authors, including Meyermans and Van Brusselen (2000a,b) and Fagan, Henry and Mestre (2001).[3]

At the end of 1996, when this research programme began, the EMU was yet to come. There were many doubts about its feasibility, and no one knew which countries would eventually take part in it (see for instance Eichengreen, 1993). The 12-country European Union was the most natural, if not the only choice for the reference European aggregate.[4] This version of the European aggregate model was published in Bagnai and Carlucci (1998, 2003) and utilized in the preliminary version of this chapter. Its theoretical reference framework is post-Keynesian: output is demand constrained and labour demand follows from cost minimization under a standard neoclassical technology; the real-wage long-run dynamics is determined by productivity and the unemployment rate, while the price dynamics follows from a set of mark-up equations; the model includes a representation of the general government sector.

Estimation was performed on annual data by a two-stage procedure allowing for the non-linearity and simultaneity of equations, for the non-stationarity of variables, as well as for the presence of structural changes in parameters. This was achieved by estimating the long-run parameters with the cointegration procedure proposed by Gregory and Hansen (1996), which detects structural breaks of unknown date in the long-run parameters of the estimated equations. The short-run parameters were then estimated using the internal instrumental variable estimator proposed by Bowden and Turkington (1981), which takes into account the non-linearity of the model.

2.2 From an area model to a global model

Developments in the European economic system, as well as the increased availability of aggregated data referring to the EMU, have prompted a thorough revision of the model.

In re-estimating the model the euro area was taken as the reference aggregate. This makes the model outputs directly comparable with published statistics for the euro area. In particular, the European exchange rate represented in the model is now the EUR/USD rate, rather than an effective exchange rate involving a mixture of 'in' and 'out' currencies.

The structure of the model was modified in four respects.

First, the supply side was respecified by representing explicitly the accumulation of business-sector capital stock. The factor demand equations are now derived by cost minimization under CES technology.[5] The dynamic labour demand equation follows from error correction around the long-run path defined by the static conditional demand function. The investment function adopts the approach of Knight and Wymer (1978), where the desired rate of growth of the real capital stock adjusts to the spread between the marginal productivity of capital and real interest rate.[6]

Secondly, while the previous versions of the model were very aggregative (considering only total output, total employment, total investment, and so on), the present version adopts a clearer distinction between the business and government sectors, thus distinguishing, for example, between government and business employment, investment, output and capital stock. The government and households appropriation accounts were also specified in more detail. This raises the number of equations from 34 to about 60, but also increases the scope for economic policy simulations and provides more meaningful estimates of the supply-side parameters.

Thirdly, trade equations were reestimated in terms of extra-EMU flows, taking into account only trade with non-EMU countries. The consolidation of the trade flows was made using the Monthly Foreign Trade Statistics database in OECD (2002). This led to more satisfactory estimates of their price elasticities and was also a prerequisite to the fourth major revision, namely the integration of the euro area model into a model of the global economy.

The present specification of this global model considers a division of the global economy into five blocks:[7] the European Monetary Union, the United States, the United Kingdom, Japan and the rest of the world.

The first four blocks share the common theoretical structure described so far and are linked through real trade flows, competitiveness and interest rates.[8] The trade and competitiveness linkages were set up as in Multimod (Laxton et al., 1998): there are two separate competitiveness measures for exports and imports, and real exports depend in each block on a trade-weighed average of real imports of the remaining blocks. The measures of competitiveness depend on prices and bilateral exchange rates. The latter are endogenized using the monetary approach of Frenkel (1976), which was recently shown by Kim and Mo (1995) to provide reliable medium-run forecasts of nominal exchange rates when implemented with cointegration estimators. Interest rate linkages occur both directly, because the US interest rate affects the monetary policy reaction function of other submodels, and indirectly, through inflation spillovers. The rest of the world is represented by a set of trade and competitiveness relations that ensures the consistency of trade flows at the global level.[9]

As a result of this extension the European economy is no longer considered as a 'small open economy' whose growth path is largely determined by a *deus ex machina* world demand variable, taken as exogenous. On the contrary, about half of world demand for European goods is now endogenous to the model. Moreover, inflation rates (hence, via monetary policy reaction functions, interest rates) are linked to the competitiveness measures. This means that the economic conditions of Europe now feed back on world demand growth, as well as on prices and interest rates of the major partner countries, thus embodying in the model a number of repercussions that should increase its reliability as an instrument of economic analysis.

3 Results

3.1 The baseline scenario

The results presented in this section are in a sense preliminary because, as mentioned above, two blocks of the model, the UK and Japan submodels, are still under construction. Therefore, the export prices, real imports and bilateral exchange rates (in terms of the US dollar) of these countries were taken as exogenous in the present simulations, which account only for the repercussions between the EMU and the United States. This is an appreciable improvement over the previous 'small open economy' version of the European model, because these repercussions are not negligible, as shown for instance by Douven and Peters (1998).

The EMU and US blocks of the model were estimated over the sample 1960–2002 using the time series provided by OECD (2002). The linkage of the EMU and US models resulted in a model of 127 equations with 80 exogenous variables, mostly related to the government sector. The main exogenous variables are the labour force, government consumption, government investment and government employment, average tax rates and average social security contribution rates.

The model was first simulated over the sample 2003–07 in order to construct a baseline scenario. The model database was extended over the simulation sample in two stages. In the first stage, the most recent OECD 'flashfile' (OECD, 2003b), supplemented with the projections provided by OECD (2003a) and IMF (2003), were used to extend the time series of the exogenous variables from 2003 to 2004. In the second stage, the exogenous variables of the two blocks were further extended over 2005–07 using the hypotheses summarized in Table 9.1.[10]

Both in the EMU and in the United States it is assumed that the labour force will evolve according to the 'discouraged worker' hypothesis, starting from low or negative growth rates and gradually reaching its long-run growth rate.

The exogenous variables pertaining to the government sector were extrapolated in both submodels under a set of 'neutral' hypotheses: average tax and social security contribution rates were held constant at their historical values, while the other revenues and transfers were expressed as a ratio to GDP, using the latest historical values. Government investment (in volume), government intermediate consumption (in value) and government employment were allowed to grow at a rate close to their average long-run growth rate.

Although this set of hypotheses appears reasonable, this scenario should not be interpreted as a 'forecast' of the European economy, but rather as a convenient benchmark against which to assess some alternative dynamic paths.

Table 9.1 The baseline scenario: percentage change in exogenous variables over the simulation period 2003–07

	2003	*2004*	*2005*	*2006*	*2007*
EMU					
Government sector					
Government investment (real)	4.0	1.0	3.0	3.0	3.0
Government intermediate consumption (nominal)	4.0	4.0	4.0	4.0	4.0
Government employment	0.1	0.1	0.1	0.1	0.1
Supply side					
Labour force	–0.04	0.04	1.0	1.0	1.0
United States					
Government sector					
Government investment (real)	4.5	4.5	4.5	4.5	4.5
Government intermediate consumption (nominal)	4.0	4.0	4.0	4.0	4.0
Government employment	0.9	0.9	0.9	0.9	0.9
Supply side					
Labour force	0.09	0.12	0.16	0.20	0.25
Other blocks					
Import volume					
Japan	3.5	4.1	4.1	4.1	4.1
UK	2.8	9.5	9.5	9.5	9.5
Rest of the world	4.5	6.0	6.0	6.0	6.0
Export prices					
Japan	2.0	2.0	2.0	2.0	2.0
UK	2.0	2.0	2.0	2.0	2.0
Rest of the world	1.0	1.0	1.0	1.0	1.0

Table 9.2 reports selected results of the simulation following from the hypotheses set out in Table 9.1. As the focus of this analysis is the euro area, we do not give here a full account of the US economy and report instead only the US variables that feed back directly on the European economy (through the €/US$ exchange rate equation or the real exports function of the euro area).

The results for the first two years are quite close to the current projections of the IMF and OECD, which is not surprising, since the simulations are based on IMF and OECD projections of the exogenous variables. The European economy is expected to grow in 2003 at a moderate rate (about 1.2 per cent), in line with the current OECD and IMF forecasts of 1.0 and 1.1 per cent respectively (see OECD, 2003; IMF, 2003); recovery starts in 2004, with a growth rate of 2.4 per cent, gradually reaching a value of about 2.8 per cent at the end of the simulation period.

Table 9.2 The baseline scenario: results

	Units	*2003*	*2004*	*2005*	*2006*	*2007*
EMU						
Real gross domestic product	*% change*	1.23	2.40	2.66	2.74	2.79
Real private consumption	*% change*	0.87	2.32	1.97	1.71	1.59
Real total investment	*% change*	−1.38	2.93	2.83	2.91	3.63
Real exports of goods and services	*% change*	3.08	7.11	8.41	8.67	8.41
Real imports of goods and services	*% change*	3.68	6.82	7.16	6.99	6.85
Private consumption deflator	*% change*	1.70	1.28	1.77	2.33	3.31
Wage rate	*% change*	4.47	2.76	2.69	3.03	4.10
Unemployment rate	*level*	8.95	8.85	8.75	8.56	7.83
Total employment	*% change*	−0.67	0.15	1.15	1.25	1.85
Deficit/GDP ratio	*level*	2.40	2.56	2.73	2.85	2.88
Short-term interest rate	*level*	3.82	3.96	4.05	4.52	5.32
Money stock	*% change*	5.61	3.02	4.01	4.51	5.75
EUR/USD exchange rate	*level*	0.99	1.02	1.05	1.08	1.09
US						
Real gross domestic product	*% change*	2.79	4.43	4.61	4.55	4.03
Real imports of goods and services	*% change*	3.78	8.37	8.97	9.06	8.18
Private consumption deflator	*% change*	0.91	1.29	2.02	2.80	3.50
Short-term interest rate	*level*	2.59	3.40	4.40	5.35	6.17
Money stock	*% change*	6.07	1.63	1.91	4.14	7.30

The recovery of EMU is fuelled mainly by real exports, whose growth rate attains 7.1 per cent in 2004 as a result of two effects: a strong growth of US real imports, at about 8.4 per cent, and a moderate devaluation of the euro. These effects both depend on the growth of US real GDP. In particular, according to the prediction of the standard flexible-price monetary model by Frenkel (1976), the positive growth differential in favour of the United States determines a devaluation of the euro of about 3.4 per cent in the first year. The exchange rate keeps increasing at a decreasing rate over the simulation period, converging to a value of about €1.1 per US$.

This devaluation feeds back on EMU domestic prices. EMU inflation starts growing in 2005 after reaching a minimum in 2004. The resurgence of inflation in the course of the simulation horizon exerts two contrasting effects on consumption and investment: the former recedes slightly, because of a slowdown in households' real disposable income; the latter increases, due to a drop in the real interest rate.

Unemployment reaches a maximum of about 9 per cent in 2003 before decreasing towards 7.8 per cent. This reflects the well-known persistence of European unemployment in response to adverse shocks (see for instance Bean, 1994).

The government balance-to-GDP ratio increases slowly, reaching 2.9 per cent at the end of the simulation horizon. This result is determined by an increase in government gross interest payments of about one GDP point, which follows from the counter-cyclical increase in interest rates.

3.2 A positive world demand shock

The remainder of this section examines the sensitivity of the model's projections to deviations from the basic assumptions set out in Table 9.1, analysing the response of the EMU economy to different paths of world demand, international prices, and the euro area interest rate.

The first counterfactual experiment simulates the effects of a more sustained increase in world demand. This was done by adding one percentage point of growth to the dynamic path of the UK and rest of the world imports volumes specified in Table 9.1. The rate of growth of Japan imports was left unaffected.

Table 9.3 and Figure 9.1 report selected results of the simulation, measured as deviations from the baseline paths reported in Table 9.2.

Table 9.3 A positive world demand shock

	2003	*2004*	*2005*	*2006*	*2007*
EMU					
Real gross domestic product	0.22	0.23	0.24	0.24	0.25
Real private consumption	0.07	0.01	−0.04	−0.09	−0.14
Real total investment	0.15	0.20	0.20	0.20	0.21
Real exports of goods and services	0.85	1.07	1.09	1.07	1.06
Real imports of goods and services	0.63	0.64	0.64	0.63	0.64
Private consumption deflator	0.15	0.34	0.56	0.81	1.09
Wage rate	0.18	0.38	0.63	0.91	1.23
Unemployment rate	−0.16	−0.34	−0.52	−0.71	−0.91
Total employment	0.18	0.19	0.20	0.21	0.21
Deficit/GDP ratio	−0.04	−0.10	−0.18	−0.26	−0.36
Short-term interest rate	0.03	0.16	0.37	0.66	1.02
Money stock	0.36	0.53	0.71	0.92	1.18
EUR/USD exchange rate (% deviations)	0.05	0.45	1.16	2.13	3.36
US					
Real gross domestic product	0.10	0.11	0.12	0.12	0.11
Real imports of goods and services	0.23	0.27	0.29	0.31	0.32
Private consumption deflator	0.02	0.06	0.11	0.18	0.26
Short-term interest rate	0.02	0.06	0.11	0.17	0.24
Money stock	0.04	0.12	0.20	0.28	0.38

Notes: Deviations from the baseline reported in Table 9.2 of some endogenous variables under the alternative hypothesis of a positive world demand shock in 2003, defined as a permanent one point increase in the rate of growth of UK and ROW import volumes. The EUR/USD exchange rate deviations are expressed in percentages.

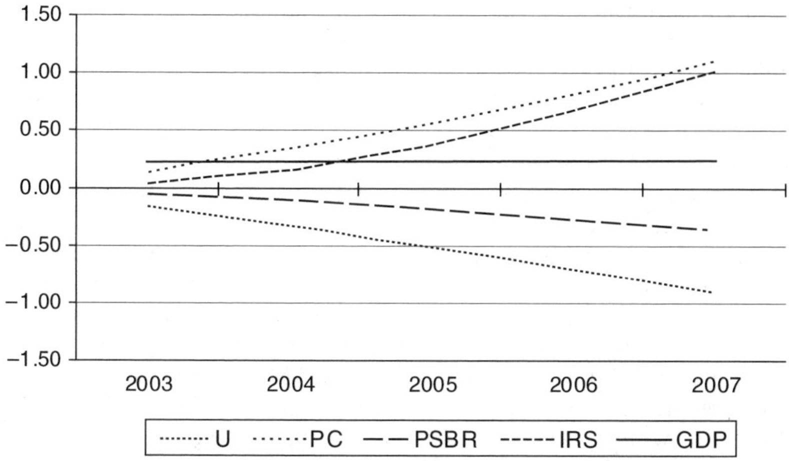

Figure 9.1 Deviations from the baseline of some endogenous variables under the alternative hypothesis of a positive world demand shock in 2003

Notes: The demand shock is defined as a permanent one point increase in the rate of growth of UK and ROW import volumes. U is the unemployment rate, PC the rate of inflation, PSBR the deficit/GDP ratio, IRS the short-term interest rate and GDP the real rate of growth.

The increase in UK and rest of the world imports exerts a stronger impact on the EMU, where the real growth rate increases permanently by about 0.2 percentage points, than on the US economy, where the real growth increase is about half this amount (0.1 percentage points). This depends partly on the relative importance of the trade shares and partly on the structure of the exchange rate and money demand equations. The share of UK imports in EMU exports is about three times greater than that in US exports, hence an increase in UK imports has a stronger effect on the EMU than on the US. Moreover, money demand has a lower impact elasticity with respect to output in the US (about 0.5) than in the EMU (about 1). This means that the impact response of the money stock is larger in the EMU area than in the US (the increases in the money stock growth rates are 0.36 and 0.04 respectively). Since the exchange rate equation has unit impact elasticity with respect to the differential in money stock growth rates, as envisaged by the standard dynamic version of the flexible-price monetary model of the exchange rate (see for instance Razzak and Grennes, 1998), the euro depreciates. This depreciation further boosts EMU real exports, whose rate of growth increases in the first year by 0.85 percentage points.

Although the output elasticity of labour demand is unity (according to the CES factor demand specification), the increase in EMU output does not translate fully into employment because of a simultaneous increase in real wages. Therefore, the rate of growth of employment in the counterfactual simulation increases by slightly less than 0.2 percentage points. This increase, however, is persistent (being determined by the persistent increase in output), and entails a fall in the unemployment rate that approaches 0.9 percentage points at the end of the simulation period.[11]

This evolution of unemployment and exchange rates affects the inflation rate in the euro area: at the end of the simulation inflation is about 1 percentage point above the baseline. The EMU monetary authorities react by increasing the short-term interest rate, whose differential with the corresponding US rate increases by about 0.77 points by the end of the simulation horizon. Since the exchange rate equation features a positive semi-elasticity of about 0.03 with respect to the EMU-US interest rate differential, this evolution of the interest rates contributes to a further depreciation of the euro, which approaches 3.4 per cent at the end of the simulation (corresponding to €1.13 per US$).[12]

This evolution of prices and interest rates involves a decrease in both the real disposable income and the real interest rate, with contrasting effects on consumption (which slows down by the end of the simulation) and investment (which increases persistently).

3.3 A positive shock to international prices

This simulation examines the impact on the recovery path of the EMU economy of a transitory increase in the export prices of the rest of the world. The size of the shock was set by analogy with those experienced in the oil-price shocks of the 1970s, considering an increase of 20 percentage points in 2003.

The main findings are summarized in Figure 9.2 and Table 9.4. This supply-side shock has a strong but transitory impact on the euro area GDP, whose growth rate decreases by 0.45 percentage point in the first year (from the baseline value of 1.23 per cent to 0.78 per cent) and then reverts to the baseline. This contraction results mainly from a fall in consumption by 0.88 percentage points (determined by a fall in real income), and by a fall in investment equal to 1.68 percentage points, fostered by an increase by about 1.4 percentage points in the long-run real interest rate. The reaction of output, prices, and interest rates determines a contraction of the nominal money stock by about 2 per cent. A similar effect occurs in the US, but its size is smaller (1.44 per cent). Therefore, the euro appreciates by about 1.5 per cent in the first year, thereby mitigating the effects of the price shock on domestic inflation.

In the first year the rate of growth of real wages drops by about one percentage point with respect to the baseline. The fall in output therefore

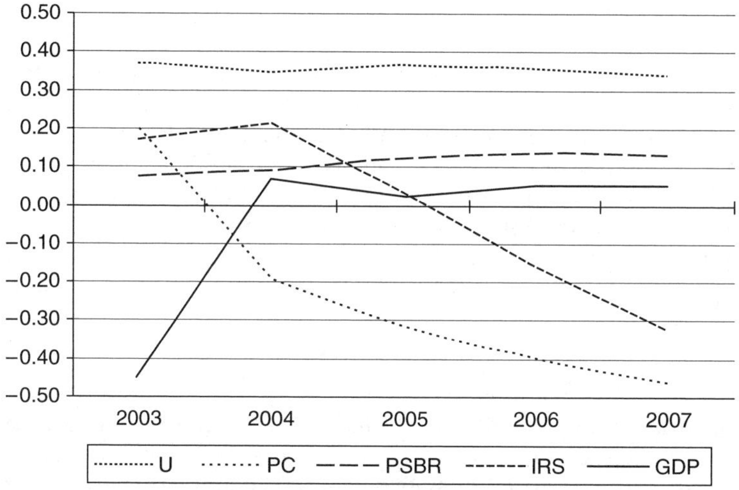

Figure 9.2 Deviations from the baseline of some endogenous variables under the alternative hypothesis of a positive shock to the export prices of the rest of the world block

Notes: The shock is defined as a temporary increase by 20 percentage points of the export prices of the rest of the world in 2003. U is the unemployment rate, PC the rate of inflation, PSBR the deficit/GDP ratio, IRS the short-term interest rate and GDP the real rate of growth.

Table 9.4 A positive shock to international prices

	2003	*2004*	*2005*	*2006*	*2007*
EMU					
Real gross domestic product	−0.45	0.07	0.02	0.05	0.06
Real private consumption	−0.88	−0.05	0.00	0.06	0.10
Real total investment	−1.68	0.12	0.07	0.11	0.20
Real exports of goods and services	−0.18	−0.13	−0.06	−0.07	−0.10
Real imports of goods and services	−1.36	0.08	−0.09	−0.01	0.00
Private consumption deflator	0.20	−0.19	−0.32	−0.40	−0.46
Wage rate	−0.45	−0.18	−0.29	−0.37	−0.45
Unemployment rate	0.37	0.35	0.36	0.36	0.34
Total employment	−0.40	0.02	−0.02	0.01	0.02
Deficit/GDP ratio	0.08	0.09	0.12	0.14	0.13
Short-term interest rate	0.17	0.21	0.03	−0.16	−0.33
Money stock	−2.05	−0.73	−0.45	−0.43	−0.38
EUR/USD exchange rate (%)	−1.55	−1.92	−3.08	−4.55	−6.04
US					
Real gross domestic product	−0.08	0.00	0.12	0.12	0.05
Real imports of goods and services	−2.19	−1.65	−0.61	−0.18	−0.10
Private consumption deflator	0.86	0.68	0.56	0.50	0.46
Short-term interest rate	0.78	0.65	0.55	0.50	0.46
Money stock	−1.44	0.18	0.82	0.97	0.92

Note: The table reports the deviations of some endogenous variables from the baseline paths (Table 9.2) under the assumption of a temporary increase of the rate of growth of the rest of the world export prices by 20 percentage points in 2003.

does not translate fully into a fall in employment: the rate of growth of employment is only 0.4 percentage points under the baseline.

After the first year the EMU economy is set on a deflationary spiral, where the fall in nominal wage rate is matched by the fall in domestic prices, favoured by a gradual appreciation of the euro with respect to the baseline, which in turn is determined by a gradually slowing monetary contraction. Therefore, real wages are unable to foster a recovery of total employment, and the temporary shock in prices results in a persistent shock to unemployment.

3.4 An expansionary monetary policy

The last simulation experiment studies the impact of an expansionary monetary policy, defined as a 100 basis points decrease of the short-run interest rate with respect to its baseline values. The simulation was performed by a Type 1 fix, namely, by 'exogenizing' the interest rate equation.

The results are reported in Table 9.5 and Figure 9.3. In the present version of the model, monetary policy exerts its effects in the real sector via both

Table 9.5 An expansionary monetary policy

	2003	*2004*	*2005*	*2006*	*2007*
EMU					
Real gross domestic product	0.10	−0.02	0.00	0.00	0.00
Real private consumption	0.16	−0.01	0.00	−0.01	−0.01
Real total investment	0.87	0.31	0.24	0.19	0.14
Real exports of goods and services	−0.07	−0.07	−0.03	0.00	0.02
Real imports of goods and services	0.30	−0.03	0.03	0.03	0.03
Private consumption deflator	−0.05	0.03	0.05	0.06	0.07
Wage rate	0.08	0.01	0.04	0.06	0.07
Unemployment rate	−0.07	−0.05	−0.05	−0.06	−0.06
Total employment	0.07	−0.02	0.00	0.00	0.00
Deficit/GDP ratio	−0.09	−0.21	−0.32	−0.41	−0.47
Short-term interest rate	−1.00	−1.00	−1.00	−1.00	−1.00
Money stock	1.22	−0.14	0.02	0.07	0.08
EUR/USD exchange rate (%)	−2.11	−1.92	−1.71	−1.51	−1.33
US					
Real gross domestic product	0.03	0.01	0.00	0.00	−0.01
Real imports of goods and services	0.04	0.00	0.01	0.00	0.00
Private consumption deflator	0.02	0.02	0.03	0.03	0.03
Short-term interest rate	0.02	0.02	0.02	0.03	0.03
Money stock	0.00	0.05	0.05	0.04	0.04

Notes: The table reports the simulation of an expansionary monetary policy, defined as a 100 basis point decrease of the short-term interest rate from its baseline value. The results are reported as deviations from the paths reported in Table 9.2.

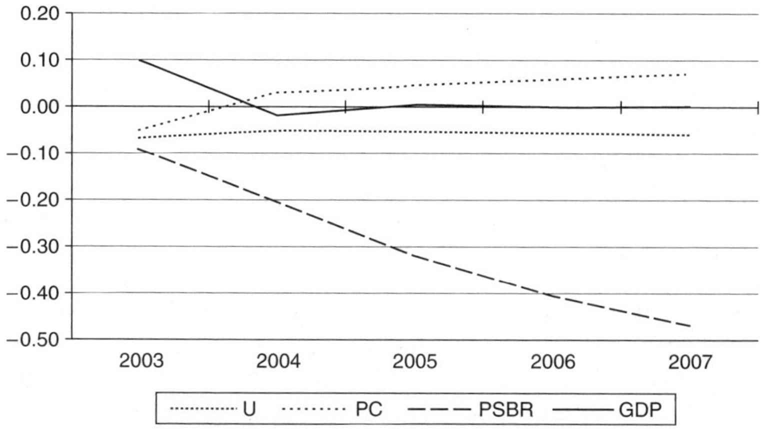

Figure 9.3 Deviations from the baseline of some endogenous variables under the alternative hypothesis of an expansionary monetary policy

Notes: An expansionary monetary policy is defined as a 100 basis points decrease in the EMU area short-term interest rate. U is the unemployment rate, PC the rate of inflation, PSBR the deficit/GDP ratio and GDP the real rate of growth.

the investment function and the exchange rate equation. Real total investment reacts quickly to the decrease in the real interest rate, with an increase of 0.87 percentage points above the baseline in the first year. This effect is partly offset by an appreciation of the euro, which results from three contrasting effects: on the one side, the fall in domestic interest rate and the increase in domestic output (which determines an appreciation of the euro), on the other side, the expansion of the nominal money stock (which brings about a devaluation of the euro). The appreciation of the euro moderates the inflationary pressure of the expansionary monetary policy: the inflation rate actually decreases in the first year, and the real wage increases slightly, thus reducing the effects on employment of the increase in output.

Starting from the second year most variables revert to their baselines, the only notable exceptions being real investment and the exchange rate (which revert slowly to the baseline), and the deficit/GDP ratio (which converges to −0.5 points under the baseline). The latter result is explained almost entirely by the evolution of the gross government interest payments, whose ratio to GDP falls at the end of the simulation horizon from 4.88 in the baseline to 4.44 in the monetary expansion scenario.

4 Conclusions

This work aims at evaluating quantitatively by simulation methods some alternative development paths for the EMU under various hypotheses involving the rate of growth of world demand and international prices, and the conduct of monetary policy in the euro area. The simulations were performed using a preliminary version of a model of the EMU as a part of the world economy, which at present accounts only for the repercussions between the EMU and the United States economy.

Several findings of these simulations are worth noting.

First, the baseline path projections show that when the exogenous variables of the model are extrapolated according to the most recent projections of multilateral agencies such as the IMF (2003) and the OECD (2003b), using a set of neutral hypotheses about the government sector variables, the aggregated deficit/GDP ratio in the euro area does not show any tendency to a 'close to balance' path, even in the presence of relatively sustained real growth (at about 2.7 per cent). This result lends some support to the view expressed by IMF (2003) that some structural fiscal tightening is needed in the larger EMU countries. At the same time, it raises the question of whether a 'close to balance' fiscal position is compatible with the structural parameters of the EMU economy. This point deserves further investigation by appropriate econometric techniques.

Secondly, the baseline path shows that, in accordance with the prediction of the monetary model of the exchange rate, the presence of a persistent growth differential in favour of the United States causes a devaluation of the euro, which converges towards a value of about €1.1 per US$, putting inflationary pressure on the euro area.

Thirdly, the monetary expansion experiment in Section 3.4 shows that, contrary to the views expressed for instance by IMF (2003) and Cotis (2003), monetary policy *per se* can play only a minor and transient role in steering the recovery. This is because a decrease in the EMU short-term interest rate exerts conflicting effects on the real interest rate, on the one hand, and competitiveness, on the other. However, monetary expansion is shown to ease considerably the burden of public debt. This means that an accurate mix of monetary and fiscal expansion could foster recovery without running into an unsustainable public debt path. This is another point for future research.

Fourth, the results of the 'oil-price shock' experiment in Section 3.3 explain the recent behaviour of the euro. In the simulation, the shock results in a monetary contraction which causes an appreciation of the domestic currency (the euro), thus partly offsetting the inflationary consequences of the shock. This mimics quite well the behaviour of the European economy in 2002, which featured a sizeable drop in the rate of growth of the broad money stock, coupled with an appreciation of the euro, in response to a rise in oil prices. The results set out in Table 9.4 show also that in the absence of active policies a supply-side shock of this kind can have persistent effects on unemployment, setting the EMU economy on a deflationary spiral.

Finally, the simulation of a persistent world demand shock in Section 3.2 shows that while an increase in world demand can actually exert persistent effects on the real growth of the euro area, it would also affect quite strongly the EMU inflation rate, both through the Phillips curve and through a devaluation of the European currency. These effects are determined by the structure of the exchange rate and money demand functions in the EMU and US models.

These results need to be evaluated carefully, especially because the estimation of the structural parameters of the aggregate European economy was carried out on the basis of data preceding the structural change caused by the inception of the EMU. Needless to say, all applied empirical work on the aggregate European economy currently shares this feature, whose impact is at present uncertain and will be empirically verifiable only when a reasonably large set of fresh (i.e. post-1999) data is available. Meanwhile, the interest and the reliability of these experiments could be improved in several ways. First, the representation of the other poles of the world economy (Japan and the European non-EMU countries, represented by the United Kingdom) should be completed. Secondly, the empirical specification of the model could be further refined, for example by considering asymmetric price effects in the Phillips curve, estimating an endogenous labour supply function, including wages and property income separately in the consumption function and so on. Thirdly, the model could be supplemented with some kind of alternative fiscal policy rule. Research on these topics is already in progress.

Notes

1. A full and updated description of the model structure can be found on the model home page http://eumodel.net
2. More exactly, the equations are 68 with 51 exogenous variables in the euro area submodel, and 59 with 47 exogenous variables in the US submodel. These small differences are explained by marginal differences in the representation of the supply side and the government sector. In the joint simulation some 'linkage' variables (such as the US and EMU trade variables, money stocks, interest and exchange rates) become endogenous, thus reducing the overall number of exogenous variables to 80.
3. Other examples of this aggregate approach are listed in Bagnai and Carlucci (2003).
4. We refer, of course, to the 'pre-EMU' EU-12, whose members were EU-15 minus Sweden, Finland, and Austria.
5. The previous version of the model assumed a Cobb-Douglas technology, because the estimates of the elasticity of substitution obtained were very close to one (as they are in most previous empirical work on the aggregate European economy). The estimation carried out on the revised dataset provided a value of $\sigma = 0.8$.
6. This approach was first applied to the aggregate European economy by Dramais (1986).
7. A similar structure was already proposed by Dramais (1986) and Meyermans and Van Brusselen (2000a,b). In the present version of the model the UK and Japan are represented only by a set of trade linkage equations, instead of a full structural model.
8. The econometric specification of the submodels may actually differ according to the empirical results and to the structure of the available data. Thus, the supply

side of the US submodel is based on a Cobb-Douglas production function, which proved superior to the CES in terms of empirical significance of the derived factor demand equations, while US government accounts consider a slightly different set of items than those of the euro area.

9. We plan to further disaggregate the rest of the world block into a number of regional submodels. This extension, however, involves considerable data issues.
10. A more detailed account of the assumptions and results of the simulations is available from the author upon request or can be downloaded from the model homepage as in note 1.
11. This effect may be overstated due to the fact that labour force is exogenous over the simulation horizon. A stronger recovery would imply a stronger growth of labour supply, which would dampen the effects on the unemployment rate. We plan to include this feature in the model in the near future.
12. The positive response (i.e., depreciation) of the exchange rate to an increase in the domestic short-term interest rate is a standard feature of Frenkel's (1976) monetary model. A similar result is reached by Razzak and Grennes (1998), who estimate a model for the trade-weighed effective exchange rate of the USD with respect to the other G7 currencies, finding an interest rate semi-elasticity of about 0.05.

References

Altavilla, C. and U. Marani (2002) 'Is There a Deflationary Bias in European Economic Policies?' *Quaderni del Dipartimento di Scienze Economiche e Sociali*, no. 15 (Naples: Frederic II University).

Bagnai, A. and F. Carlucci (1998) 'Un modello econometrico aggregato dell'Unione Europea', *Quaderni di Studi Europei*, no. 1, University of Rome 'La Sapienza', pp. 13–85.

Bagnai, A. and F. Carlucci (2003) 'An Aggregate Model for the European Union', *Economic Modelling*, vol. 20, pp. 623–49.

Bean, C.R. (1994) 'European Unemployment: a Survey', *Journal of Economic Literature*, vol. 32, pp. 573–619.

Bowden, R. and D. Turkington (1981) 'A Comparative Study of Instrumental Variable Estimators for Nonlinear Simultaneous Models', *Journal of the American Statistical Society*, vol. 76, pp. 985–96.

Cotis, J.P. (2003) 'Editorial: a Progressive but Unspectacular Recovery', *OECD Economic Outlook*, no. 73, pp. vii–viii.

Douven, R. and M. Peters (1998) 'GDP-spillovers in Multi-country Models', *Economic Modelling*, vol. 15, pp. 163–95.

Dramais, A. (1986) 'COMPACT – A Prototype Macroeconomic Model of the European Community in the World Economy', *European Economy*, vol. 27, pp. 111–60.

Eichengreen, B. (1993) 'European Monetary Unification', *Journal of Economic Literature*, vol. 31, pp. 1321–57.

Fagan, G., J. Henry and R. Mestre (2001) 'An Area-wide Model (AWM) for the Euro Area', European Central Bank Working Paper, no. 42.

Frenkel, J. (1976) 'A Monetary Approach to the Exchange Rate: Doctrinal Aspects and Empirical Evidence', *Scandinavian Journal of Economics*, vol. 78, pp. 200–24.

Gregory, A.W. and B.R. Hansen (1996) 'Residual-based Tests for Cointegration in Models with Regime Shifts', *Journal of Econometrics*, vol. 70, pp. 99–126.

IMF (2003) *World Economic Outlook – Growth and Institutions* (Washington DC: IMF).

Kim, B.J. and S. Mo (1995) 'Cointegration and the Long-run Forecast of the Exchange Rate', *Economics Letters*, vol. 48, pp. 353–9.
Knight, M.D. and C. Wymer (1978) 'A Macroeconomic Model of the United Kingdom', *IMF Staff Papers*, vol. 25(4), pp. 742–78.
Laxton, D., P. Isard, H. Faruquee, E. Prasad and B. Turtelboom (1998) 'MULTIMOD Mark III, The core dynamic and steady-state models', IMF Occasional Paper no. 164.
Meyermans, E. and P. Van Brusselen (2000a) 'The NIME Model – Specification and Estimation of the Demand Equations of the Household Sector', Federal Planning Bureau Working Paper, Brussels, no. 8.
Meyermans, E. and P. Van Brusselen (2000b) 'The NIME Model – Specification and Estimation of the Enterprise Sector', Federal Planning Bureau Working Paper, Brussels, no. 10.
OECD (2002) *OECD Statistical Compendium*, 2002/2 (Paris: OECD).
OECD (2003a) *OECD Statistical Compendium*, 2003/1 (Paris: OECD).
OECD (2003b) Flashfile to the *OECD Economic Outlook*, no. 73, http://www.oecd.org/xls/M00040000/M00040707.xls
Razzak, W.A. and T. Grennes (1998) 'The Long-run Nominal Exchange Rate: Specification and Estimation Issues', *Reserve Bank of New Zealand Discussion Paper*, no. 98/5.
Taylor, J. (1993) 'Discretion versus Policy Rules in Practice', *Carnegie-Rochester Conference on Public Policy*, vol. 39, pp. 195–214.

10

Towards a European National Economy? Lessons from the Economic History of Europe

Nuno Valério
ISEG, Technical University of Lisbon, Portugal

1 Introduction

The institutional framework of the European Union has been the subject of much debate. The proposals presented to the European Convention, meeting during 2002 and the first half of 2003,[1] illustrate the diversity of positions concerning this institutional framework. It is possible to divide these positions into three main groups:

(a) Those that support the transformation of the European Union into a true federal state (i.e. a state with its own constitution, as distinct from a treaty among the member states, and its own government independent of the governments of the federated national states belonging to it), even if they admit that it should be a confederation (i.e. a federal state in which federated states retain their own separate role in international relations and have the right to leave the union).

(b) Those that support the idea that the European Union, which is neither a federal state nor an intergovernmental international organization, should maintain its present institutional arrangements based on a significant role for supranational elements, without upgrading them into a federal state.

(c) Those that support the transformation of the European Union into an intergovernmental international organization, by reducing the role of supranational elements in its institutional structure, or even suppressing them.

The debate over these alternatives will certainly continue in the future, whatever the results of the European Convention and the political decisions that will follow. This chapter tries to draw some conclusions about the feasibility of these alternatives through a consideration of several experiences from the economic history of Europe.

2 National states and national economies

It is widely accepted that one particular feature of the history of Europe during the last few centuries of the second millennium AD was the development of a political geography based on national states (defined as politically independent areas that ideally correspond to nations, that is, culturally distinct and homogeneous communities) (Kennedy, 1987; Fèbvre, 1999). Of course, reality often differed from the ideal, because feudal remnants (micro-states such as Andorra, Monaco or San Marino), imperial powers (such as Austria, Germany, Russia and Turkey until the First World War) and culturally heterogeneous states (such as Belgium, Spain and Switzerland) always co-existed with true national states. However, there is no doubt that Europe avoided both extreme feudal division and imperial unification. France and England may be seen as early prototypes of national states, but the model spread, through different political processes, to the whole continent, from Iberia and Italy to Scandinavia and the Balkans. The inter-war period in the first half of the twentieth century was perhaps the epoch in which this correspondence between states and national communities was taken even further, in the wake of the collapse of the Austrian, German, Russian and Turkish empires as a result of their defeat in the First World War.

To say that this was a particular feature of Europe does not mean that national states did not exist in the rest of the world. However, while they tended to be the typical political unit in Europe, the political geography of the rest of the world tended to be dominated until the nineteenth century by other types of political units. Tribal states (defined as politically independent areas devoid of any elaborate bureaucratic apparatus) were the typical political unit of non-literate societies (in Northern and Central Asia, Sub-Saharan Africa, non-colonial America, Australasia and the islands of the Pacific Ocean); huge empires (defined as politically independent areas that involve the dominance of one national community over other communities) were the typical political unit of sophisticated societies such as China, India, and the Moslem world; feudal states (defined as politically independent areas that correspond to communities smaller than nations) were often the result of the collapse of empires; and a special type of empire, colonial empires made up of plantation colonies, emigration colonies and conquest colonies, proved to be the typical formula found in the early days of European expansion. Japan was perhaps the only country in the world that developed a stable national state in the European sense throughout the whole of the second half of the second millennium AD, although other examples, less stable because of imperial interferences, might be mentioned (Korea, always under pressure from China, Japan – and later Russia and the United States of America – and still divided into two states in the early twenty-first century is a case in point).

The model of the European national state was exported to the rest of the world as a result of the political hegemony of Europe during the late nineteenth and early twentieth centuries. This implied the destruction of different arrangements that prevailed in other parts of the world, at least in formal terms. Although these different previous arrangements were often replaced by temporary situations of European colonial domination, later decolonization processes swept away almost all these temporary situations. The independence of American colonies in the late eighteenth and early nineteenth centuries and the decolonization of Asia and Africa during the third quarter of the twentieth century, together with the peace agreements signed after the First World War, represented the most important waves in the creation of formal national states.

Together with a political geography based on national states, Europe developed an economic geography based on national economies corresponding to these same national states. During the nineteenth century and the first half of the twentieth century, these national economies stabilized as customs areas, monetary areas and fiscal areas (in the sense that they were homogeneous and distinct from other national economies as far as these aspects of economic life were concerned). At the same time, these areas also corresponded to the areas where the same economic laws applied and common economic policies were implemented. This economic map of Europe was the product of both a very long-term institutional evolution that gradually destroyed local particularisms (Braudel, 1979) and of the possibilities opened up by the technological revolutions of the epoch of modern economic growth (Kuznets, 1966). The double impact of the institutional measures arising from the French Revolution (such as the abolition of internal customs, or the general spread of the metric system), together with the transportation and communication possibilities arising from the spread of railways and the electrical telegraph, perhaps amounted to the last decisive step in this process, first in France and then later all over the European continent (and the British Isles, unified under English hegemony).

The institutional arrangements of national economies were exported to other regions of the world, as was the model of the national state. Thus, national economies and the international economy, that is, the interplay of national economies to form a world economy (Foreman-Peck, 1995), came to be seen as standard features of economic life. As a consequence, other institutional arrangements, such as quasi-closed world-economies corresponding to political units of the imperial type, or quasi-closed local economies corresponding to political units of the tribal type, became things of the past.

Of course, border changes, processes leading to the merger of previously separate national economies into one single national economy, and processes involving the splitting of previously united national economies into separate national economies, were far from unknown. The immediate post-First World War arrangements may again be seen as a very important example of these processes. However, these processes did not change the main relevant economic spaces from being a basic framework of national economies and an international economy.

3 The changing economic geography of Europe

There is no doubt that the second half of the twentieth century witnessed significant changes in the economic geography of Europe (El-Agraa, 1998).

The late 1940s and the 1950s were characterized by the split between the market economies gathered together under the umbrella of the OEEC – Organisation of European Economic Cooperation (formed in 1948 by Austria, Belgium, Denmark, France, the Federal Republic of Germany, Great Britain, Greece, Iceland, Ireland, Italy, Luxembourg, Netherlands, Norway, Portugal, Sweden, Switzerland and Turkey), to which could be added Finland and Spain,[2] and the centrally planned economies gathered together in Comecon – Council for Mutual Economic Assistance (formed in 1949 by Bulgaria, Czechoslovakia, Hungary, Poland, Romania and the USSR, joined subsequently by Albania, Cuba, the German Democratic Republic, Mongolia and Vietnam), to which could be ideologically added Yugoslavia.[3] This corresponded to a political split between what may be termed the American and Soviet zones of influence in Europe, which lasted until the late 1980s.

The late 1950s and the 1960s were characterized by a further split within the OEEC between the customs and economic union of the European Communities – the European Coal and Steel Community + the European Atomic Energy Community + the European Economic Community (formed in 1958[4] by Belgium, France, the Federal Republic of Germany, Italy, Luxembourg and the Netherlands) and the free trade zone of EFTA – European Free Trade Association (formed in 1960 by Austria, Denmark, Great Britain, Norway, Portugal, Sweden and Switzerland). This division corresponded to different perspectives concerning the future of Europe. The countries that chose the European Communities attached greater importance to European integration than to relations with the rest of the world. Great Britain, which opposed the European Communities project and led the process for the formation of EFTA, gave preference to its links with the British Commonwealth over European integration. Those states which joined EFTA had a variety of motivations: Denmark, Norway, Sweden and Portugal sought to maintain their important economic relations with the UK; Austria, Sweden and Switzerland mistrusted political links with the European Communities; and Portugal gave special preference to colonial projects.[5]

In a certain sense, both the European Communities and EFTA were successes, but, by the late 1960s, it had become clear that European integration was a much more successful project than the maintenance of overseas ties, and Great Britain was soon applying for membership in the European Communities. In 1969, the Hague Summit of the European Communities made the solemn declaration that the integration of the European Communities was irreversible and paved the way for the enlargement of the European Communities to include Denmark, Great Britain, Ireland and Norway (a process that was concluded in 1973 without Norway) and the signing of free trade agreements with the remaining EFTA members. At the same time, the first attempts were made to start a European monetary union, which failed, leaving in its place the so-called snake monetary arrangements, which was upgraded in 1979 to give birth to the European Monetary System.

From then on, the European Communities became the undoubted core of the process of European integration, which was taken further with the twin measures of its deepening and enlargement. The 1980s witnessed the so-called Mediterranean enlargement to include Greece (1981), Portugal and Spain (1986), the merger of the European Communities into one single European Community (1987) and the drawing up of plans to resume the process of European economic and monetary union (1989). The turn of the decade brought the collapse of the centrally planned economies, which immediately implied a fourth enlargement of the European Community with the reunification of Germany (1990). The 1990s saw decisive steps being taken towards the full economic union of the twelve members of the European Community (Belgium, Denmark, France, Germany, Great Britain, Greece, Ireland, Italy, Luxembourg, Netherlands, Portugal and Spain), with the abolition of all obstacles to the free movement of goods, services, people and capital (1993); the transformation of the European Community into the European Union through the addition of the pillars of justice and home affairs, as well as foreign and security policy, to the European Community (1993); the formation of a European Economic Area bringing together the countries of the European Union and EFTA (1994, with the formal self-exclusion of Switzerland[6]); the fifth enlargement of the European Union to include Austria, Finland and Sweden (1995); the beginning of negotiations leading to a sixth enlargement involving twelve candidates (Bulgaria, Cyprus, Czech Republic, Estonia, Hungary, Latvia, Lithuania, Malta, Poland, Romania, Slovakia and Slovenia);[7] and the conclusion of the European monetary union between eleven countries (Austria, Belgium, Finland, France, Germany, Ireland, Italy, Luxembourg, Netherlands, Portugal and Spain) in 1999, joined by Greece in 2001 (and by Monaco, San Marino and the Vatican as passive members in 2002).

The evolution of most of the old national economies of Europe during the second half of the twentieth century may be summarized as shown in Table 10.1.

The future evolution of this complex group centred around the European Union is far from clear, as pointed out above. From an economic point of view, it is possible to summarize the main possibilities corresponding to the

Table 10.1 Evolution of the national economies of Europe during the second half of the twentieth century

Immediately after the Second World War	*At the beginning of the twenty-first century*
Separate customs areas	Members of a fifteen-country customs union
Separate monetary areas	Members of a twelve-country monetary union
Separate fiscal areas	Separate fiscal areas but involved in fiscal harmonization
Different economic laws	Different economic laws but an increasing role for Community law
Autonomous economic policies	Some autonomous economic policies but development of common policies and coordination of economic policies

institutional alternatives mentioned as follows:

(a) The formation of a single European national economy, of which the old European national economies will become mere regional economies – this corresponds to the so-called federalist institutional alternative.

(b) Stabilization at an intermediate situation such as the one prevailing today, in which some of the traditional characteristics of the national economies belong to the European Union (or to zones within it such as Euroland), whilst other traditional characteristics of the national economies belong to the old national economies of the member countries of the European Union – this corresponds to the intermediate (and mildly supranational) institutional alternative.

(c) The partial or complete reversal of the evolution of the last decades, with the old European national economies asserting themselves again as the key relevant spaces – this corresponds to the intergovernmental institutional alternative.

4 Lessons from the economic history of Europe

It may seem that European integration is completely different from the economic processes of the past, and thus that it is impossible to infer from previous experience what are its most likely (or desirable) outcomes. Of course, European integration has many particular characteristics. In this sense, it is a unique event, in the technical parlance of historians. However, the economic history of Europe during the nineteenth and twentieth centuries witnessed a number of processes that presented many analogies with it. This also means that it is a repetition (in the same technical parlance of historians). Thus, it is possible to draw some interesting conclusions from comparisons with these other processes.

Table 10.2 Chronology of German Unification

Year	*Event*
1815	German Confederation (38 members)
1818	Prussian customs union
1828	North German customs union (7 members, increasing to 15 members by 1831), South German customs union (2 members) and Central German trade union (10 members)
1834	German customs union (18 members, increasing to 31 members by 1867)
1837	Munich Coinage Treaty: monetary union of Southern Germany
1838	Dresden Coinage Convention: monetary union of Northern Germany
1848	Failed liberal-nationalist attempt to form a German Empire
1857	Treaty of Vienna: monetary union of Southern and Northern Germany
1867	Dissolution of German Confederation; North German Confederation (21 members corresponding to 31 members of the German Confederation + Schleswig); Austria excluded from monetary union; customs union of all Germany except for Austria, Hamburg and Bremen
1871	(Second) German Empire (25 members corresponding to 35 members of the German Confederation; Austria excluded; Alsace-Lorraine included)
1876	1 January: complete monetary union of German Empire: German mark (Law of 22 September 1875) + Reichsbank (Law of 14 March 1875)
1888	Complete customs union of German Empire

The most important of these processes was, perhaps, the German unification of the nineteenth century (Deutsche Bundesbank, 1976; Hahn, 1984; Sprenger, 1991; Holtfrerich, 1993). This was a fairly protracted process, the chronology of which is summarized in Table 10.2. It started in the second decade of the century, with an almost ineffective political construction (the German Confederation) and the decision of Prussia to establish a customs union between the various states that were united under its sovereignty. During the 1820s, three separate trade blocks emerged within the German Confederation.[8] These trade blocks merged in 1834, and it soon became clear that these trade arrangements needed to be completed by monetary arrangements, which were set up during the late 1830s. Although these monetary arrangements meant that different monetary units were maintained in Northern and Southern Germany, they provided a common silver standard. The process came to the verge of full political unification in 1848, but it failed, hesitating during most of the 1850s and 1860s on the issue of Grossdeutsche extension (including Austria, which would need an Austrian-Prussian compromise) versus Kleindeutsche extension (excluding Austria, which would allow for complete Prussian hegemony), leaping forward (in the Kleindeutsche version) in the late 1860s and early 1870s and being concluded in the 1880s. By then, a full customs and monetary union (now with a gold standard) had been established among the states that had become the German Empire in 1871.

The main difference between German unification and European integration is, of course, a cultural one. Germany is a nation in a cultural sense, Europe is not (the language test is decisive in forming this judgement). Another difference is to be found in the fact that Germany already had some kind of loose political structure (the German Confederation). A third point to be noted is the fact that Prussia played a dominant role in the process, which no national state is able to play in the case of European integration. This even led to the exclusion of the other main German state (Austria) from German unification because of internal political rivalries (with Prussia) and external imperial ambitions (over the non-German part of the Austrian Empire). However, the time periods and the political and economic issues involved in the process of German unification present striking similarities with the issues that have come to the forefront in the process of European integration. The leading role of economy over politics, the inescapable need to set up unwarranted institutions to overcome gaps in the administrative process, the doubts about the characteristics that the final stage of the process should present in terms of geographical extension and institutional depth, the uneasy tension between large and small participant states and the resulting compromises between centralization and the preservation of local particularities are cases in point.

Two other important cases, the Italian unification in the nineteenth century (Zamagni, 1993) and the German unification of 1990 are, perhaps, less interesting for our purposes, especially because they were much quicker processes, involving a much more pronounced asymmetry between participants. As a matter of fact, Piedmont-Sardinia in the case of the Italian unification in the nineteenth century and the Federal Republic of Germany in the case of the German unification of 1990 played a clearly dominant role. Moreover, the cultural homogeneity and the leading role of politics to be noted in these two cases also differ from the case of European integration. This makes the absence of previous formal ties of a political and economic nature clearly less relevant, even though this amounts to a significant similarity.

In any case, there is at least one very important similarity among all the cases considered: the outcome was one single state (a federal state in the case of Germany, a unitary state in the case of Italy), and one single national economy. Is it possible to infer that this must also occur in the case of European integration? Are there any counter-examples to be found in the history of nineteenth and twentieth-century Europe?

As a matter of fact, almost all integration schemes that did not involve some kind of political unification failed in the long run. Informal monetary arrangements such as the international gold standard, formal monetary arrangements such as the Latin Union or the Scandinavian Union, intermediate complex schemes such as the Austro-Hungarian Dual Monarchy between 1867 and 1918 are cases in point. The exceptions are few and show very peculiar characteristics. The most important case is perhaps the monetary union that has existed between Belgium and Luxembourg since 1921. It is a situation where one small country has surrendered part of its economic sovereignty to its larger neighbour, in exchange for a greater capacity to ensure monetary stability.[9]

The Austro-Hungarian Dual Monarchy[10] deserves some further attention because it was a case in which two powers (Austria and Hungary) engaged in a process of shared sovereignty, subject to a formal revision of its statutes every ten years. At the same time, there was a situation of imperial dominance over several weaker nations and provinces – the present-day Czech Republic, Slovenia, Dalmatia and South Tyrol, allotted to Austria; Croatia and Slovakia, allotted to Hungary.[11] The result was an uneasy common life for nearly half a century and a collapse as soon as a really challenging test (the First World War) arrived. The experience is very important for three reasons. First, the successive Intergovernmental Conferences to revise the institutional framework of the European Union mirror the regular revision of the statutes of the Austro-Hungarian Dual Monarchy. Secondly, there are signs that some groups within the European Union dream of something akin to the imperial structure of the Austro-Hungarian Dual Monarchy: a directorate of great powers ruling over Europe as a whole. Neither of these schemes seems to have been really favourable to the stability of the whole. Thirdly, the aftermath of the collapse of the Austro-Hungarian Dual Monarchy brought the dismal story of the so-called successor states in the twentieth-century interwar period, something that may threaten Europe in the event of a reversal of the process of European integration. The economic rationale for this is clear. Once integration has proceeded and economic life has adapted to it, there is a change in economic structures, which allows the production possibility frontier to be expanded further. To reverse the process means to revert to economic structures with a contracted production possibility frontier, something that cannot be done in a strictly symmetrical manner, not least because of the technological changes that have occurred in the meantime.

Three other recent cases (in the 1990s) of a break-up of federal states that were linked to fully integrated national economies should be mentioned here: the Union of Soviet Socialist Republics, Yugoslavia and Czechoslovakia. These cases prove that the formation of a federal state and a single national economy may also be reversible when an adverse short-term situation combines with ethnic and cultural heterogeneity. They also seem to confirm the idea that a break-up is not favourable to the economic performance of the successor states, although the short time that has elapsed since secession and the influence of relations with the European Union may disturb this assessment.

5 Conclusions

The preceding section seems to lead to the following conclusions:

(i) It is very unlikely that the process of European integration will settle in a stable manner into the intermediate model at which it stands now: limited supranational institutions and a division of the characteristics of national economies between the European Union as a whole and the old European national economies.

(ii) The formation of a federal state (even of the confederate type) and a European economy with all the traditional characteristics of a national economy seems a much safer outcome for the peace and prosperity of Europe than a partial or complete reversal of the process of European integration.

6 A note on monetary arrangements

A further reflection on the stability of intermediate schemes may come from an examination of the present situation of the European monetary union.

During the nineteenth and twentieth centuries, the typical monetary framework of a national economy came to involve the existence of a national currency unit and a system of national means of payment jointly managed by two monetary authorities: a central bank, responsible for the issue of money and monetary policy (by means of interest rate and exchange rate manipulation, open market operations, minimum reserve requirements, and banking supervision); and a government agency (usually a Ministry of Finance), able to implement an active budget policy.[12] Such an institutional framework developed in almost all European economies and elsewhere (for instance, in the United States with the development of the Federal Reserve System).[13]

The European Monetary Union, as it was set up in the late 1990s, lacks such a balanced dual structure. As a matter of fact, the European System of Central Banks, and particularly the European Central Bank, have acquired a clear superiority over the so-called Ecofin (Council of the Ministers of Economy and Finance of the European Union), not only because of the radical central bank independence schemes provided for in the statutes of the European System of Central Banks appended to the Maastricht Treaty, but especially because of the lack of significant budget instruments available to Ecofin (or any other organ of the European Union). It may be questioned if this is also a possible stable solution, or if the development of an effective counterpart to the European System of Central Banks of the Ministry of Finance type is likely or desirable. Of course, the development of a true European federal state would provide such a counterpart.

Notes

1. Available at the Convention Internet site (http://european-convention.eu.int).
2. Finland was absent from the OEEC because of the interference from the Soviet Union that gave rise to the term 'Finlandization'. Spain was absent from the OEEC because of the links its government had maintained with the regimes of Germany

and Italy, defeated in the Second World War. Spain was to join the OEEC later in 1959.

3. Yugoslavia was absent from Comecon because of the political split between its leaders and Soviet leaders within the international communist movement.
4. The European Coal and Steel Community had existed since 1952.
5. Among the OEEC members, Greece, Iceland, Ireland, Spain and Turkey remained absent from both trade blocks. These countries corresponded to the group of the less developed economies of the OEEC, with the exception of Portugal. Fears about the damaging impact of free trade with highly developed economies were decisive in shaping this division. However, Ireland had had preference arrangements with Great Britain since its independence in 1921, and attempts soon began to strengthen relations between these countries and the two trade blocks. Greece and Turkey became associated to the European Communities during the 1960s, Ireland signed a free trade treaty with Great Britain in 1966, and Iceland became an EFTA member in 1970. Notice also that Finland signed a free trade treaty with EFTA in 1961, although it only became a member in 1986.
6. This led Liechtenstein, which since the post-First World War years had relied on its economic union with Switzerland for negotiating its foreign economic agreements, to reassert its autonomy in these matters (1995).
7. Turkey was also accepted as a candidate, but, for political reasons, negotiations did not start until the early twenty-first century. By then (2003), Croatia had also applied for membership.
8. Two of these blocks were customs unions: the North German customs agreement (Norddeutsche Zollvertrag), between Prussia and Hesse-Darmstadt, soon afterwards extended to ten other states, and the South German customs union (Süddeutsche Zollvereiningung), between Bavaria and Württemberg. The other one, the Central German trade union (Mitteldeutsche Handelsverein), was just a most favoured nation agreement between ten small states. It began to falter in 1831, when Hesse-Kassel left to join the North German customs agreement as its twelfth member, and broke up in 1834, when the North and South German customs unions merged to form the German customs union (Deutscher Zollverein) and most of its members decided to join the new trade block. The remaining members of the Central German trade union and the German states that did not belong to any of the trade blocks formed during the 1820s later joined the German customs union, with the exceptions of Austria and Liechtenstein, which formed a separate customs union until 1912.
9. Luxembourg had been a member of the German Confederation and participated in the German customs union before 1867, although it did not belong to the German Empire. It also participated in the Latin Union monetary scheme, together with France, Belgium, Italy and Switzerland.
10. This was established in 1867 and may be seen as a by-product of the Austrian failure to combine participation in the process of German unification with control of its non-German empire.
11. To these, common control of Bosnia-Herzegovina was added from 1878 onwards.
12. This was the result of the replacement of traditional metallic monetary systems, which could be controlled by the government through minting activities, with modern fiduciary monetary systems, which are crucially dependent on bank activity. Of course, this process cannot be considered here in detail. See Friedman and Schwarz (1971) and Goodhart (1987).

13. This dual structure gave rise to the problem of the independence of central banks from the interference of government agencies, which cannot be considered here in detail. See Cukierman (1992) and Eijfinger (1997).

References

Braudel, Fernand (1979) *Civilisation matérielle, économie et capitalisme XVe-XVIIIe siècles* (3 volumes) (Paris: Armand Colin).

Cukierman, A. (1992) *Central Bank Strategy, Credibility and Independence* (Cambridge MA: MIT Press).

Deutsche Bundesbank (1976) *Währung und Wirtschaft in Deutschland 1876–1975* (Frankfurt-am-Main: Deutsche Bundesbank).

Eijfinger, S. (ed.) (1997) *Independent Central Banks and Economic Performance* (Cheltenham: Edward Elgar).

El-Agraa, Ali (1998) *The European Union – History, Institutions, Economics and Politics* (London: Prentice Hall Europe).

Fèbvre, Lucien (1999) *L'Europe – Génèse d'une Civilisation* (Paris: Librairie Académique Perrin).

Foreman-Pack, James (1995) *A History of the World Economy – International Economic Relations Since 1850* (2nd edn) (Hemel Hempstead: Harvester Wheatsheaf).

Friedman, Milton and Anna Schwarz (1971) *A Monetary History of the USA 1867–1960* (Princeton: Princeton University Press).

Goodhart, Charles (1987) 'Central banking', in John Eatwell, Murray Milgate and Peter Newman (eds), *The New Palgrave. A Dictionary of Economics* (London: Macmillan), vol. 1, pp. 385–7.

Hahn, Hans-Werner (1984) *Geschichte des Deutschen Zollverein* (Göttingen: Vanderhoeck & Ruprecht).

Holtfrerich, Carl-Ludwig (1993) 'Did Monetary Unification Precede or Follow Political Unification of Germany in the 19th Century?' *European Economic Review*, vol. 37(2/3), pp. 518–24.

Kennedy, Paul (1987) *The Rise and Fall of the Great Powers* (New York: Random House).

Kuznets, Simon (1966) *Modern Economic Growth – Rate, Structure and Spread* (New Haven: Yale University Press).

Sprenger, Bernd (1991) *Das Geld der Deutschen: Geldgeschichte Deutschlands von den Anf ängen bis zur Gegenwart* (Paderborn: Verlag Ferdinand Schömingh).

Zamagni, Vera (1993) *The Economic History of Italy, 1860–1990* (Oxford: Clarendon Press).